001

ZWORD ART ONLINE phantom bullet

ART: koutarou yamada
original story: Reki kawahara
character design: abec

D1117123

stage.001

THIS MIGHT BE A GAME, BUT IT'S NOT SOMETHING YOU PLAY.

—*AKIHIKO KAYABA*, SWORD ART ONLINE *PROGRAMMER*

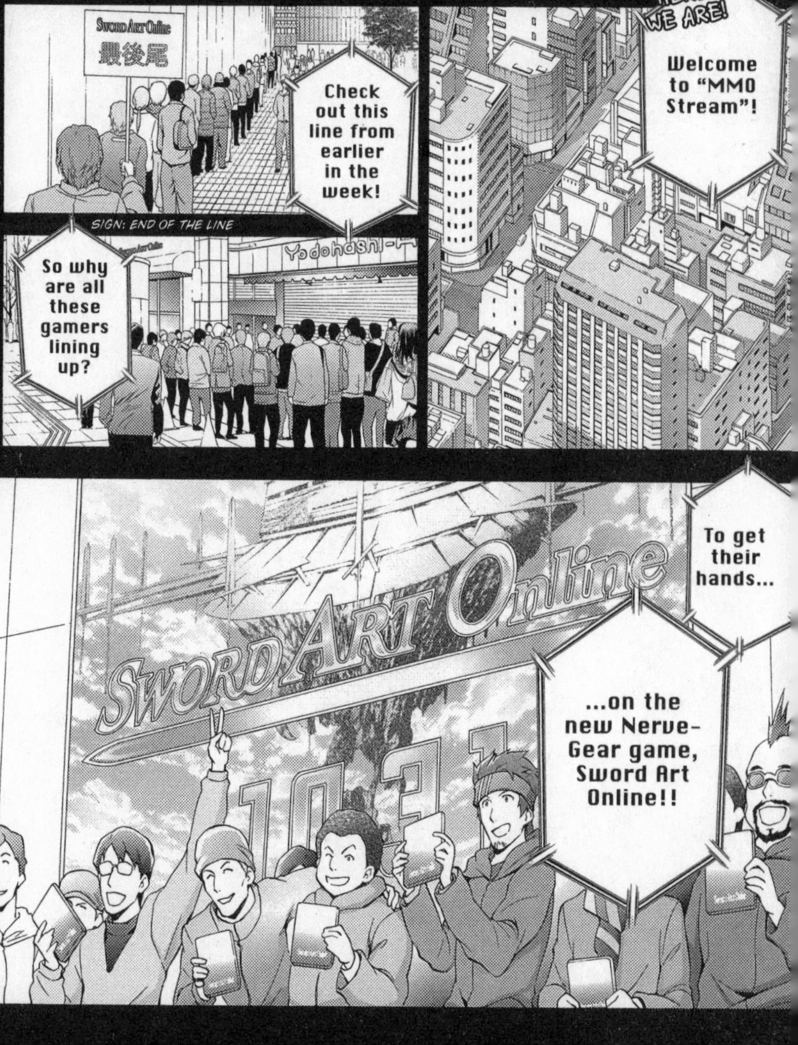
HERE WE ARE!
Welcome to "MMO Stream"!
Sword Art Online
最後尾
Check out this line from earlier in the week!
SIGN: END OF THE LINE
Yodohashi
So why are all these gamers lining up?
To get their hands...
SWORD ART Online
...on the new Nerve-Gear game, Sword Art Online!!

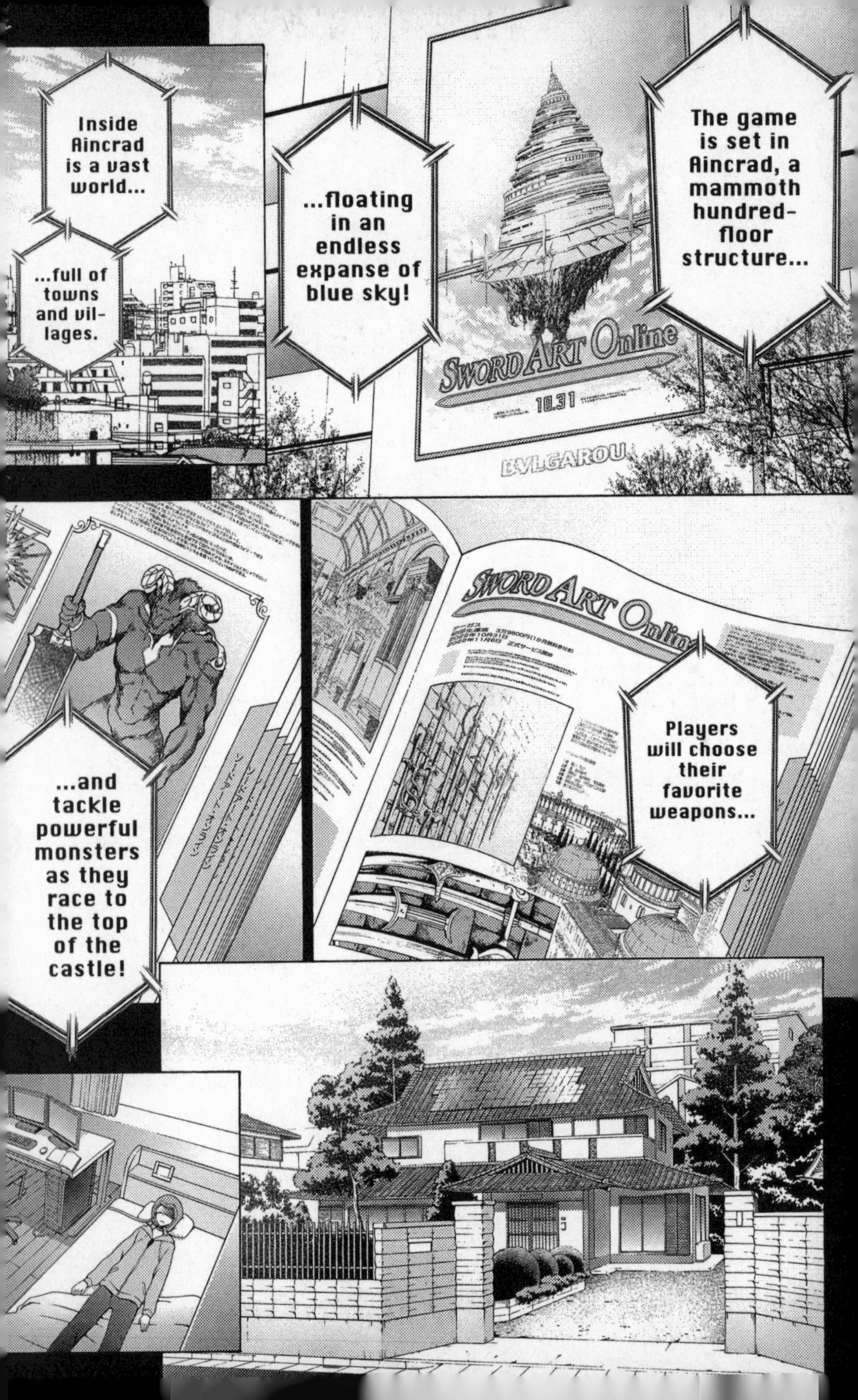
The game is set in Aincrad, a mammoth hundred-floor structure...
SWORD ART Online
10.31
...floating in an endless expanse of blue sky!
Inside Aincrad is a vast world...
...full of towns and villages.
SWORD ART Online
Players will choose their favorite weapons...
...and tackle powerful monsters as they race to the top of the castle!

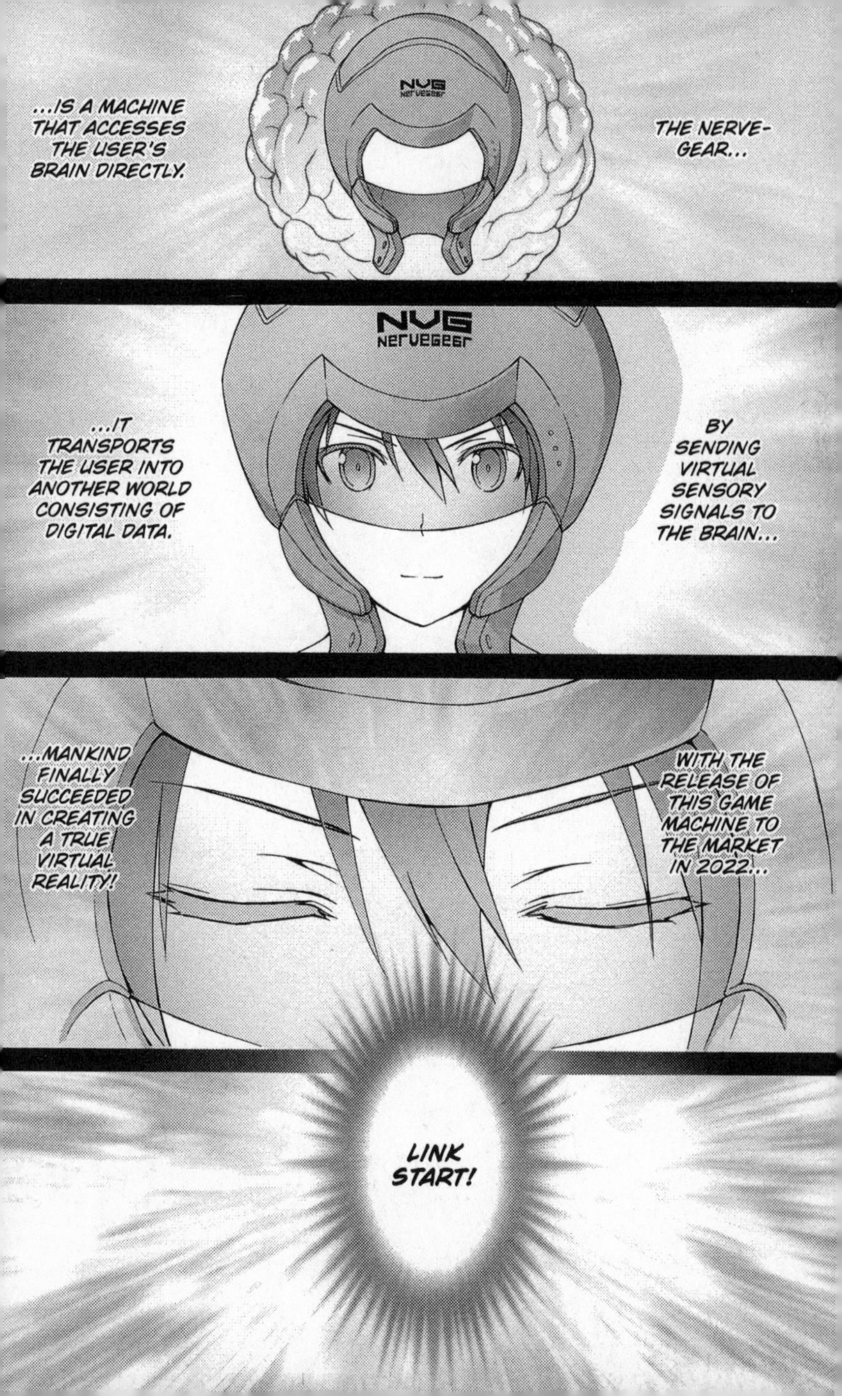
THE NERVE-GEAR...
NVG nervegear
...IS A MACHINE THAT ACCESSES THE USER'S BRAIN DIRECTLY.
BY SENDING VIRTUAL SENSORY SIGNALS TO THE BRAIN...
...IT TRANSPORTS THE USER INTO ANOTHER WORLD CONSISTING OF DIGITAL DATA.
WITH THE RELEASE OF THIS GAME MACHINE TO THE MARKET IN 2022...
...MANKIND FINALLY SUCCEEDED IN CREATING A TRUE VIRTUAL REALITY!
LINK START!

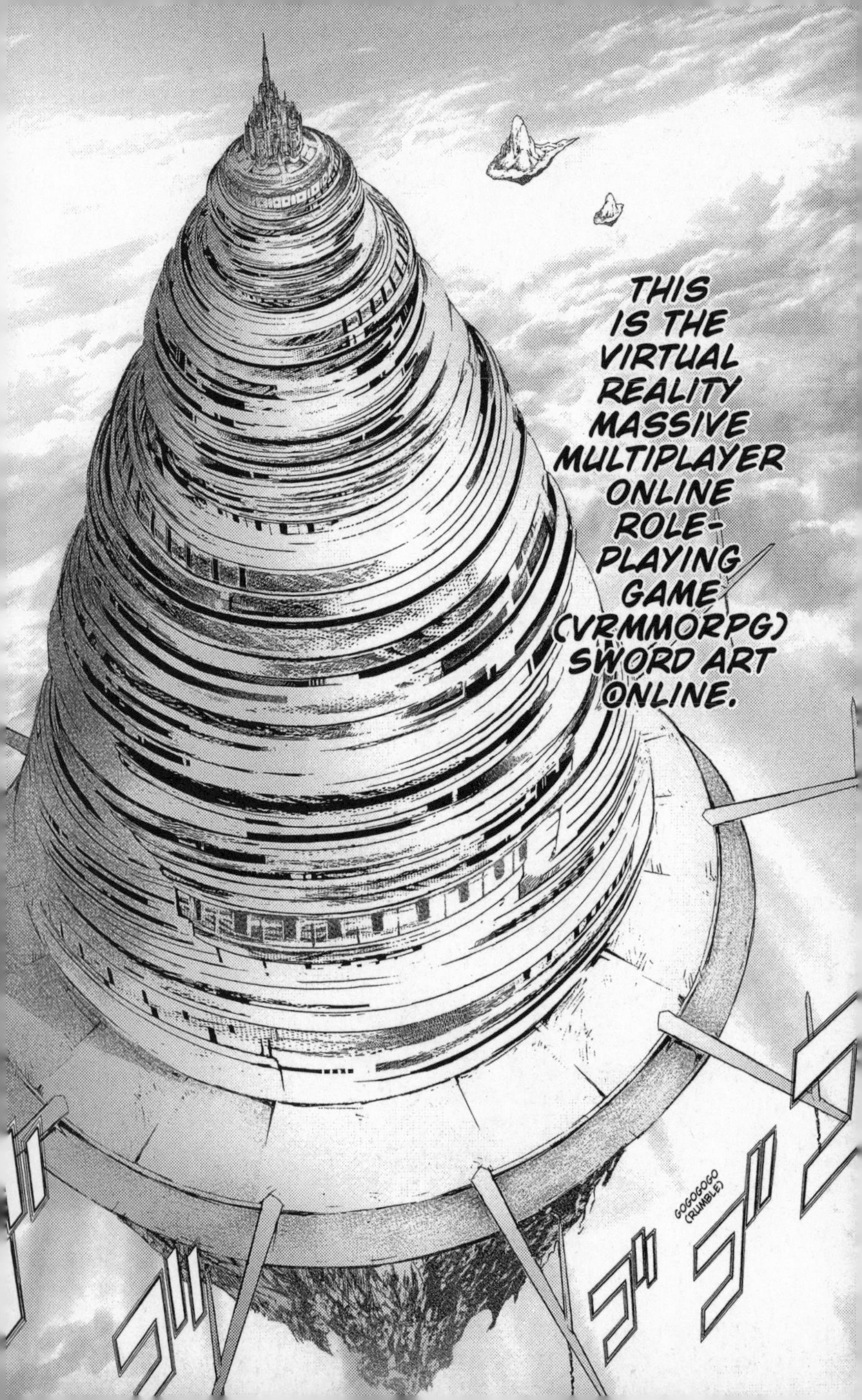
THIS IS THE VIRTUAL REALITY MASSIVE MULTIPLAYER ONLINE ROLE-PLAYING GAME (VRMMORPG) SWORD ART ONLINE.
GOGOGOGO (RUMBLE)

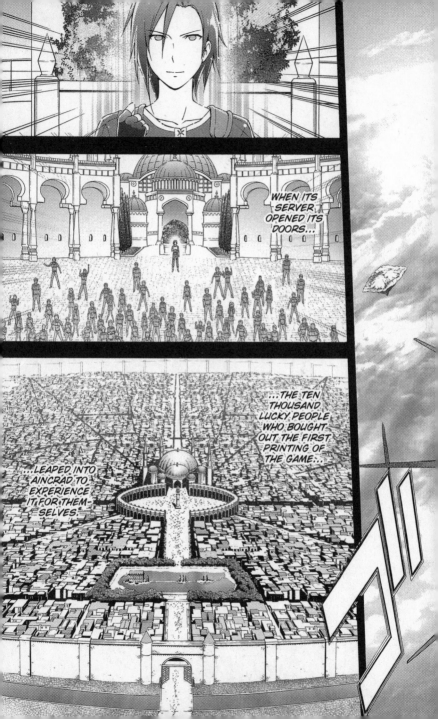

WHEN ITS
SERVER
OPENED ITS
DOORS...

...THE TEN
THOUSAND
LUCKY PEOPLE
WHO BOUGHT
OUT THE FIRST
PRINTING OF
THE GAME...

...LEAPED INTO
AINCRAD TO
EXPERIENCE
IT FOR THEM-
SELVES.

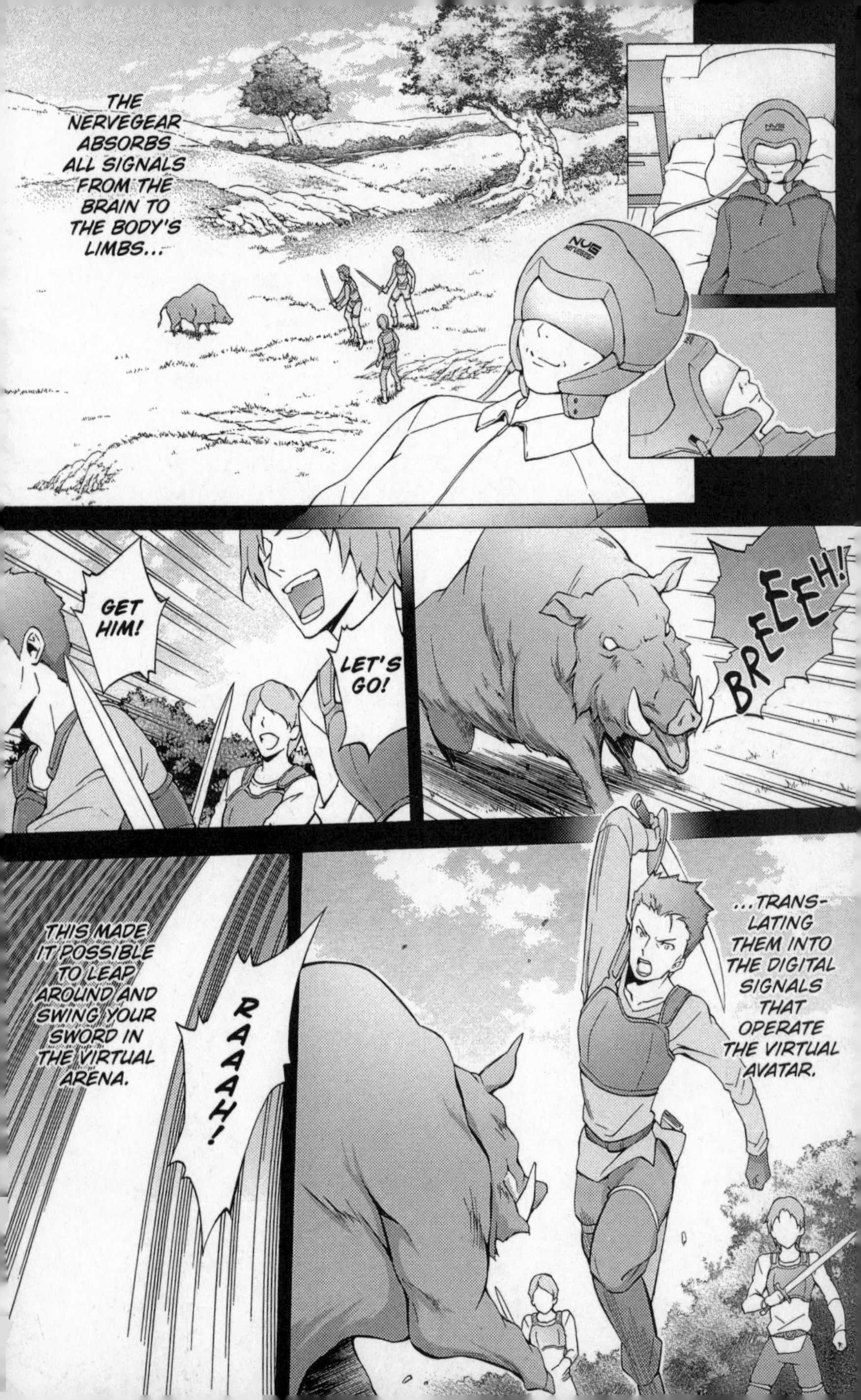
THE NERVEGEAR ABSORBS ALL SIGNALS FROM THE BRAIN TO THE BODY'S LIMBS...
BREEEH!
GET HIM!
LET'S GO!
...TRANS-LATING THEM INTO THE DIGITAL SIGNALS THAT OPERATE THE VIRTUAL AVATAR.
THIS MADE IT POSSIBLE TO LEAP AROUND AND SWING YOUR SWORD IN THE VIRTUAL ARENA.
RAAAAH!

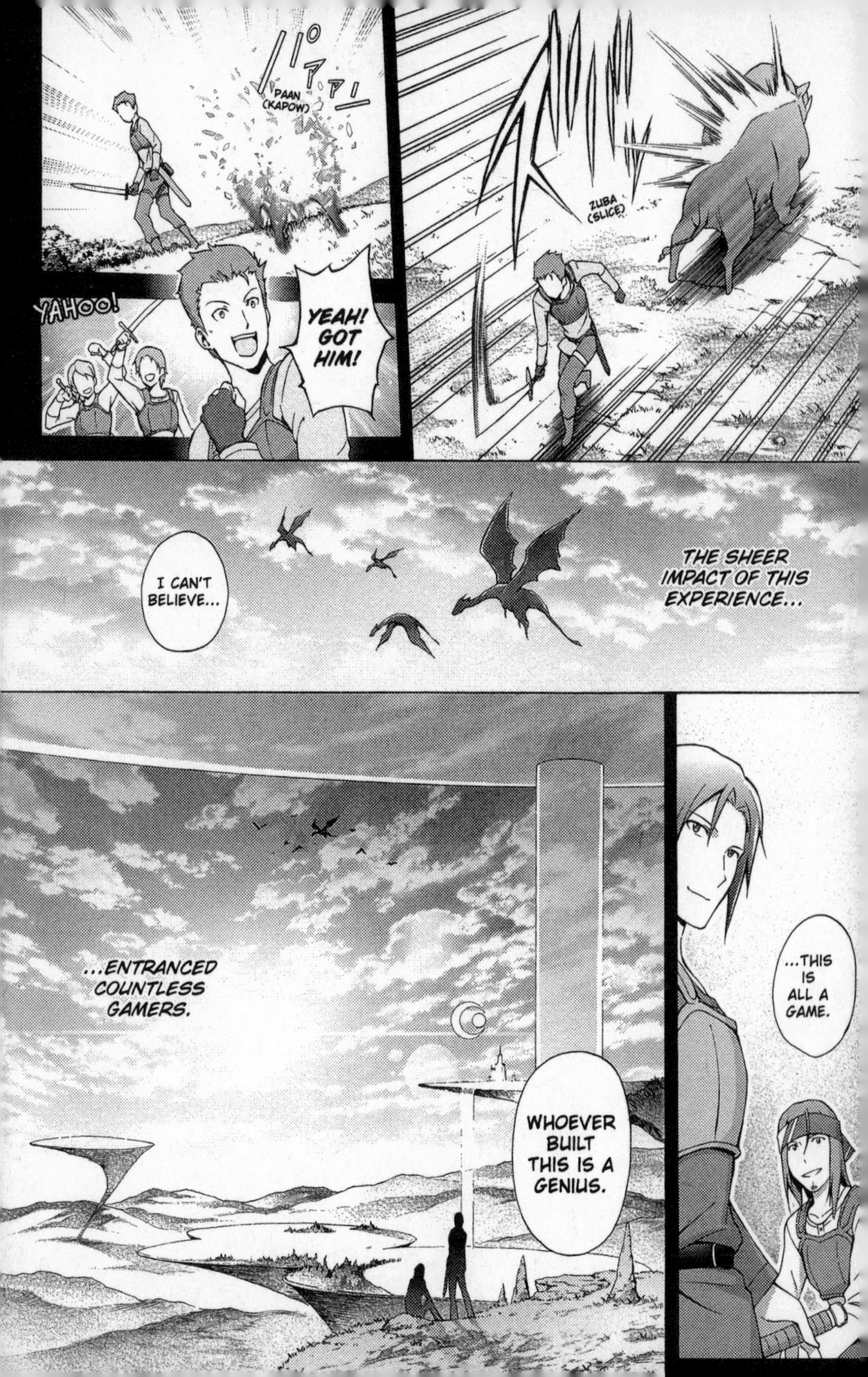
ZUBA (SLICE)
PAAN (KAPOW)
YEAH! GOT HIM!
YAHOO!
THE SHEER IMPACT OF THIS EXPERIENCE...
I CAN'T BELIEVE...
...THIS IS ALL A GAME.
WHOEVER BUILT THIS IS A GENIUS.
...ENTRANCED COUNTLESS GAMERS.

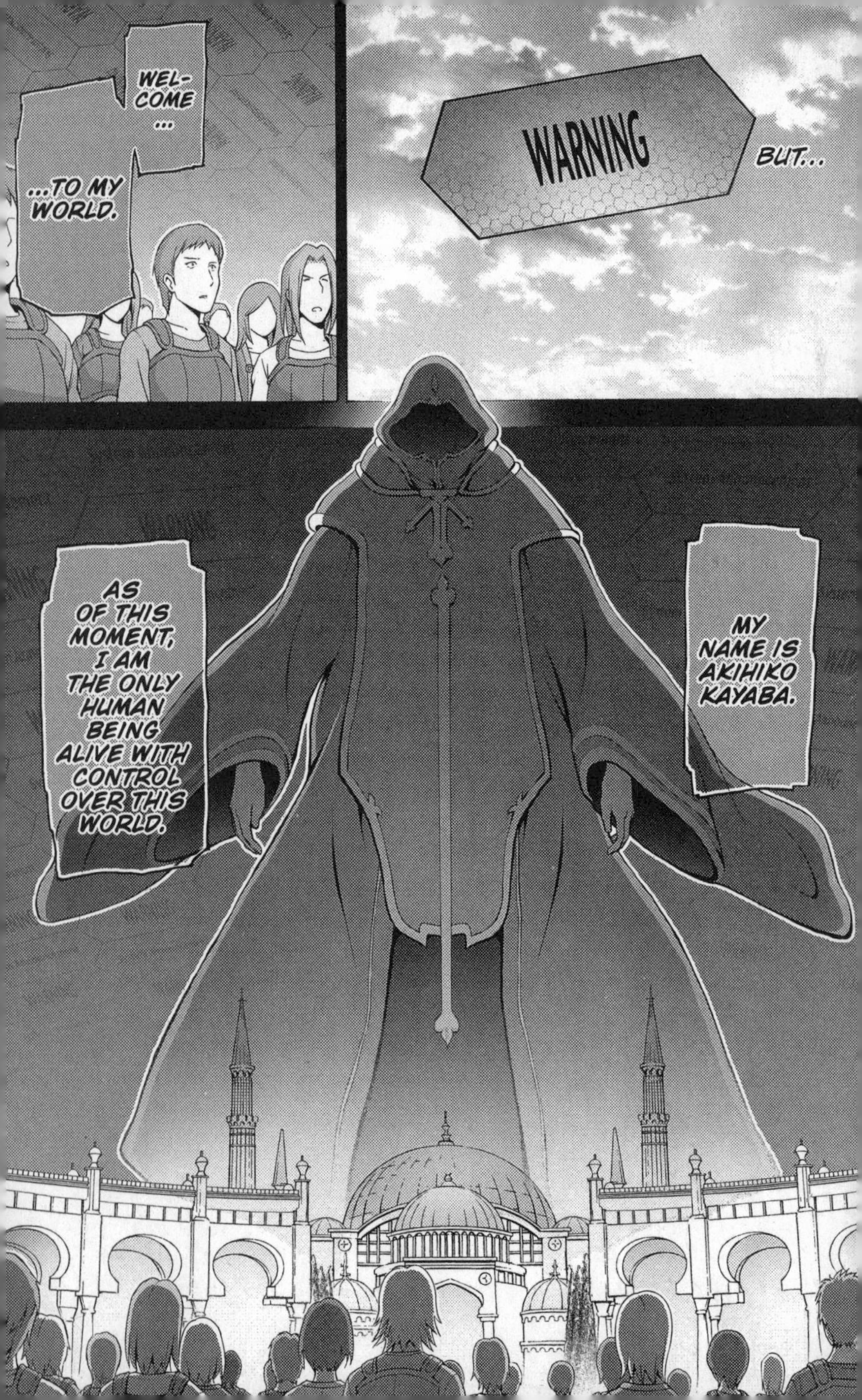
BUT...
WARNING
WEL-COME...
...TO MY WORLD.
MY NAME IS AKIHIKO KAYABA.
AS OF THIS MOMENT, I AM THE ONLY HUMAN BEING ALIVE WITH CONTROL OVER THIS WORLD.

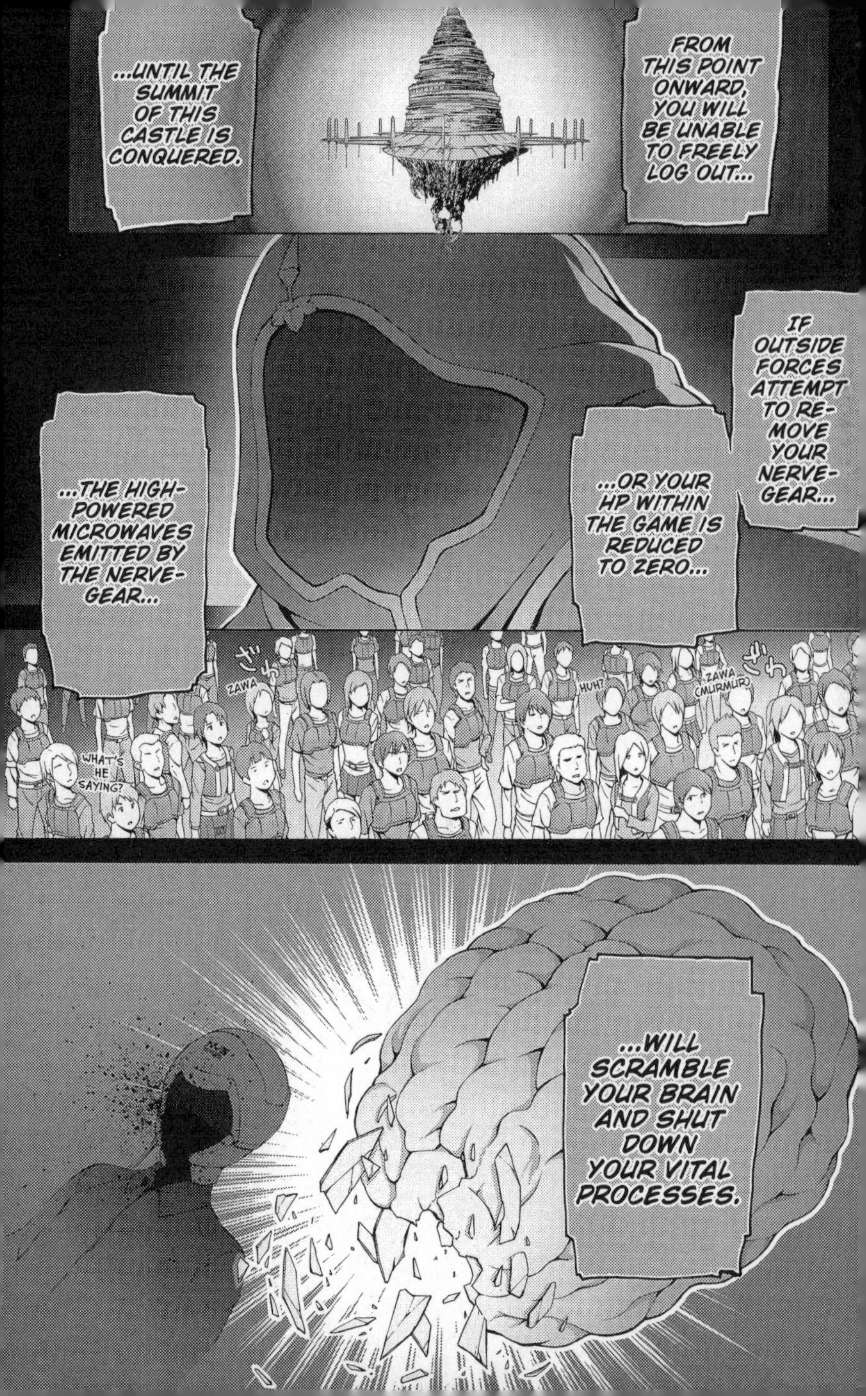
FROM THIS POINT ONWARD, YOU WILL BE UNABLE TO FREELY LOG OUT...
...UNTIL THE SUMMIT OF THIS CASTLE IS CONQUERED.
IF OUTSIDE FORCES ATTEMPT TO RE-MOVE YOUR NERVE-GEAR...
...OR YOUR HP WITHIN THE GAME IS REDUCED TO ZERO...
...THE HIGH-POWERED MICROWAVES EMITTED BY THE NERVE-GEAR...
ZAWA (MURMUR)
HUH?
ZAWA
WHAT'S HE SAYING?
...WILL SCRAMBLE YOUR BRAIN AND SHUT DOWN YOUR VITAL PROCESSES.

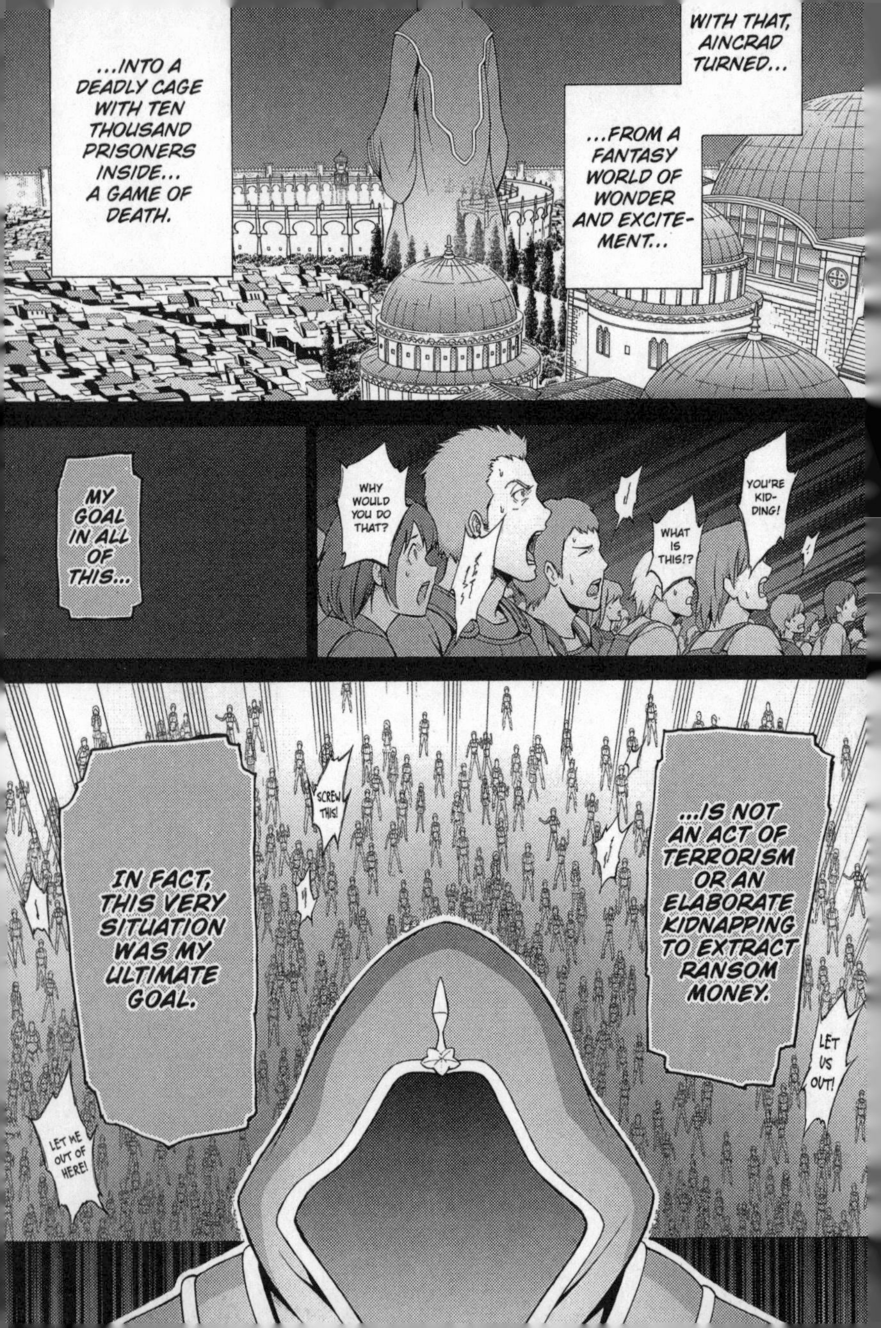
WITH THAT, AINCRAD TURNED...
...FROM A FANTASY WORLD OF WONDER AND EXCITEMENT...
...INTO A DEADLY CAGE WITH TEN THOUSAND PRISONERS INSIDE... A GAME OF DEATH.
YOU'RE KID-DING!
WHAT IS THIS!?
WHY WOULD YOU DO THAT?
MY GOAL IN ALL OF THIS...
...IS NOT AN ACT OF TERRORISM OR AN ELABORATE KIDNAPPING TO EXTRACT RANSOM MONEY.
LET US OUT!
SCREW THIS!
IN FACT, THIS VERY SITUATION WAS MY ULTIMATE GOAL.
LET ME OUT OF HERE!

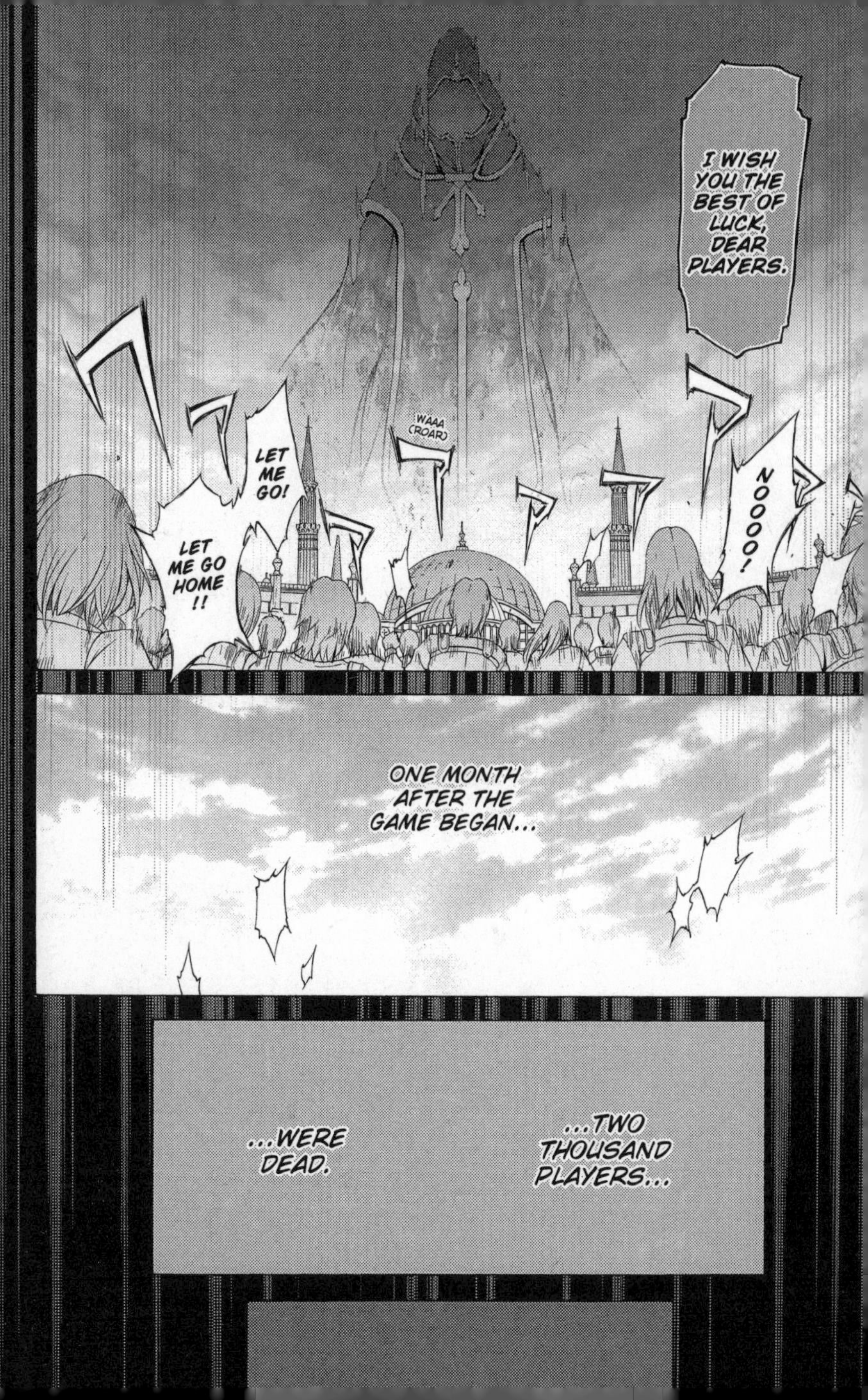
I WISH YOU THE BEST OF LUCK, DEAR PLAYERS.
NOOOOO!
WAAA (ROAR)
LET ME GO!
LET ME GO HOME!!
ONE MONTH AFTER THE GAME BEGAN...
...TWO THOUSAND PLAYERS...
...WERE DEAD.

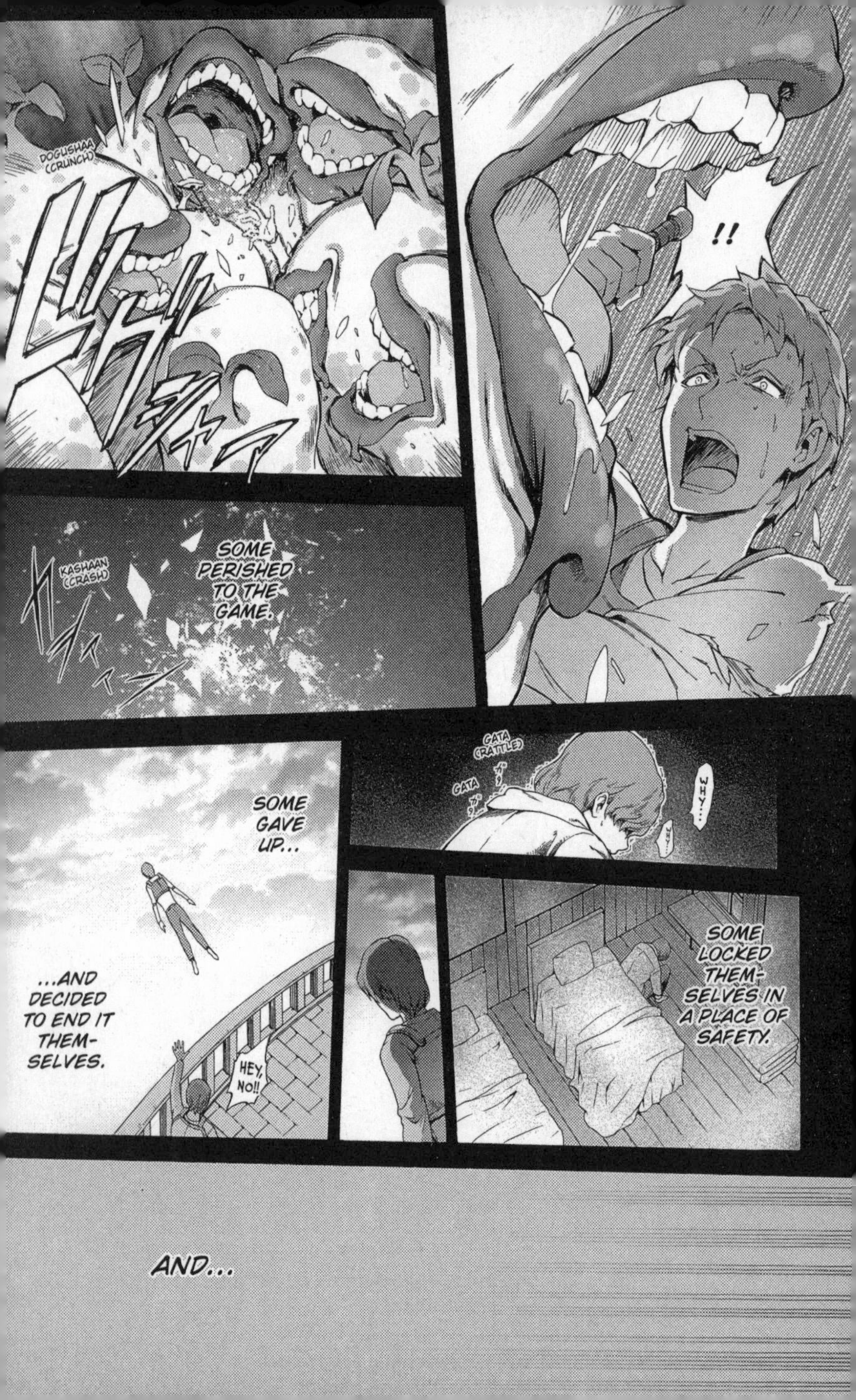
!!
DOGUSHAA (CRUNCH)
KASHAAN (CRASH)
SOME PERISHED TO THE GAME.
GATA (RATTLE)
GATA
WHY...
WHY...
SOME LOCKED THEM-SELVES IN A PLACE OF SAFETY.
SOME GAVE UP...
...AND DECIDED TO END IT THEM-SELVES.
HEY, NO!!
AND...

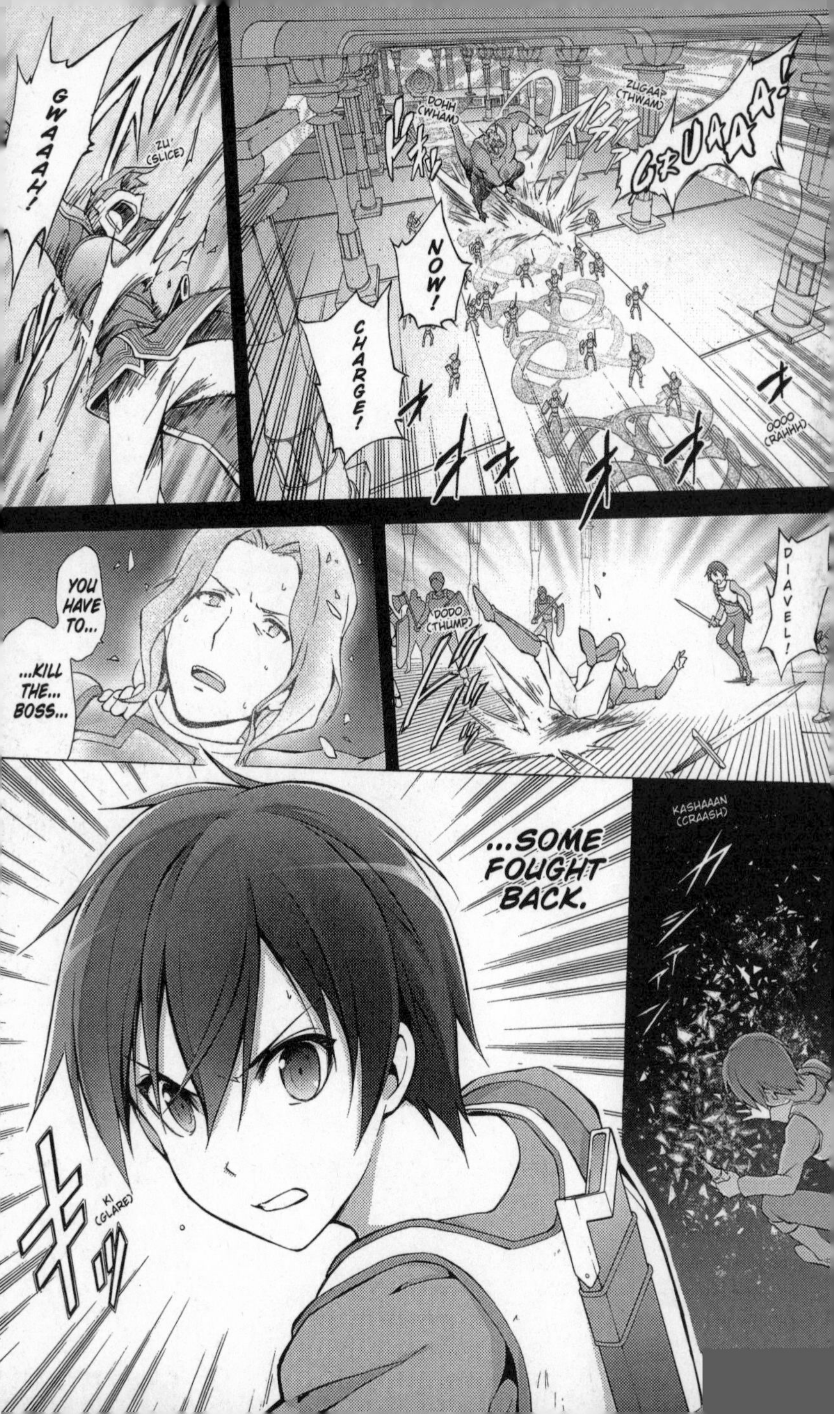
GRUAAA!
ZUGAAP (THWAM)
DOHH (WHAM)
NOW!
CHARGE!
OOOO (RAHHH)
ZU' (SLICE)
GWAAAH!
DIAVEL!
DODO (THUMP)
YOU HAVE TO...
...KILL THE... BOSS...
KASHAAAN (CRAASH)
...SOME FOUGHT BACK.
KI (GLARE)

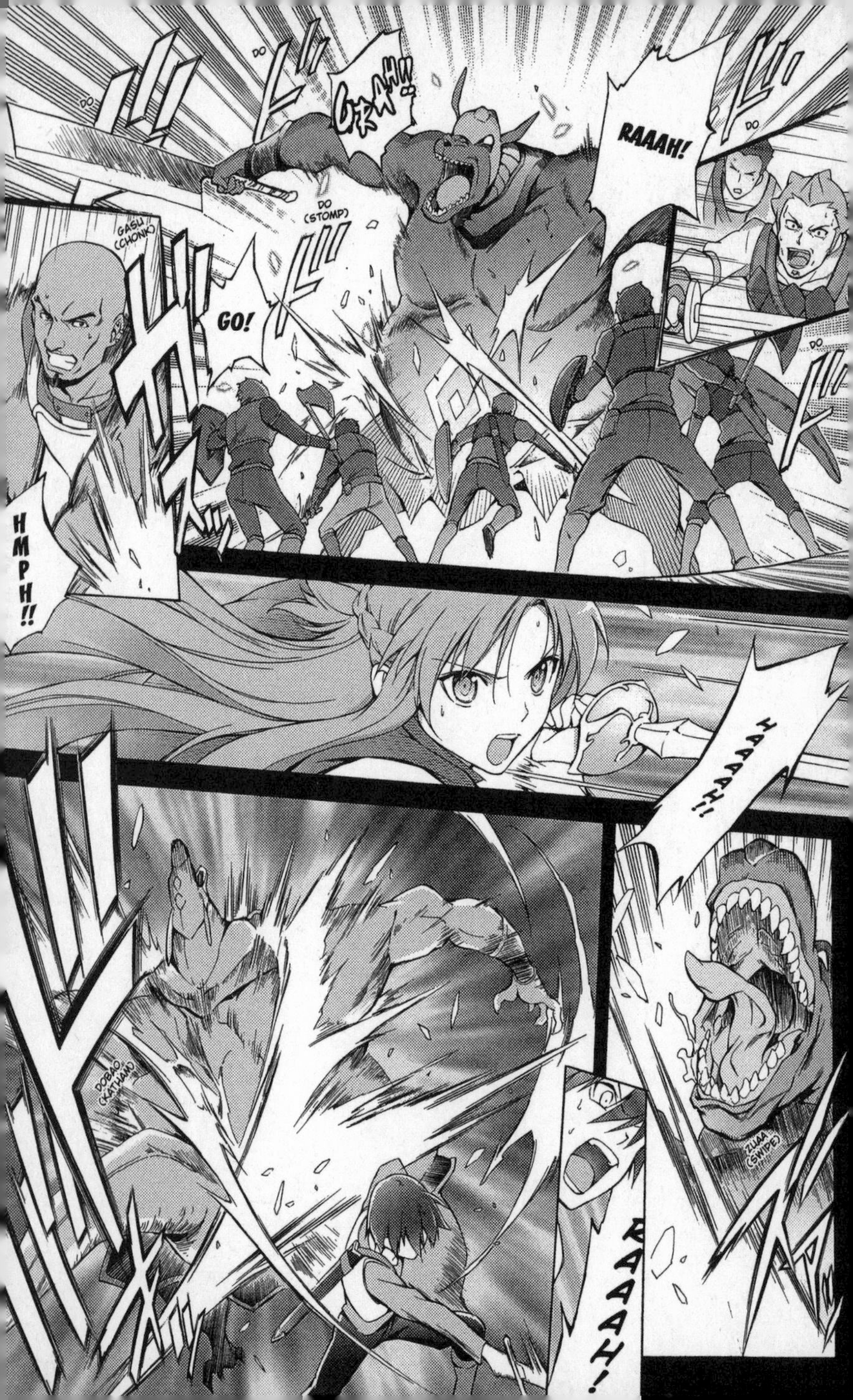
DO
RAAAH!
DO
GRAH!!
DO
DO
DO (STOMP)
GASU (CHONK)
GO!
HMPH!!
HAAAAH!!
ZUAA (SWIPE)
RAAAAH!
DOBAO (KATHAM)

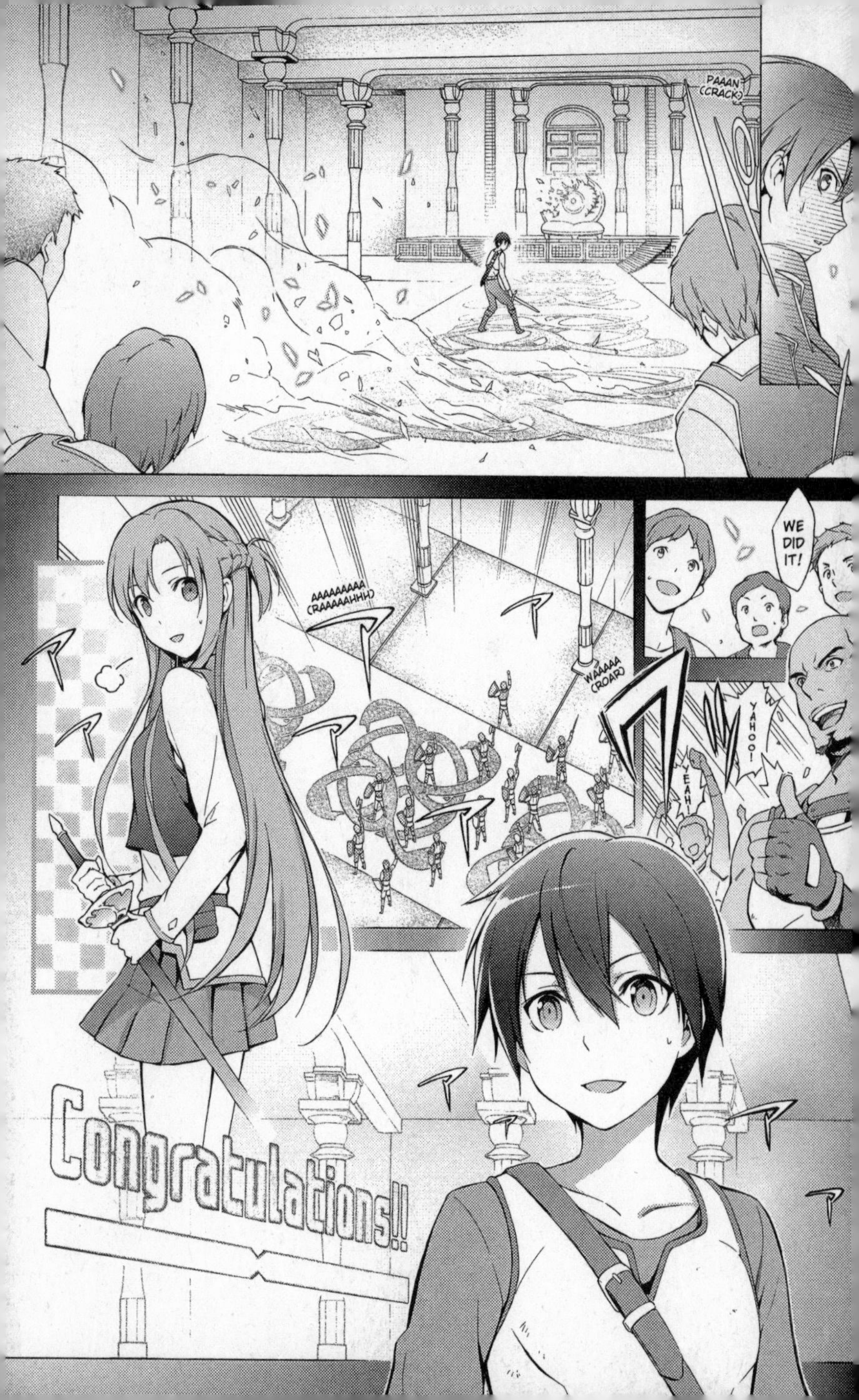
PAAAN (CRACK)
WE DID IT!
YAHOO!
YEAH!
AAAAAAAAA (RAAAAAHHH)
WAAAAA (ROAR)
Congratulations!!

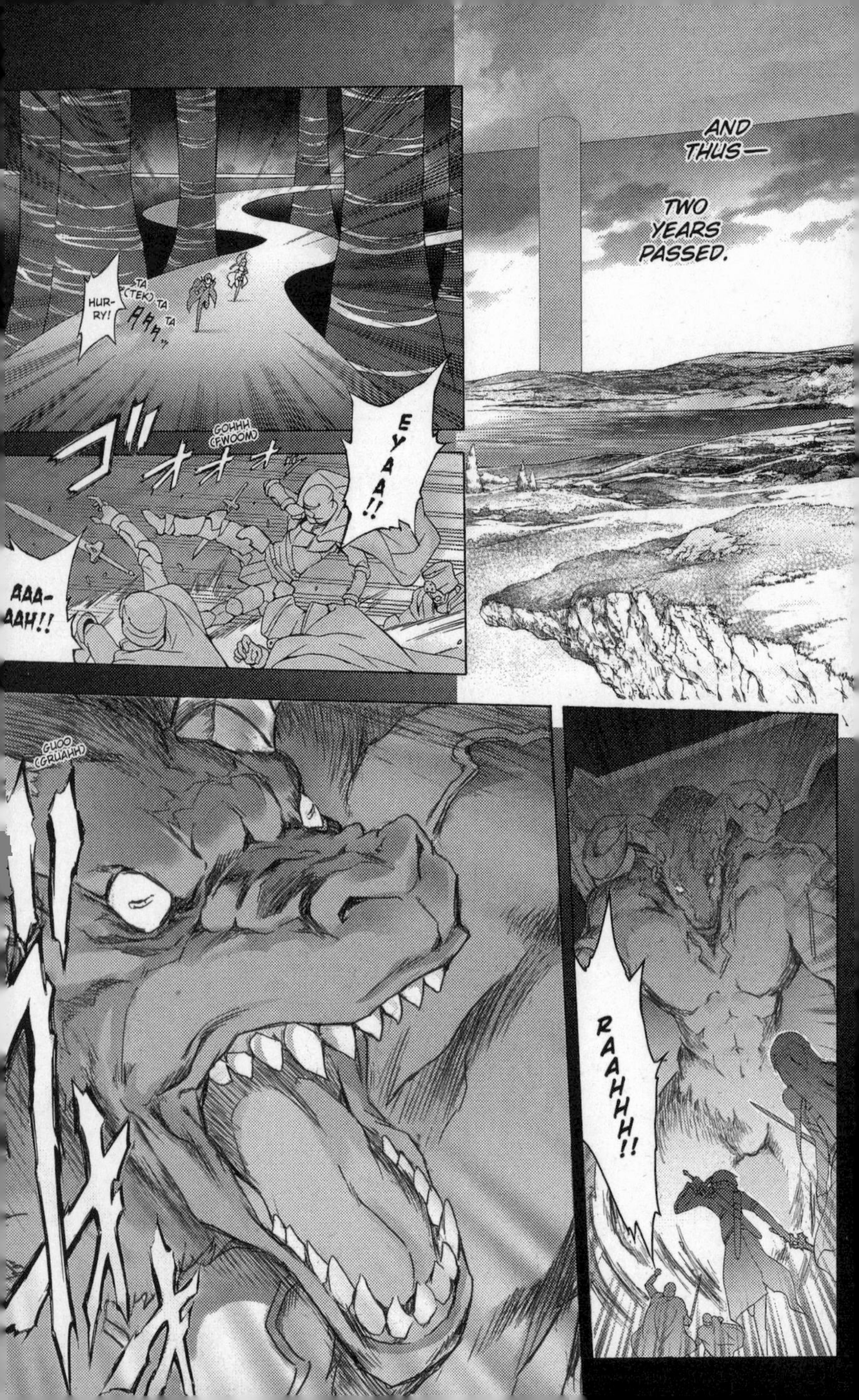
AND THUS—
TWO YEARS PASSED.
HURRY!
TA (TEK) TA TA
EYAAA!!
GOHHH (FWOOM)
AAA-AAH!!
RAAHHH!!
GUOO (GRUAHH)

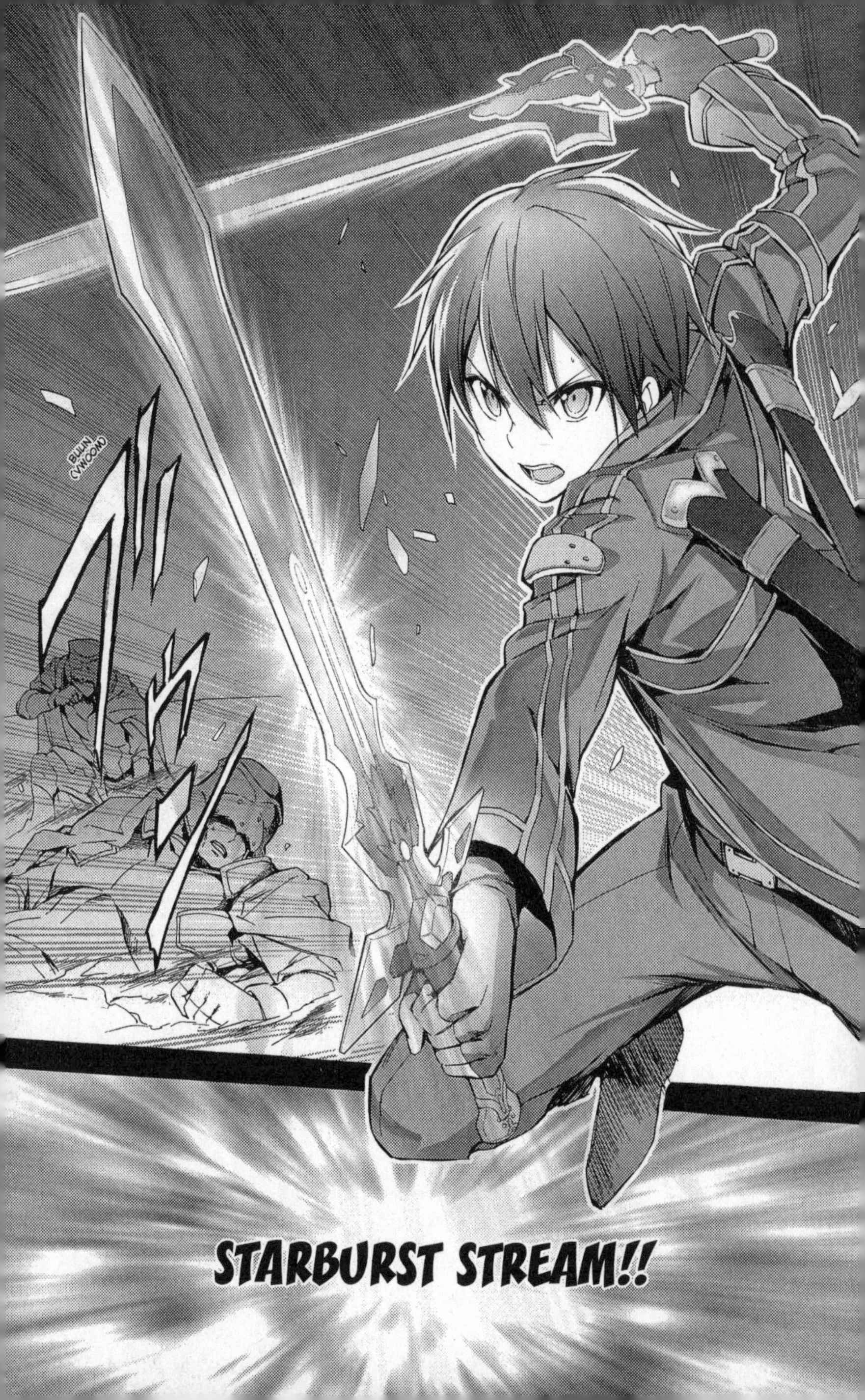
BUUN (VWOOM)
STARBURST STREAM!!

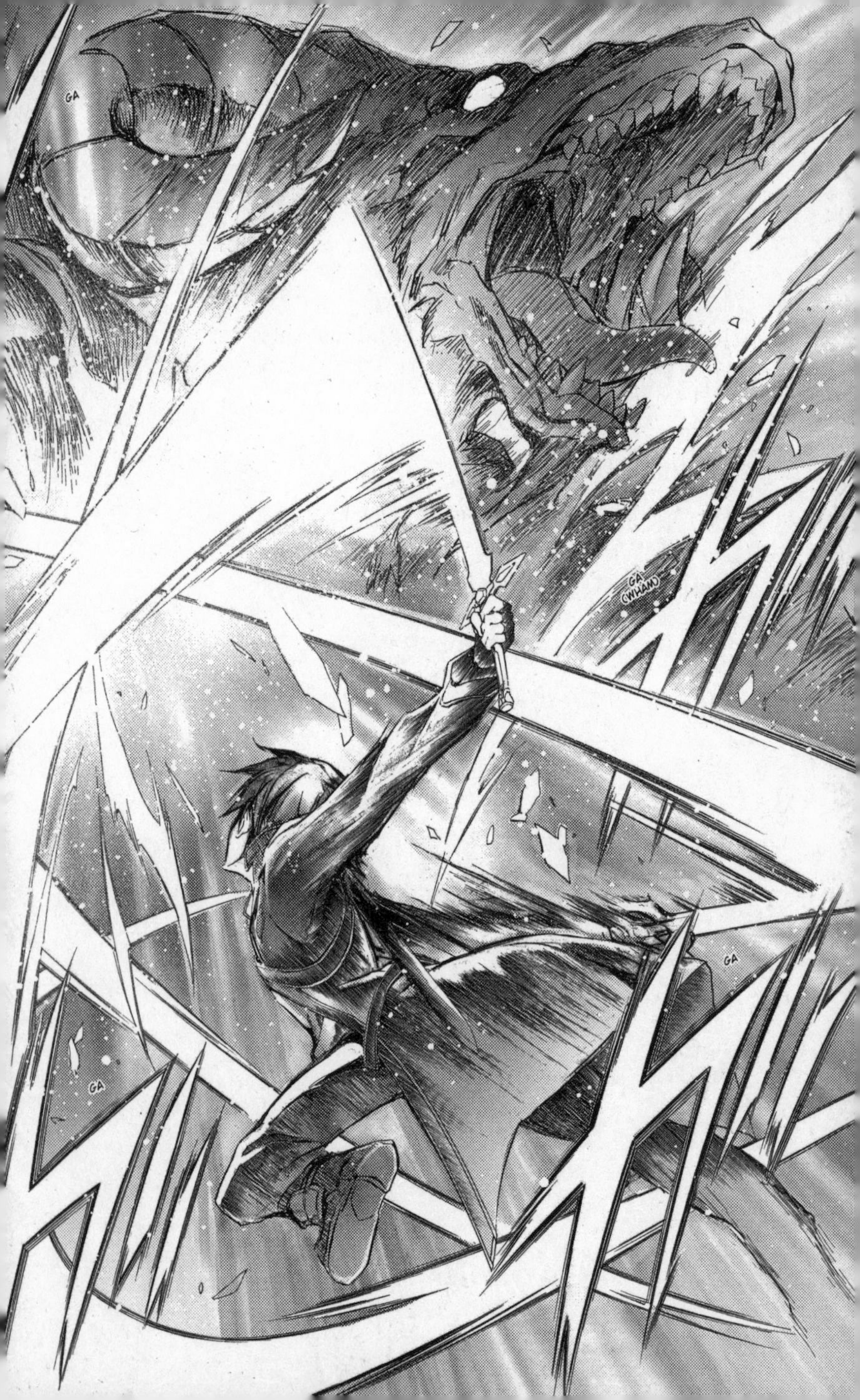
GA
GA
(WHAM)
GA
GA

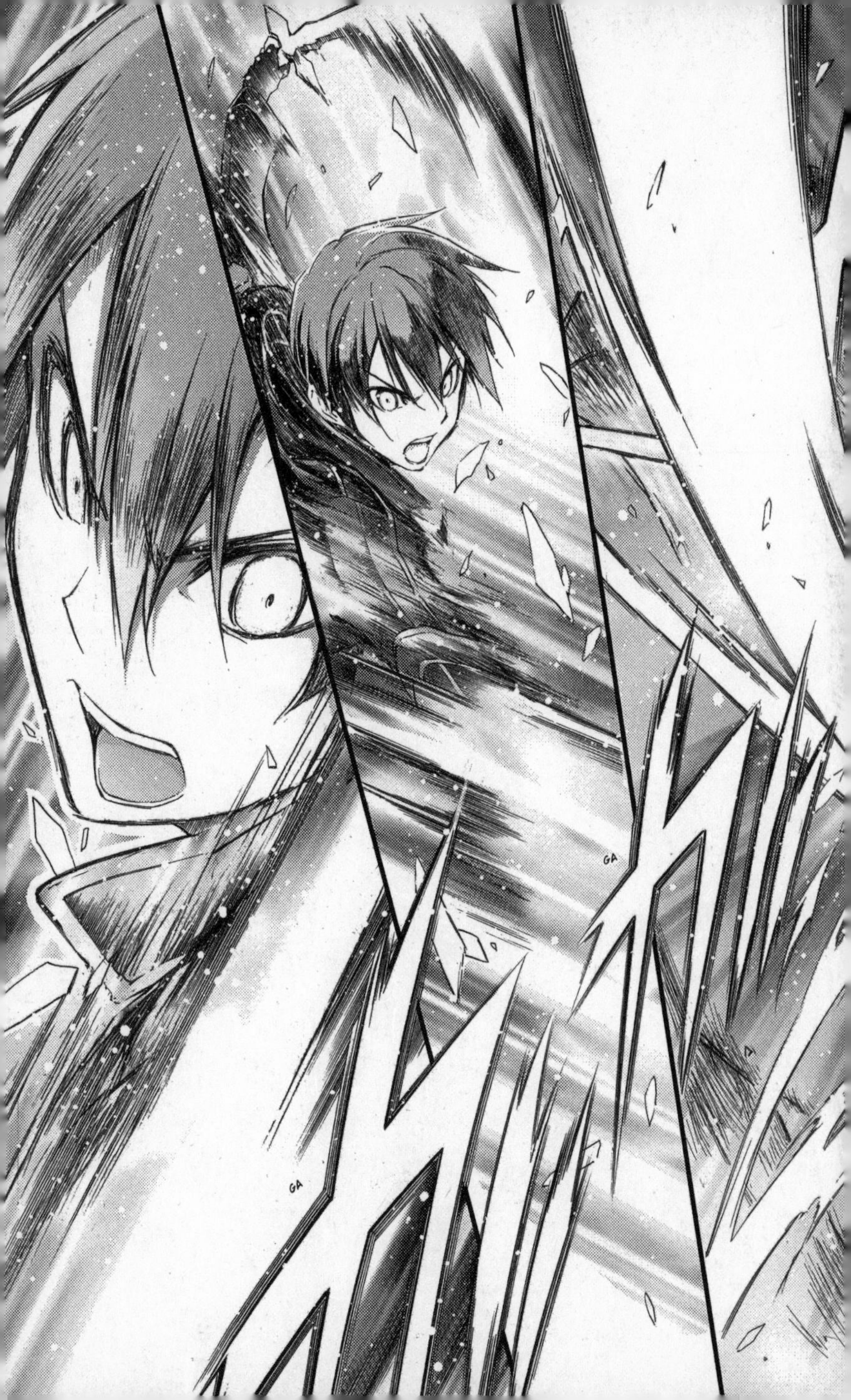
GA
GA

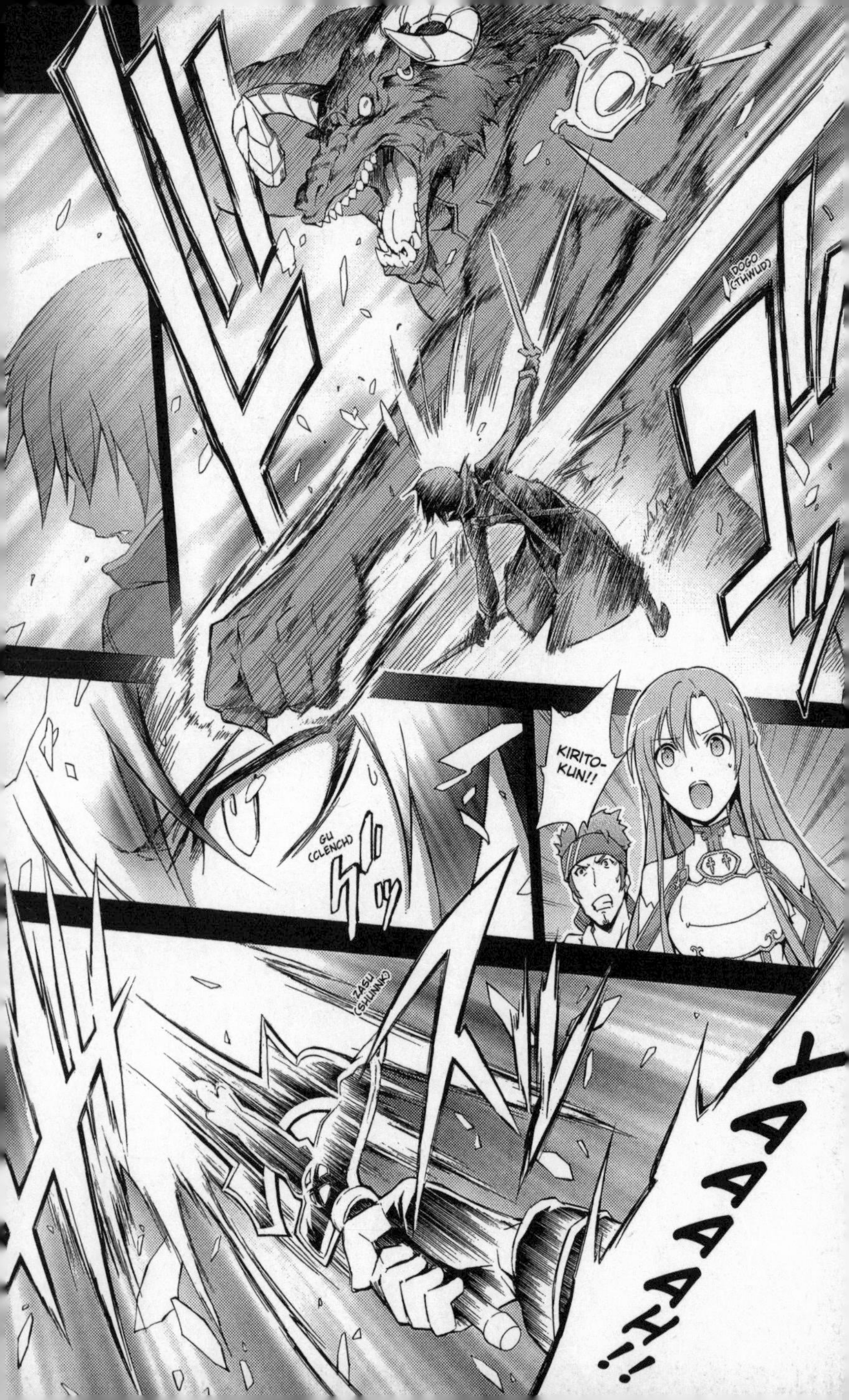
DOGO (THWUD)
KIRITO-KUN!!
GU (CLENCH)
ZASU (SHUNK)
YAAAAAH!!

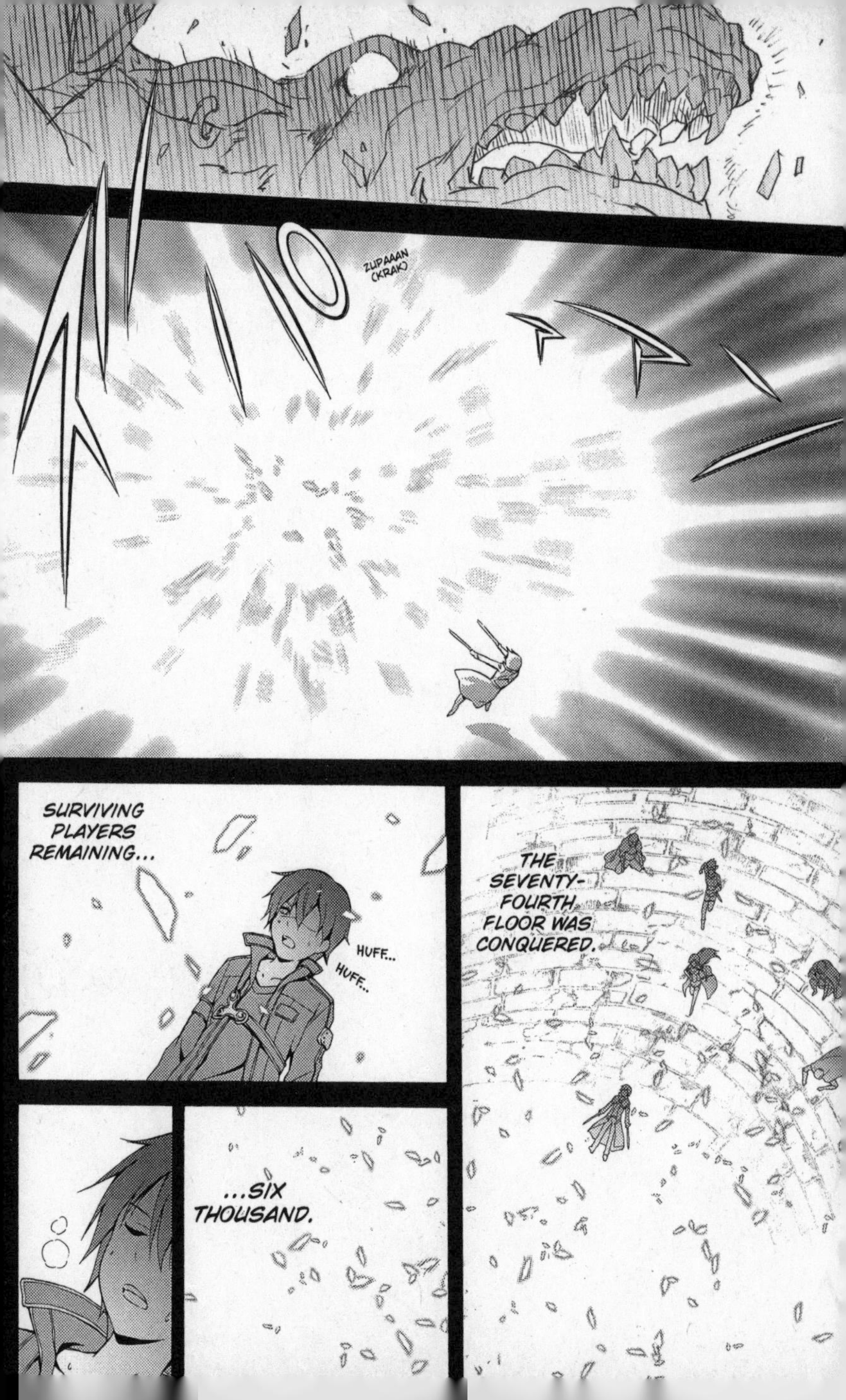
ZUPAAAN (KRAK)
THE SEVENTY-FOURTH FLOOR WAS CONQUERED.
SURVIVING PLAYERS REMAINING...
HUFF... HUFF...
...SIX THOUSAND.

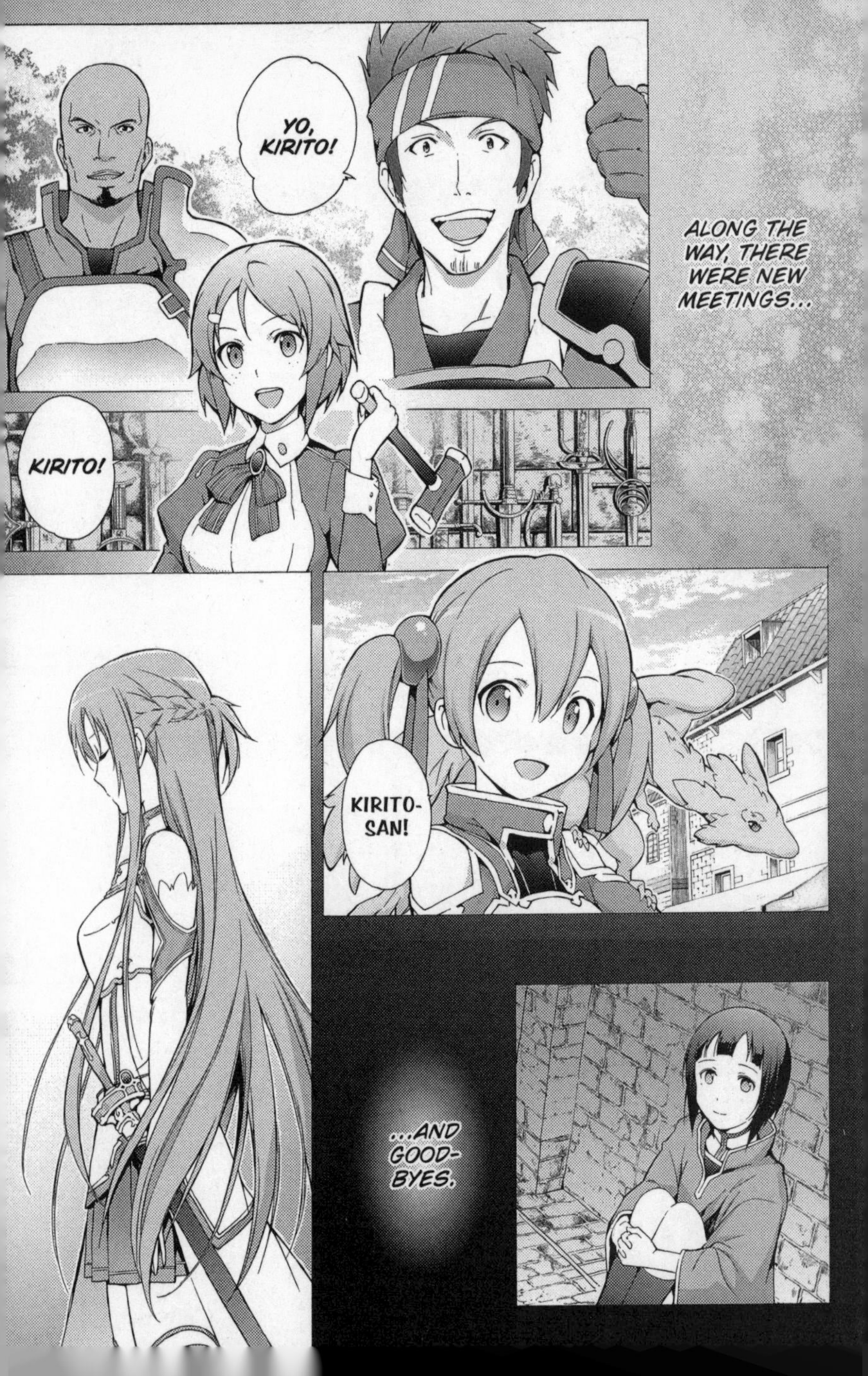
ALONG THE WAY, THERE WERE NEW MEETINGS...
YO, KIRITO!
KIRITO!
KIRITO-SAN!
...AND GOOD-BYES.

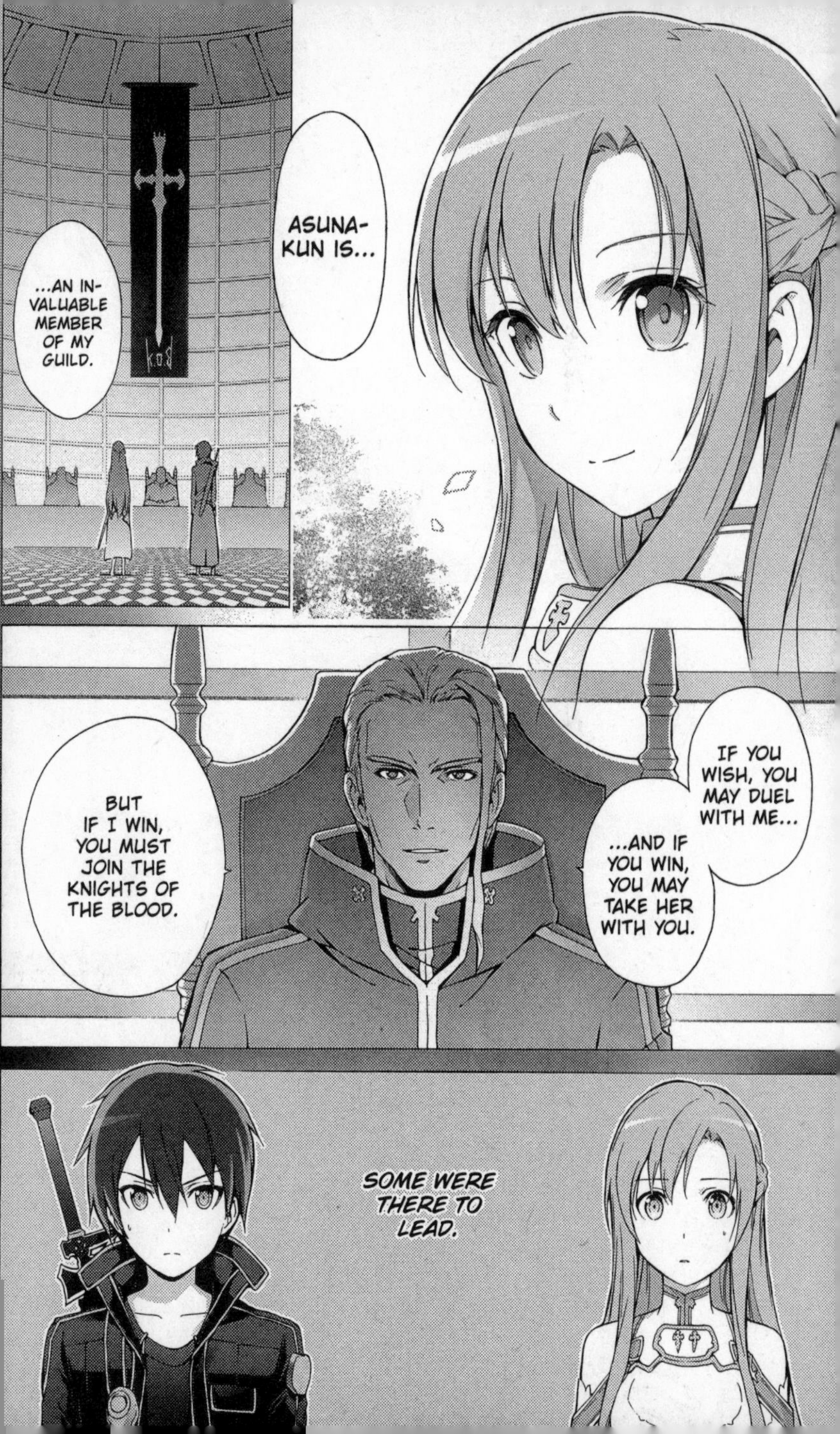
ASUNA-KUN IS...
...AN INVALUABLE MEMBER OF MY GUILD.
IF YOU WISH, YOU MAY DUEL WITH ME...
...AND IF YOU WIN, YOU MAY TAKE HER WITH YOU.
BUT IF I WIN, YOU MUST JOIN THE KNIGHTS OF THE BLOOD.
SOME WERE THERE TO LEAD.

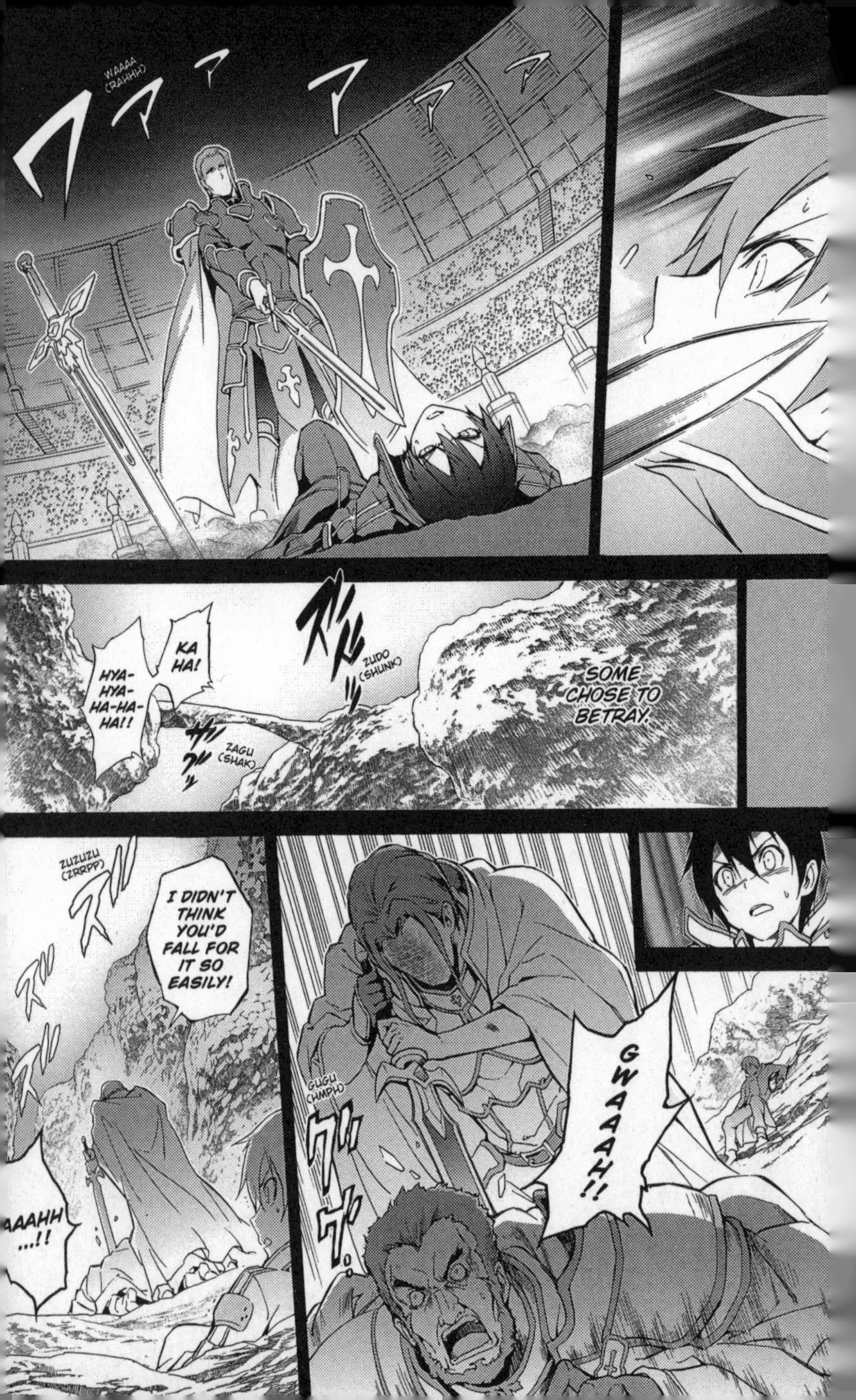
WAAAA (RAHHH)
ZUDO (SHUNK)
SOME CHOSE TO BETRAY.
ZAGU (SHAK)
KA HA!
HYA-HYA-HA-HA!!
GUGU (HMPH)
GWAAAAH!!
ZUZUZU (ZRRPP)
I DIDN'T THINK YOU'D FALL FOR IT SO EASILY!
AAAHH ...!!

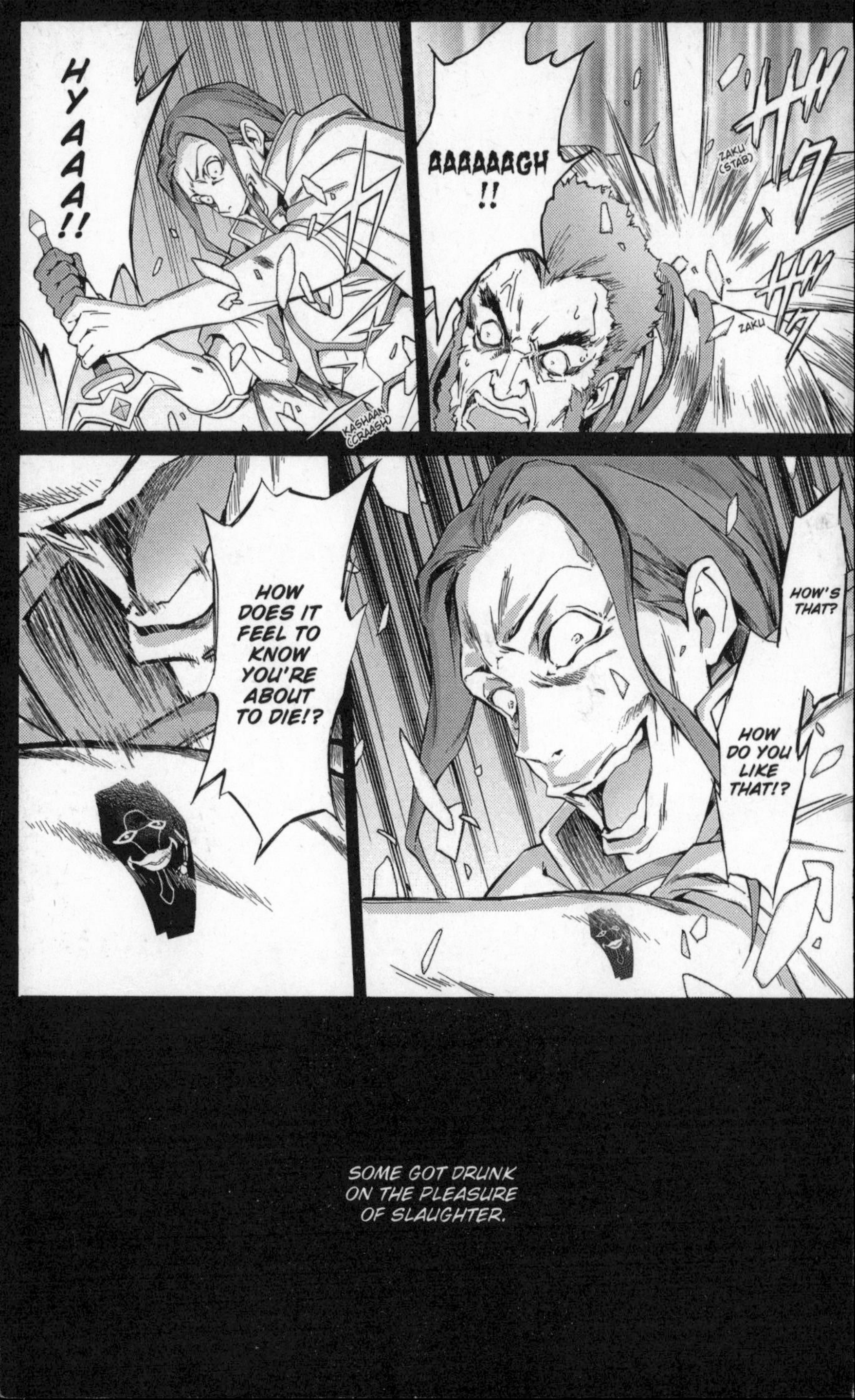
ZAKU (STAB)
ZAKU
AAAAAAGH!!
HYAAAA!!
KASHAAN (CRAASH)
HOW'S THAT?
HOW DO YOU LIKE THAT!?
HOW DOES IT FEEL TO KNOW YOU'RE ABOUT TO DIE!?

SOME GOT DRUNK ON THE PLEASURE OF SLAUGHTER.

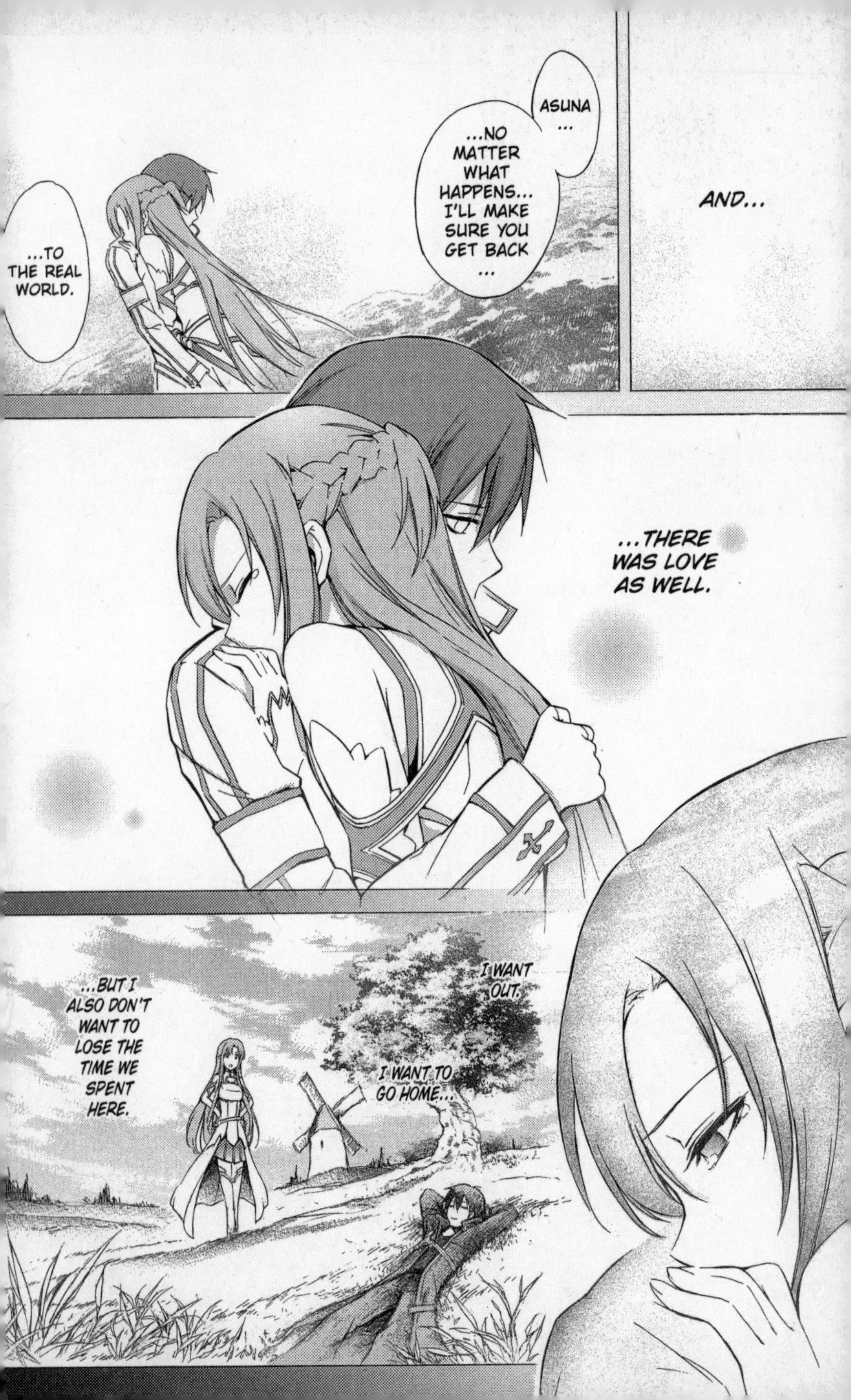
AND...
ASUNA...
...NO MATTER WHAT HAPPENS... I'LL MAKE SURE YOU GET BACK...
...TO THE REAL WORLD.
...THERE WAS LOVE AS WELL.
I WANT OUT.
I WANT TO GO HOME...
...BUT I ALSO DON'T WANT TO LOSE THE TIME WE SPENT HERE.

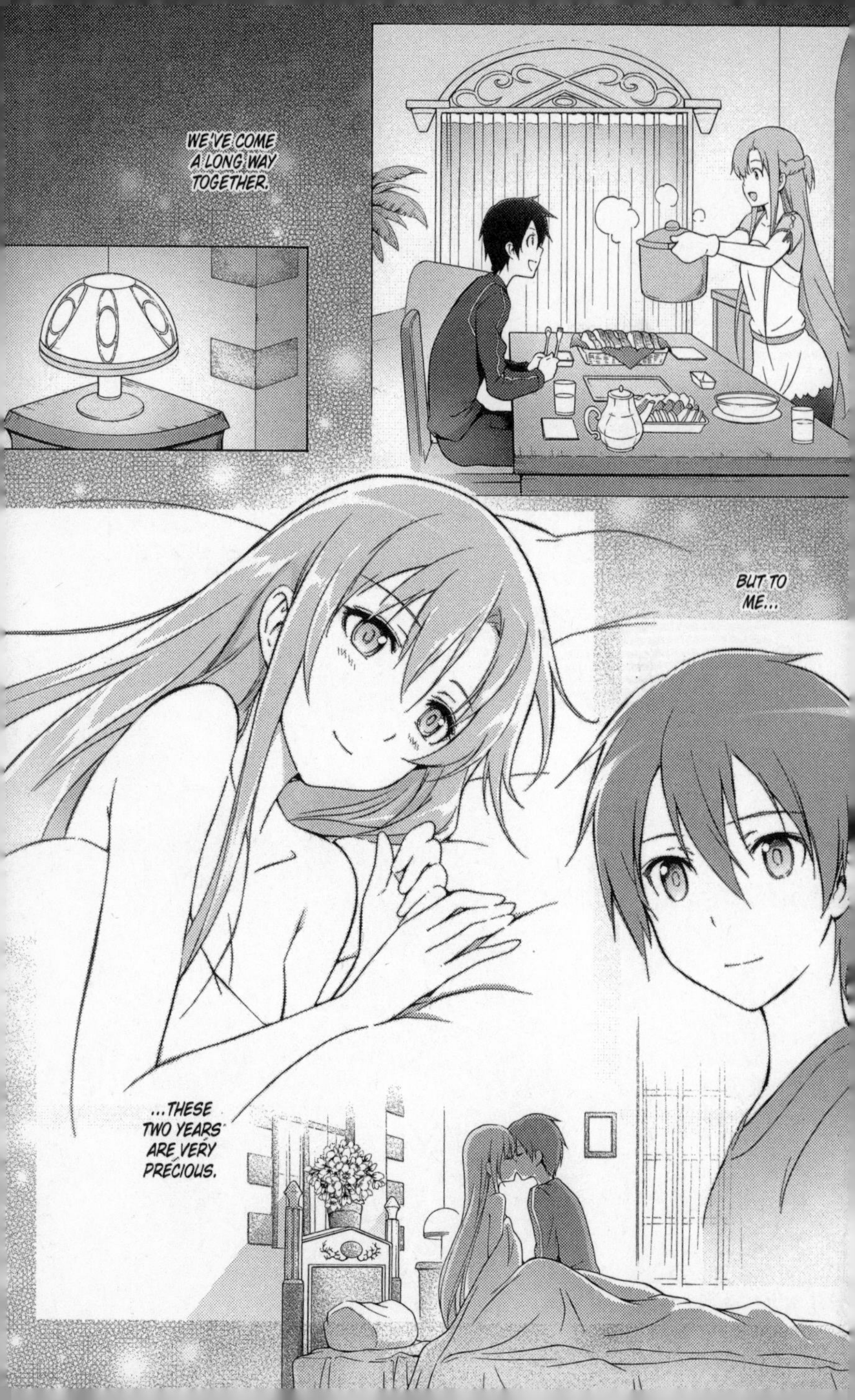
WE'VE COME A LONG WAY TOGETHER.
BUT TO ME...
...THESE TWO YEARS ARE VERY PRECIOUS.

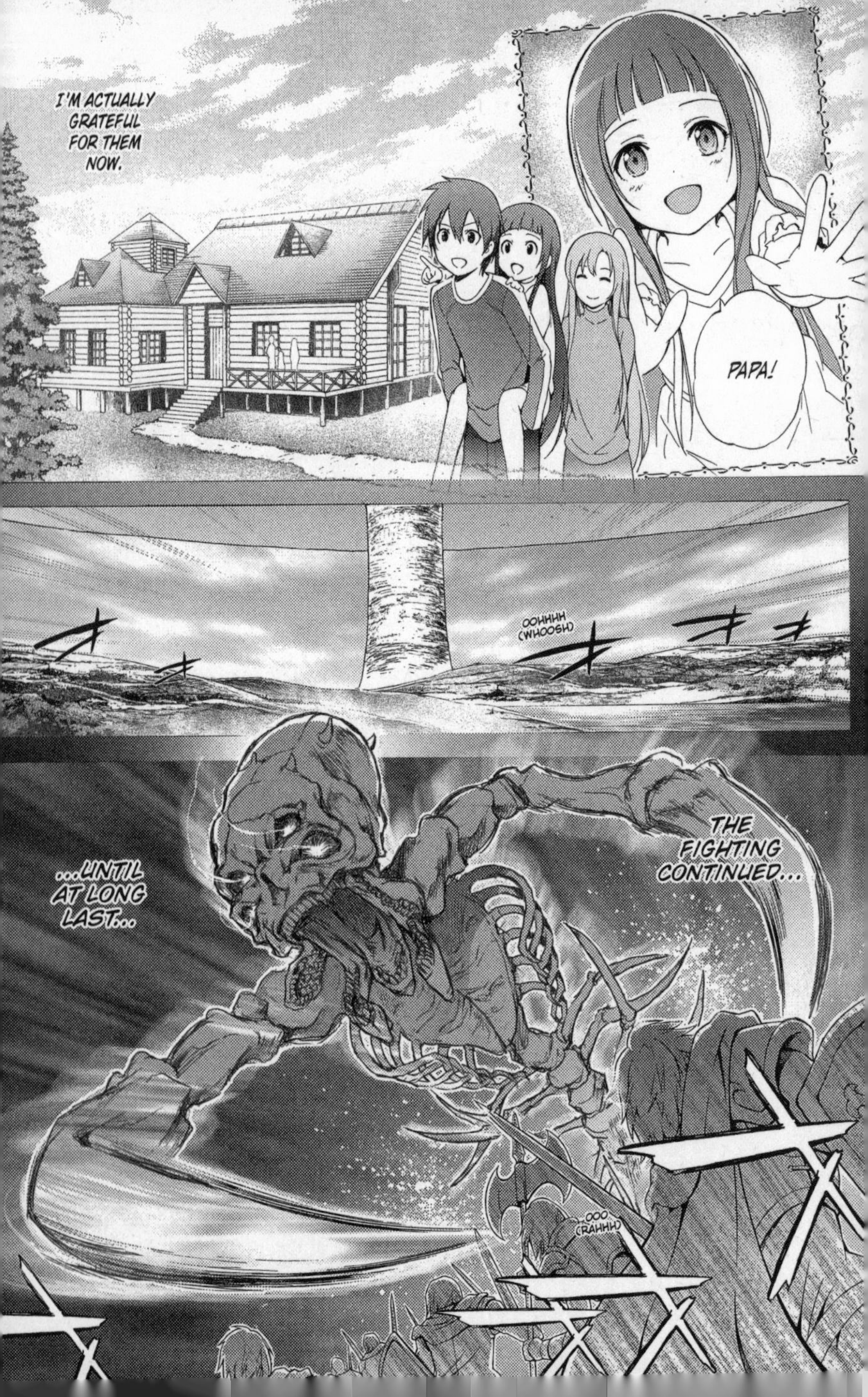
PAPA!
I'M ACTUALLY GRATEFUL FOR THEM NOW.
OOHHHH (WHOOSH)
THE FIGHTING CONTINUED...
...UNTIL AT LONG LAST...
OOO (RAHHH)

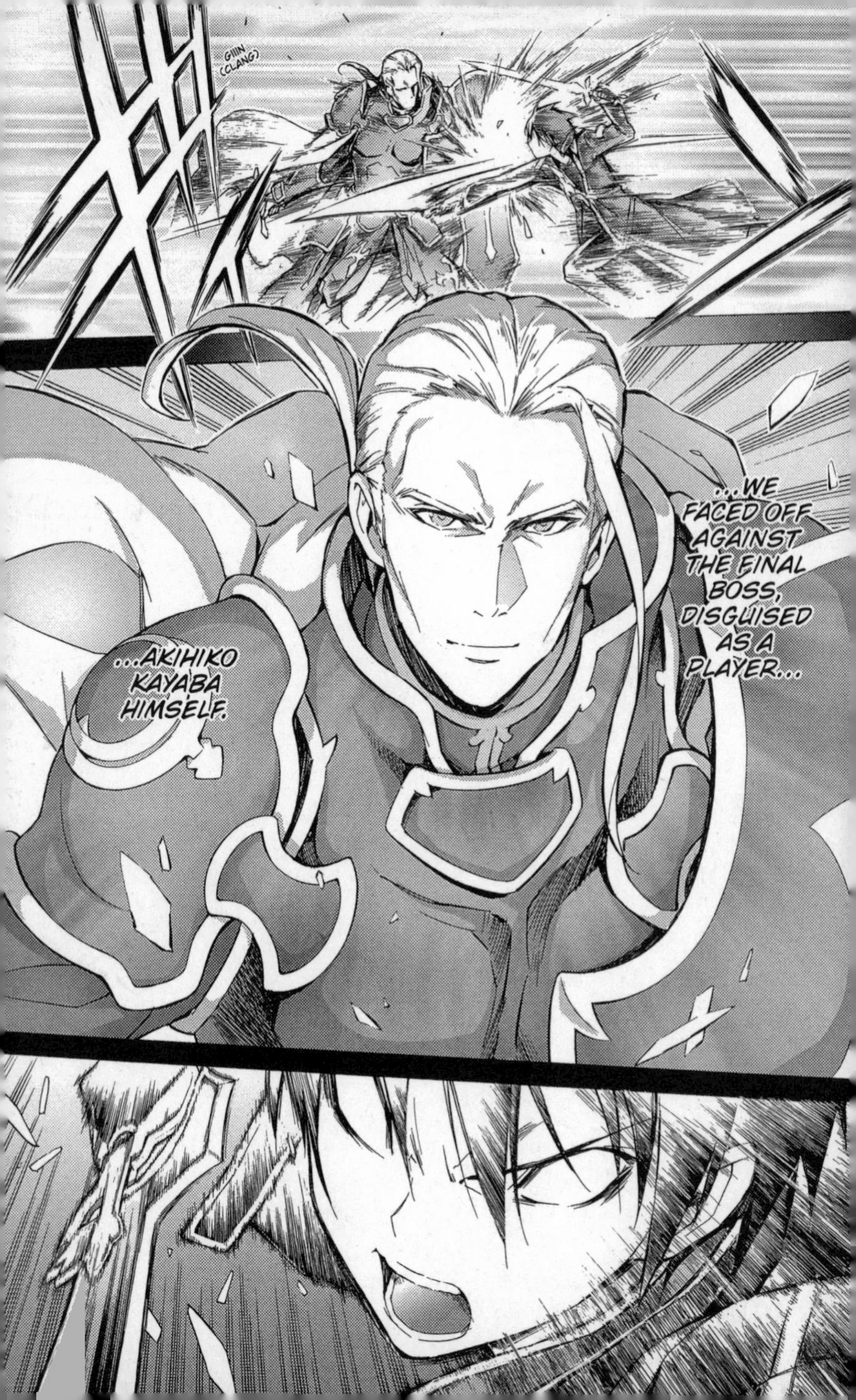
GIIN (CLANG)
...WE FACED OFF AGAINST THE FINAL BOSS, DISGUISED AS A PLAYER...
...AKIHIKO KAYABA HIMSELF.

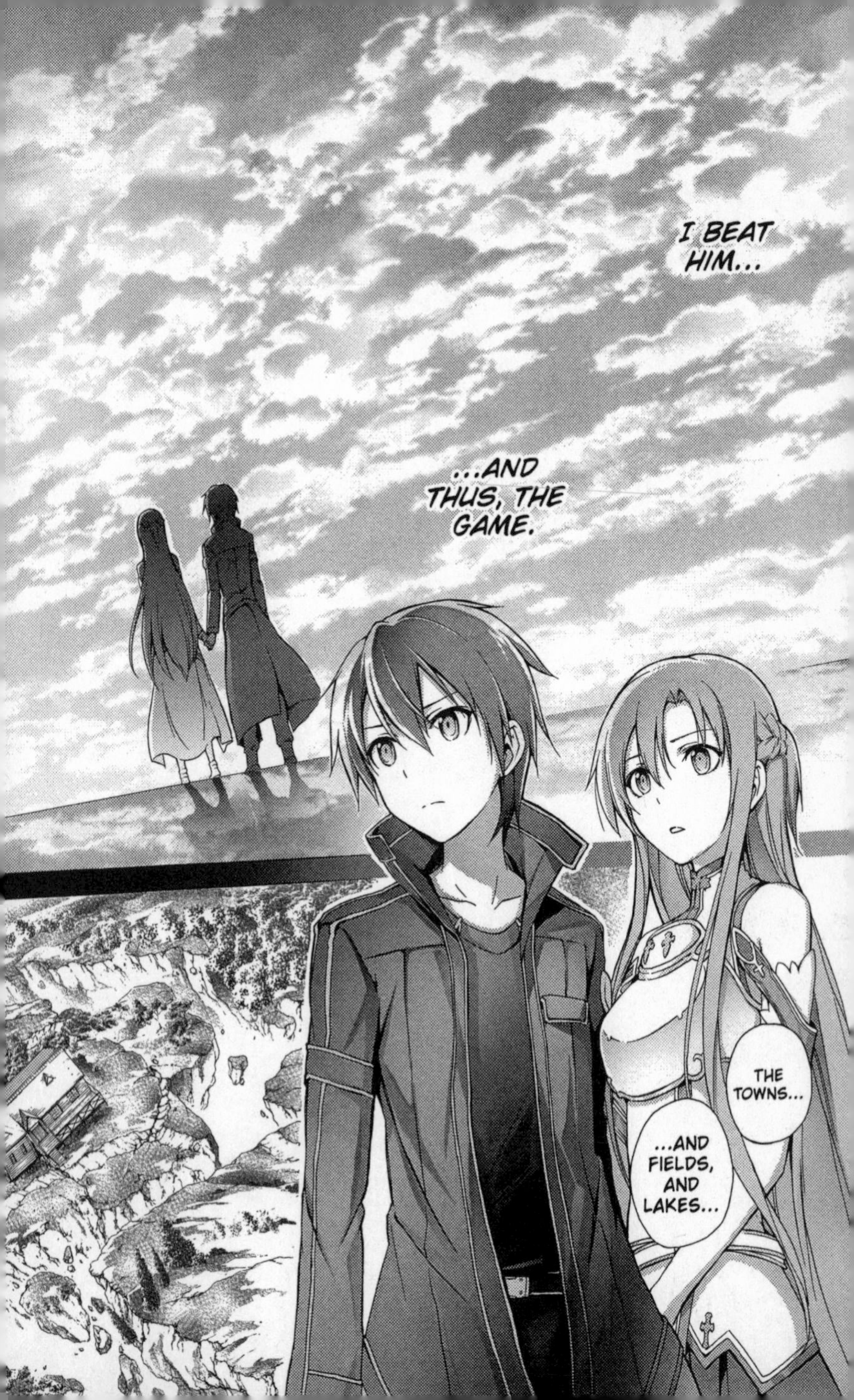
I BEAT HIM...
...AND THUS, THE GAME.
THE TOWNS...
...AND FIELDS, AND LAKES...

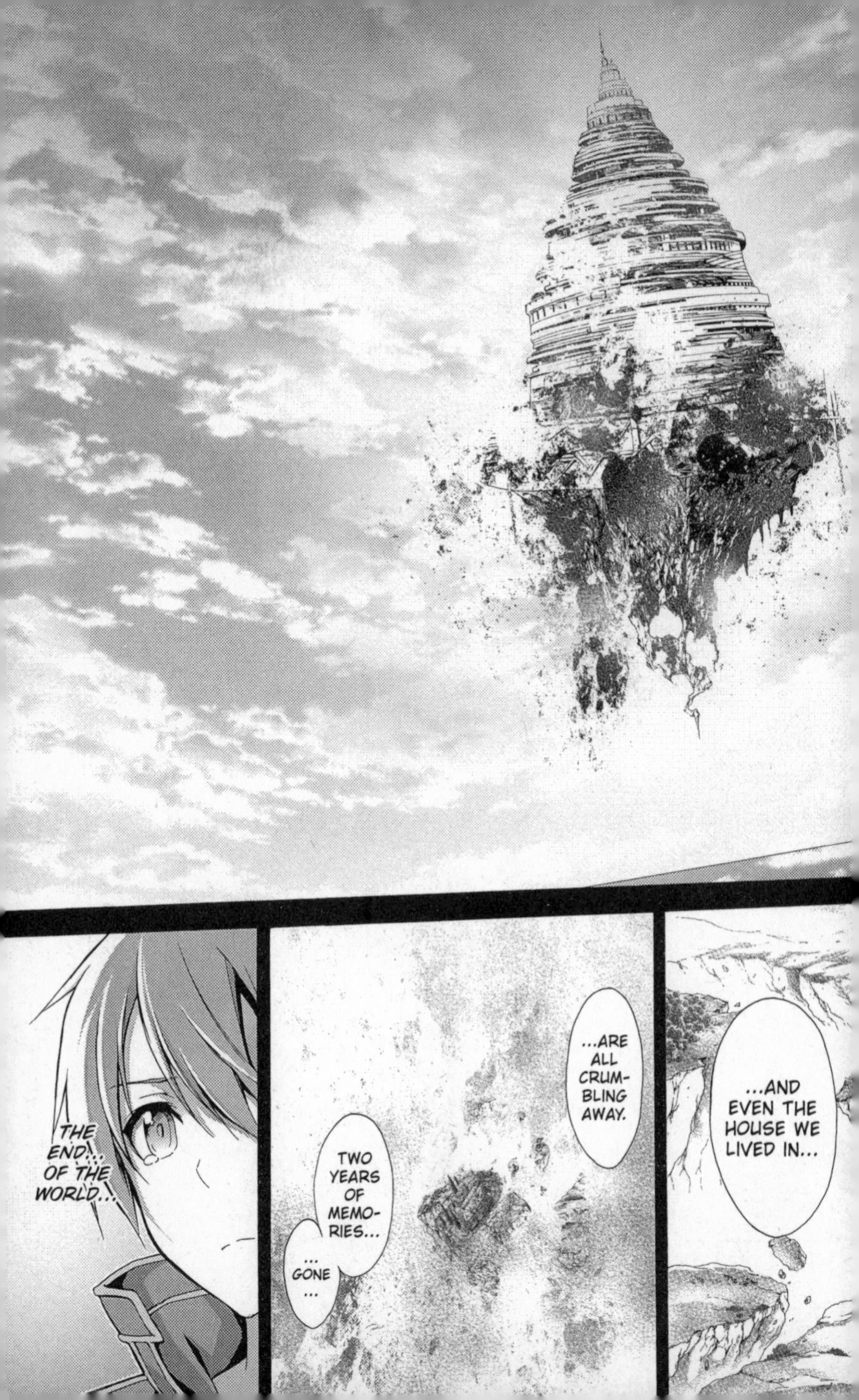
...AND EVEN THE HOUSE WE LIVED IN...
...ARE ALL CRUM-BLING AWAY.
TWO YEARS OF MEMO-RIES...
...GONE...
THE END... OF THE WORLD...

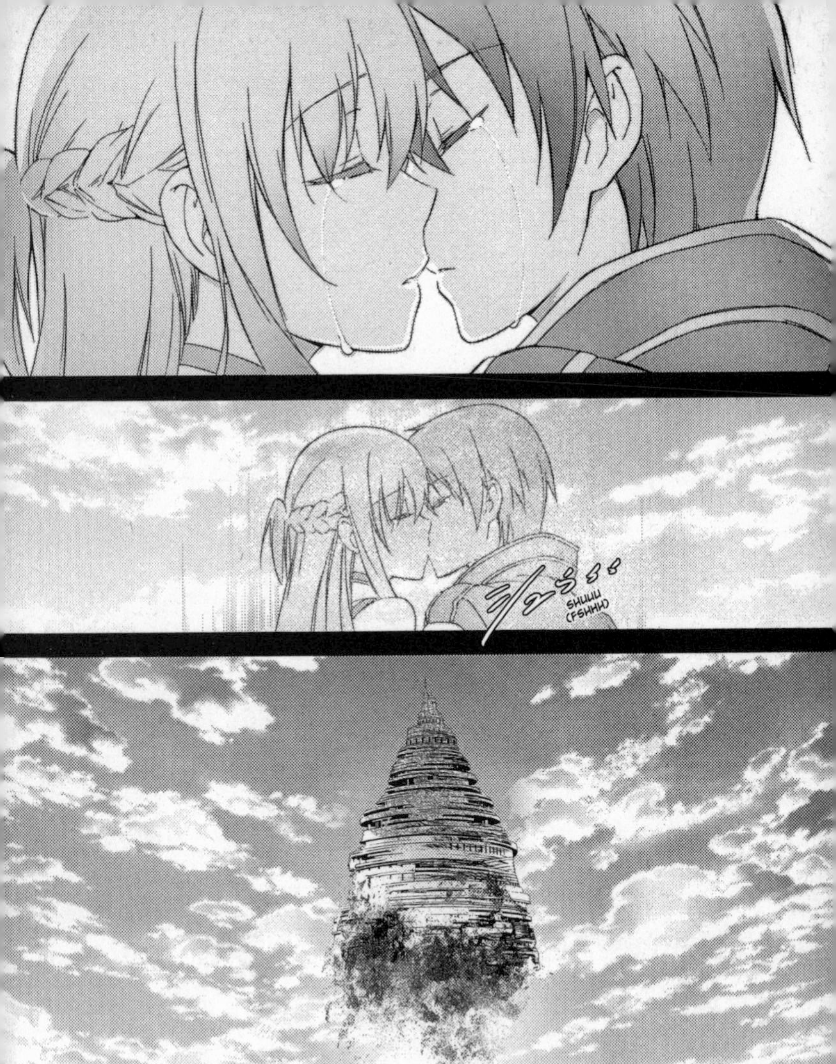
シュゥゥゥ
SHUUU
(FSHHH)
フッ
FU
(FFT)

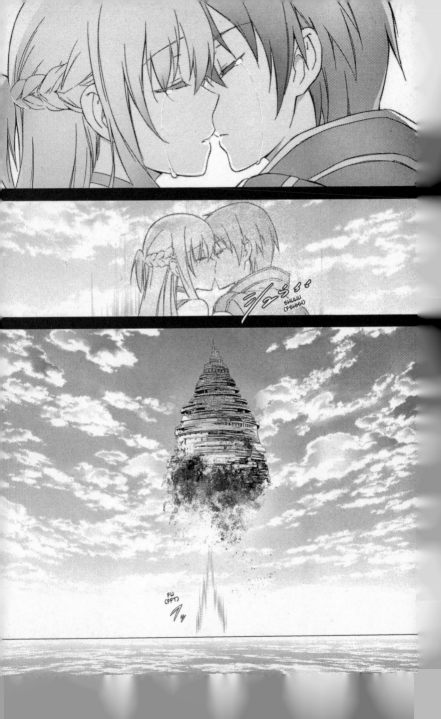

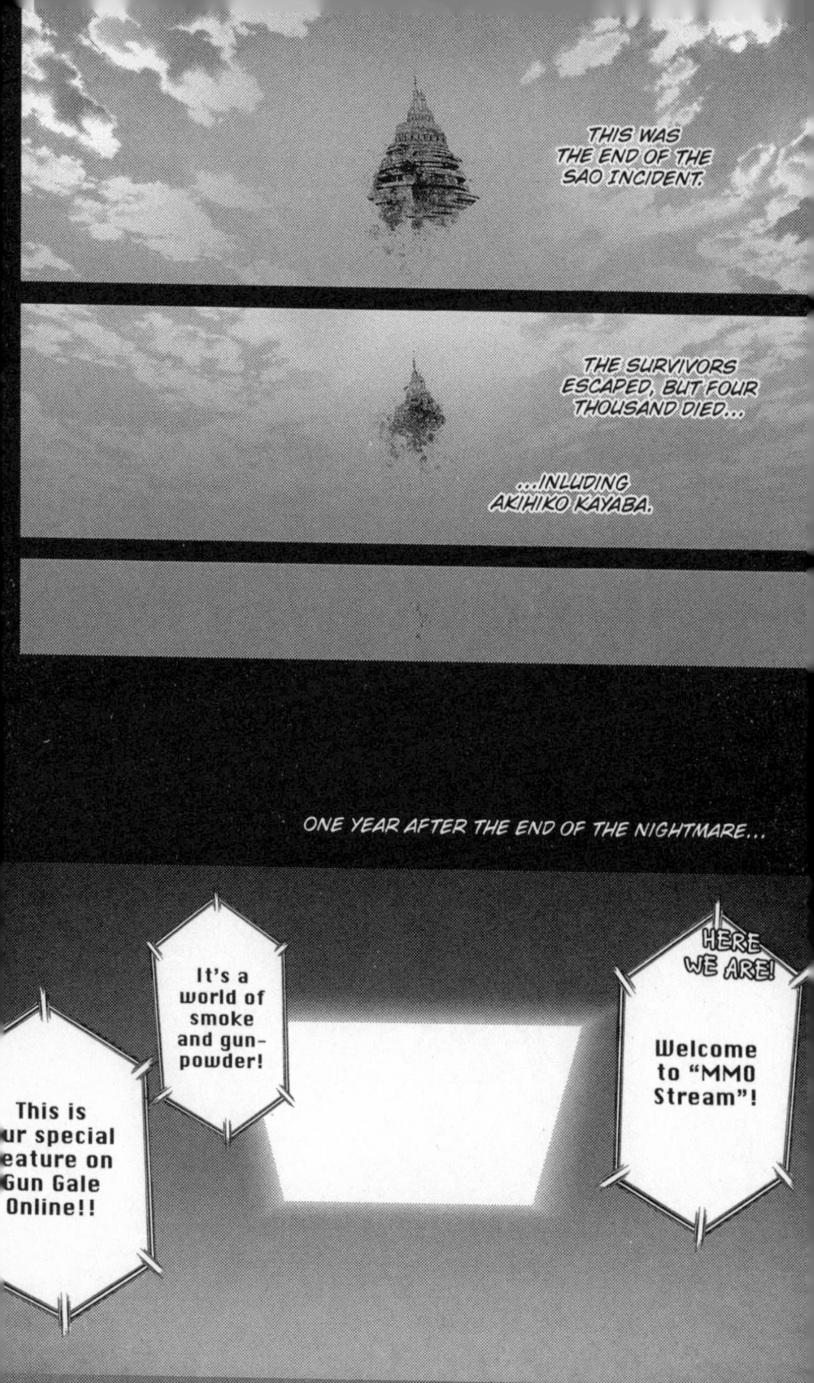
THIS WAS THE END OF THE SAO INCIDENT.
THE SURVIVORS ESCAPED, BUT FOUR THOUSAND DIED...
...INLUDING AKIHIKO KAYABA.
ONE YEAR AFTER THE END OF THE NIGHTMARE...
HERE WE ARE!
Welcome to "MMO Stream"!
It's a world of smoke and gun-powder!
This is ur special eature on Gun Gale Online!!

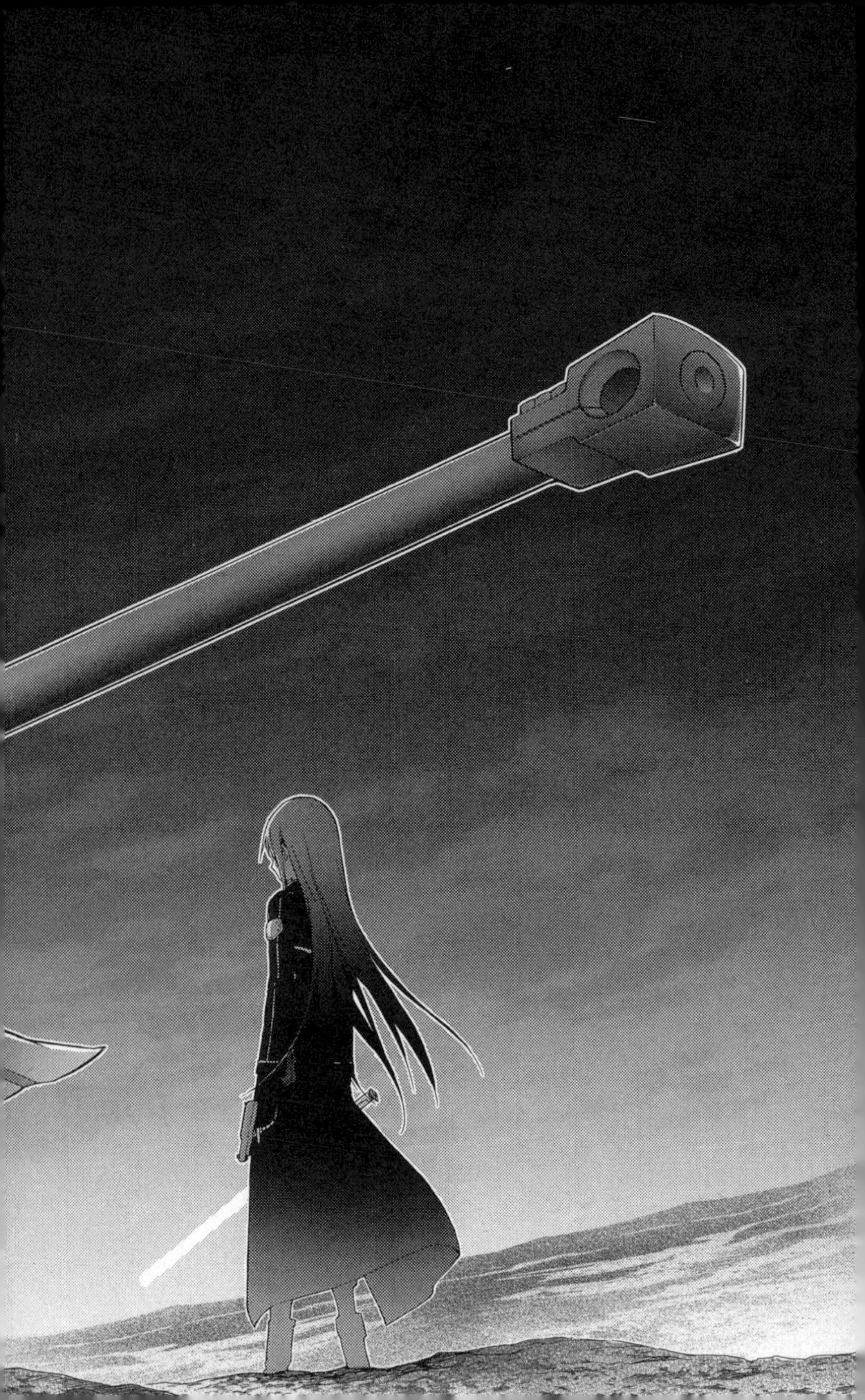

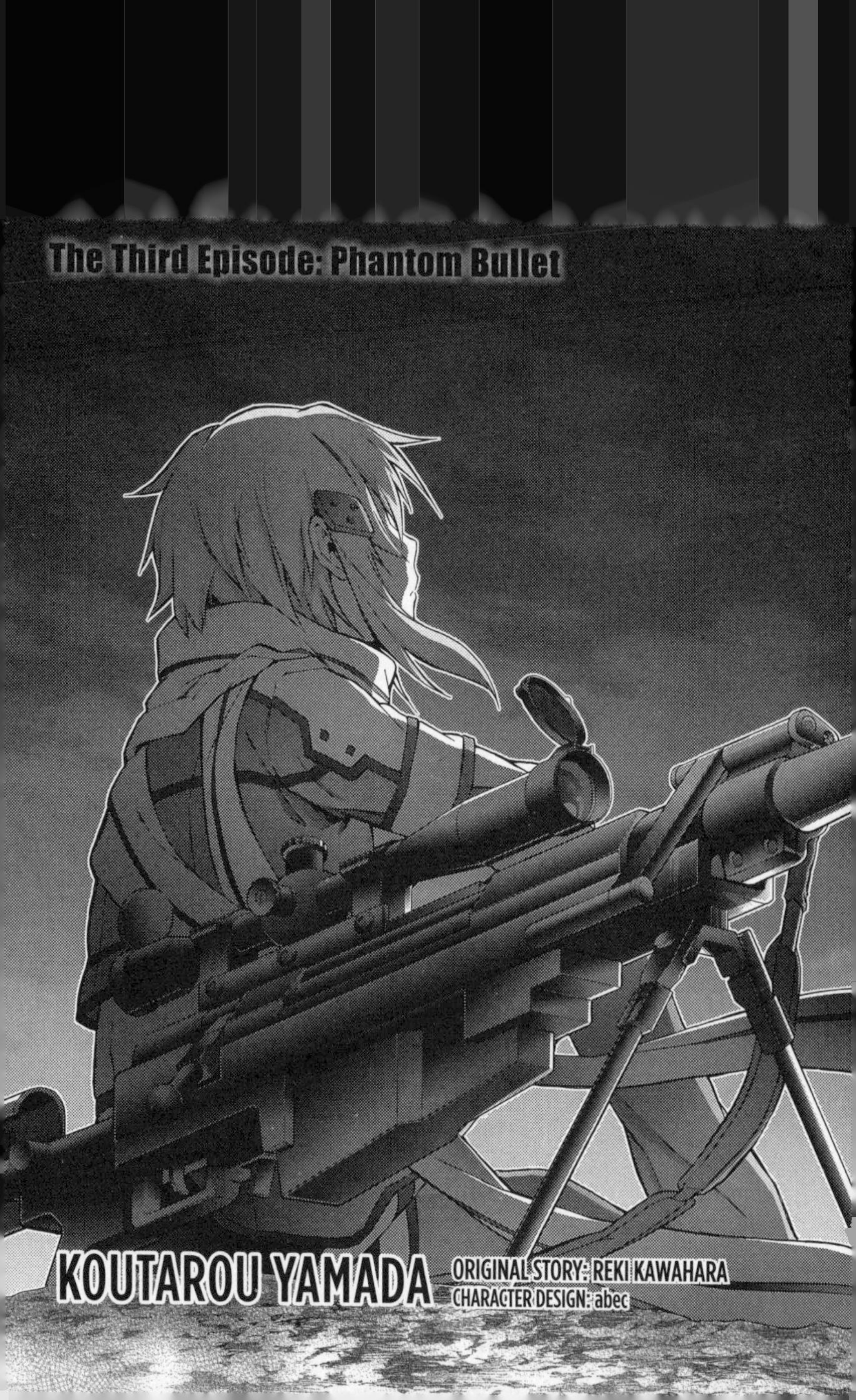
The Third Episode: Phantom Bullet
KOUTAROU YAMADA
ORIGINAL STORY: REKI KAWAHARA
CHARACTER DESIGN: abec

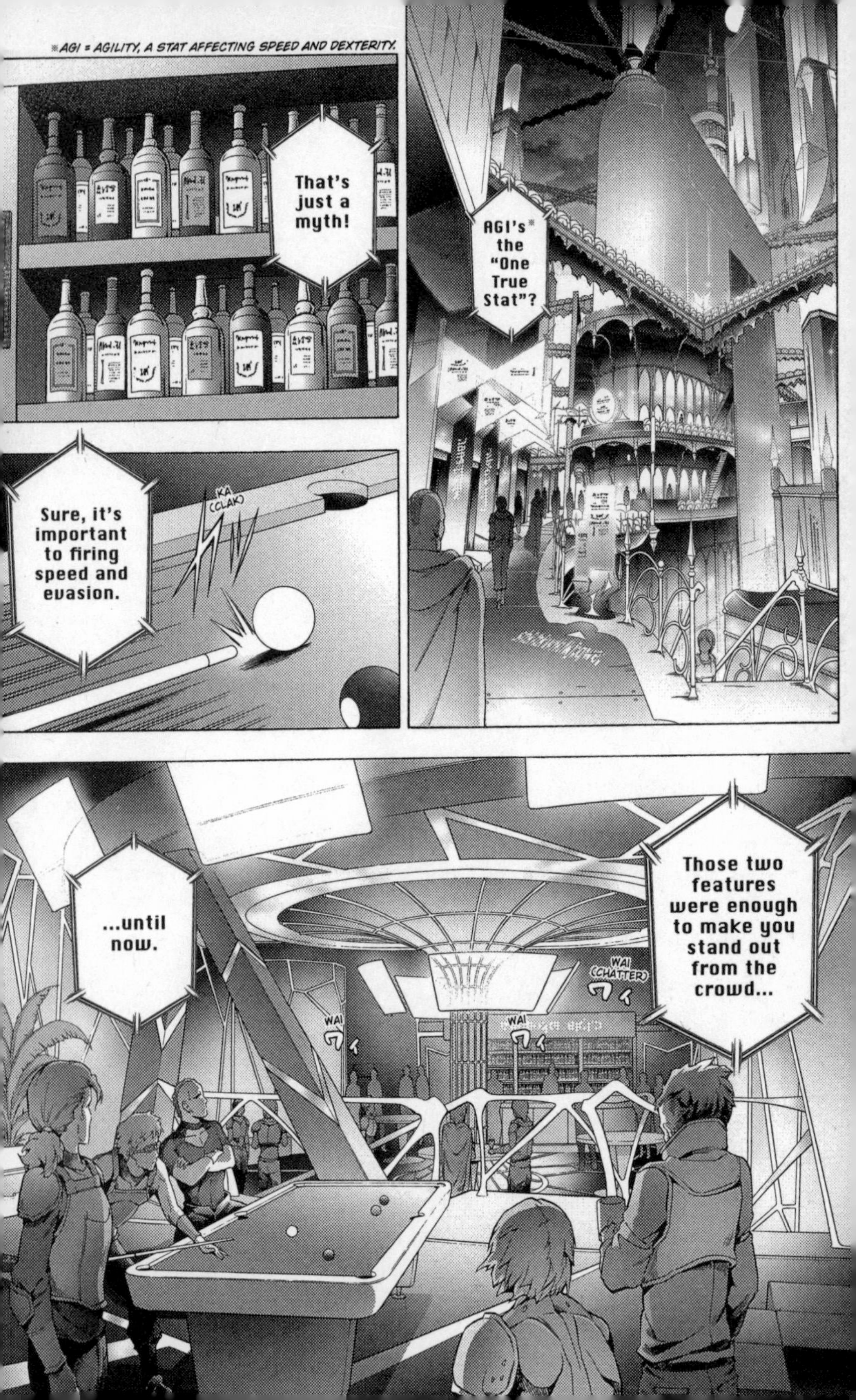
AGI's※ the "One True Stat"?
※AGI = AGILITY, A STAT AFFECTING SPEED AND DEXTERITY.
That's just a myth!
KA (CLAK)
Sure, it's important to firing speed and evasion.
Those two features were enough to make you stand out from the crowd...
WAI (CHATTER)
WAI
WAI
...until now.

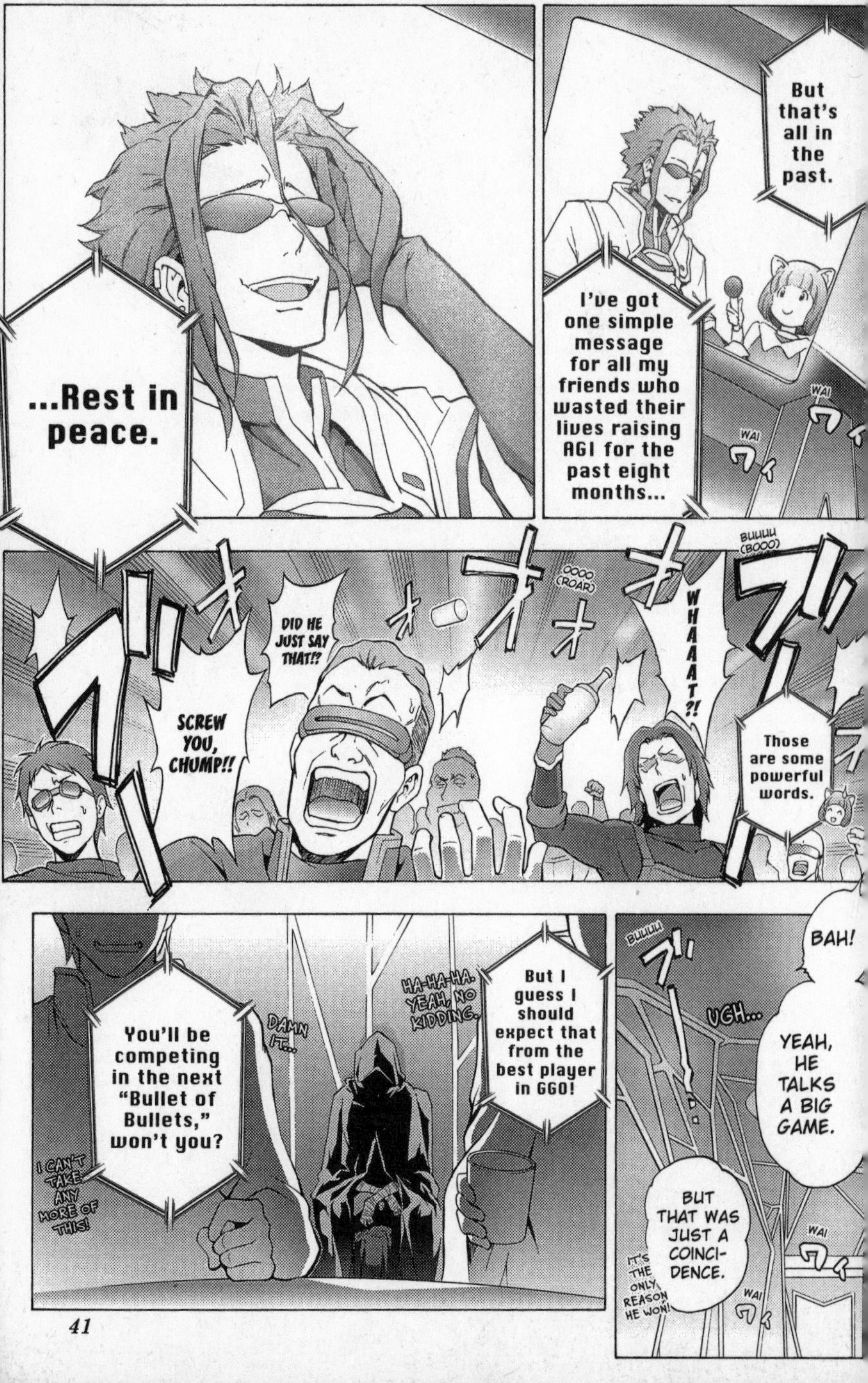
But that's all in the past.
I've got one simple message for all my friends who wasted their lives raising AGI for the past eight months...
WAI
WAI
...Rest in peace.
BUUUU (BOOO)
Those are some powerful words.
WHAAAAT?!
OOOO (ROAR)
DID HE JUST SAY THAT!?
SCREW YOU, CHUMP!!
BAH!
BUUUU
UGH...
YEAH, HE TALKS A BIG GAME.
BUT THAT WAS JUST A COINCI-DENCE.
IT'S THE ONLY REASON HE WON!
WAI
WAI
But I guess I should expect that from the best player in GGO!
HA-HA-HA. YEAH, NO KIDDING.
DAMN IT...
You'll be competing in the next "Bullet of Bullets," won't you?
I CAN'T TAKE ANY MORE OF THIS!

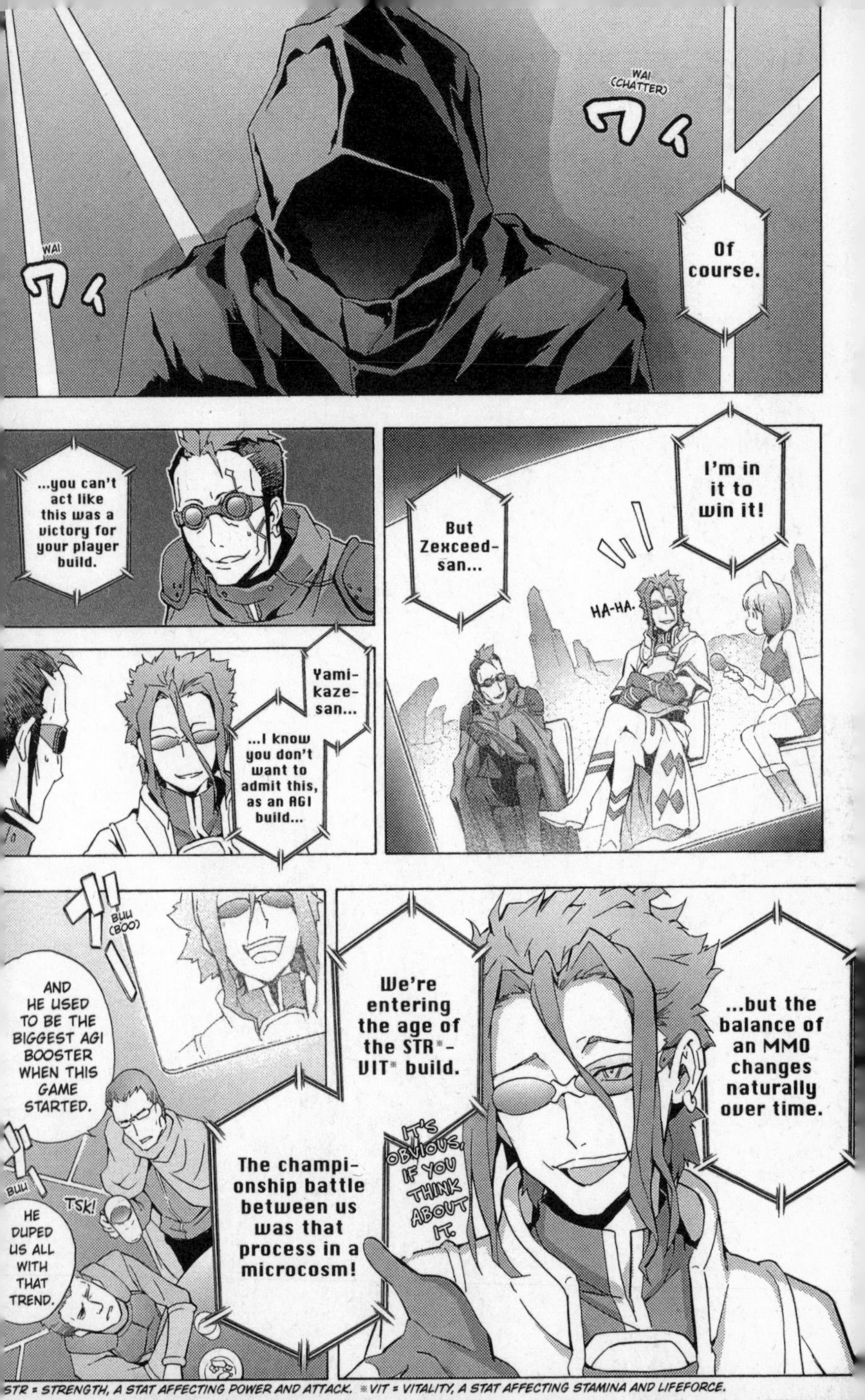
WAI (CHATTER)
Of course.
WAI
I'm in it to win it!
But Zexceed-san...
HA-HA.
...you can't act like this was a victory for your player build.
Yami-kaze-san...
...I know you don't want to admit this, as an AGI build...
...but the balance of an MMO changes naturally over time.
We're entering the age of the STR*-VIT* build.
IT'S OBVIOUS, IF YOU THINK ABOUT IT.
The champi-onship battle between us was that process in a microcosm!
BUU (BOO)
AND HE USED TO BE THE BIGGEST AGI BOOSTER WHEN THIS GAME STARTED.
BUU
TSK!
HE DUPED US ALL WITH THAT TREND.

STR = STRENGTH, A STAT AFFECTING POWER AND ATTACK. ※VIT = VITALITY, A STAT AFFECTING STAMINA AND LIFEFORCE.

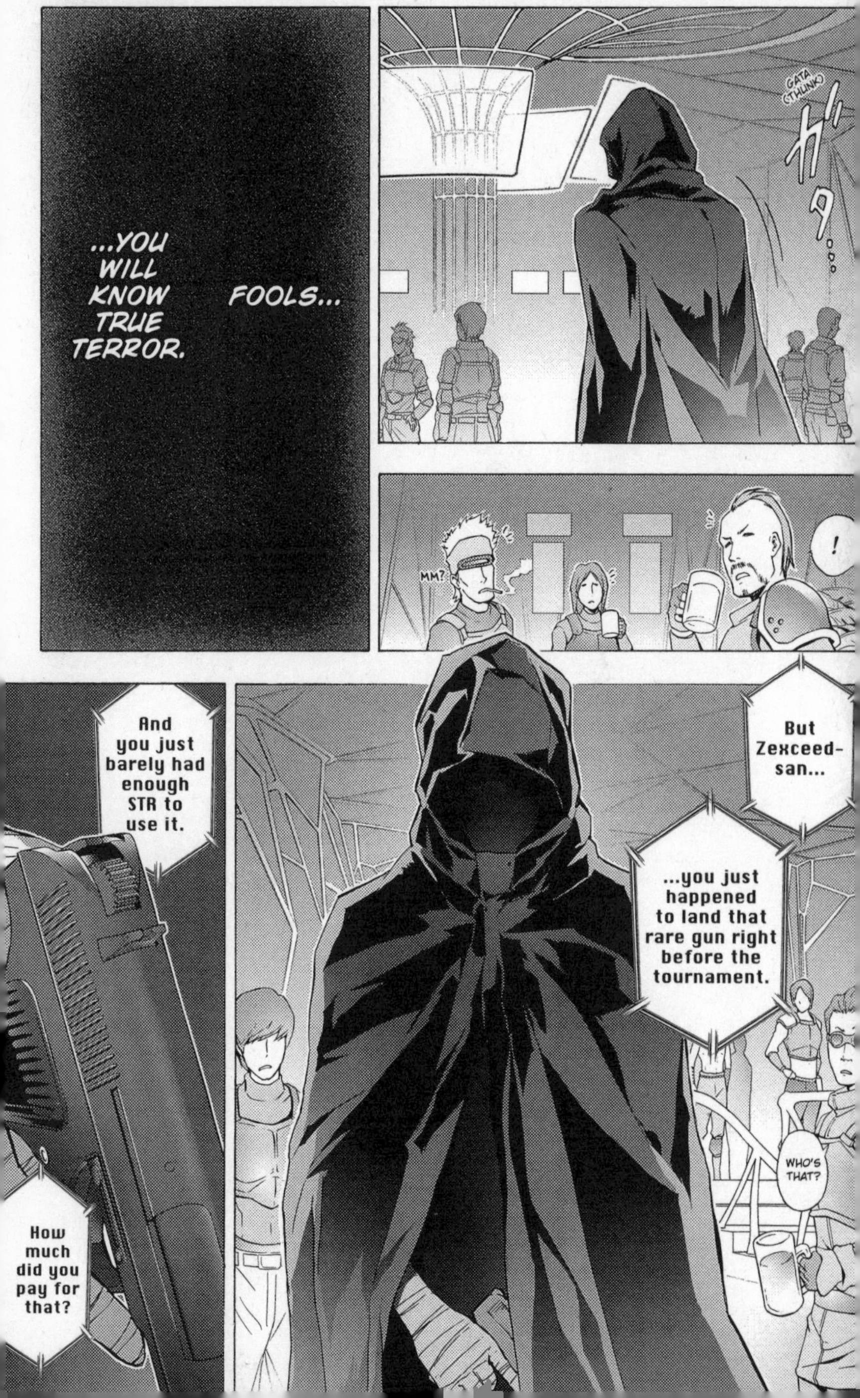
GATA (THUNK)
MM?
!
FOOLS...
...YOU WILL KNOW TRUE TERROR.
But Zexceed-san...
...you just happened to land that rare gun right before the tournament.
WHO'S THAT?
And you just barely had enough STR to use it.
How much did you pay for that?

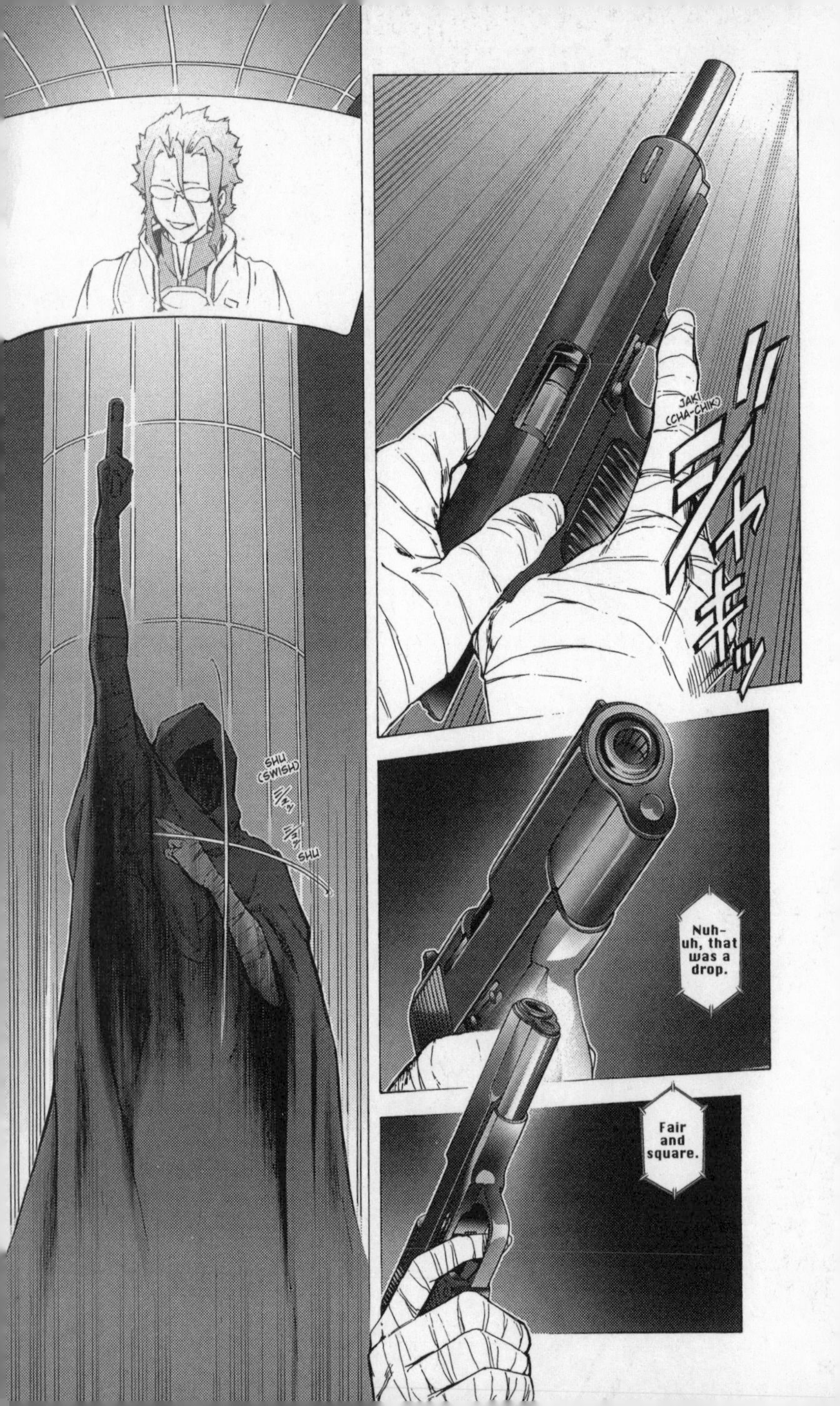
JAKI (CHA-CHIK)
Nuh-uh, that was a drop.
Fair and square.
SHU (SWISH)
SHU

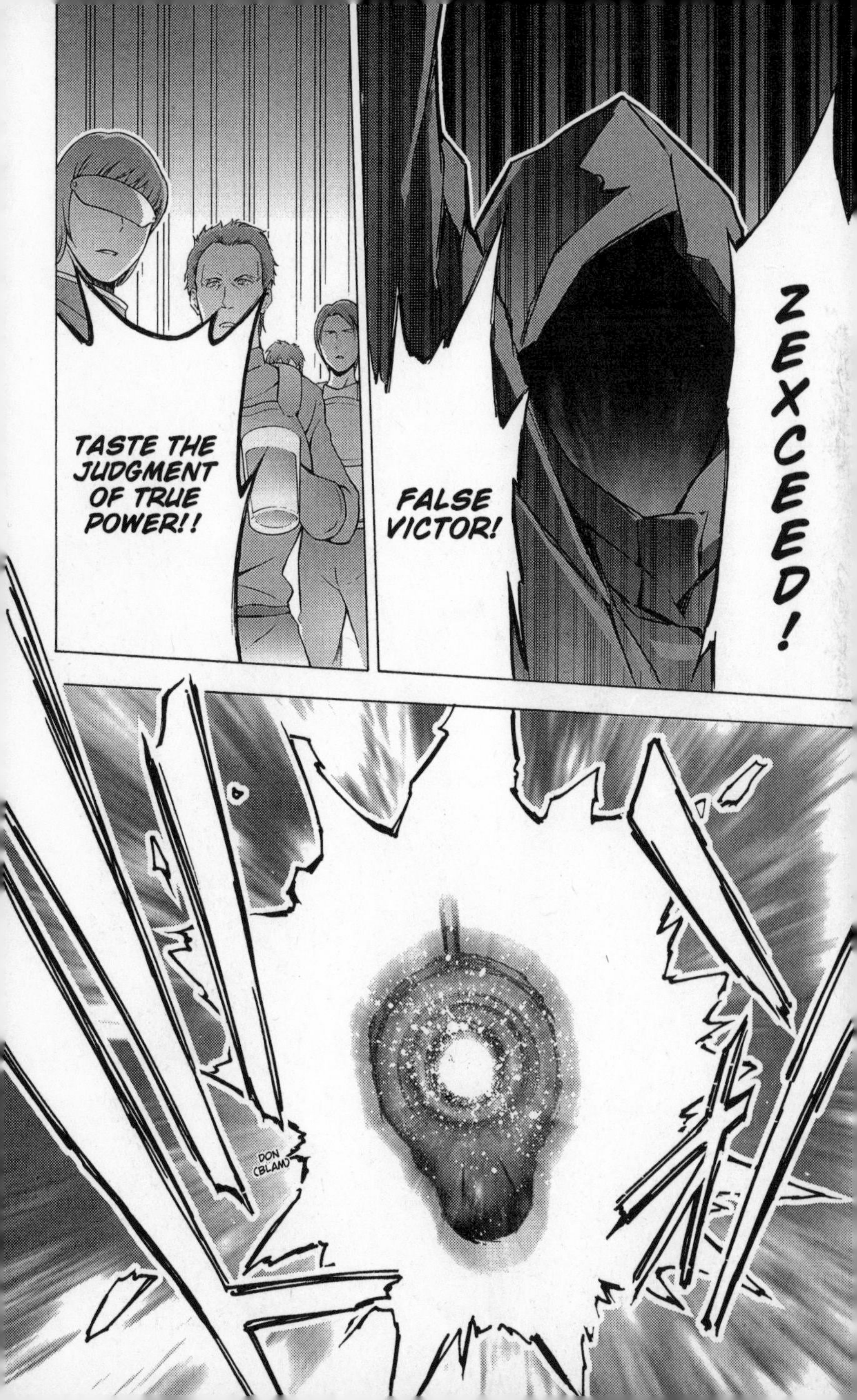
ZEXCEED!
FALSE VICTOR!
TASTE THE JUDGMENT OF TRUE POWER!!
DON (BLAM)

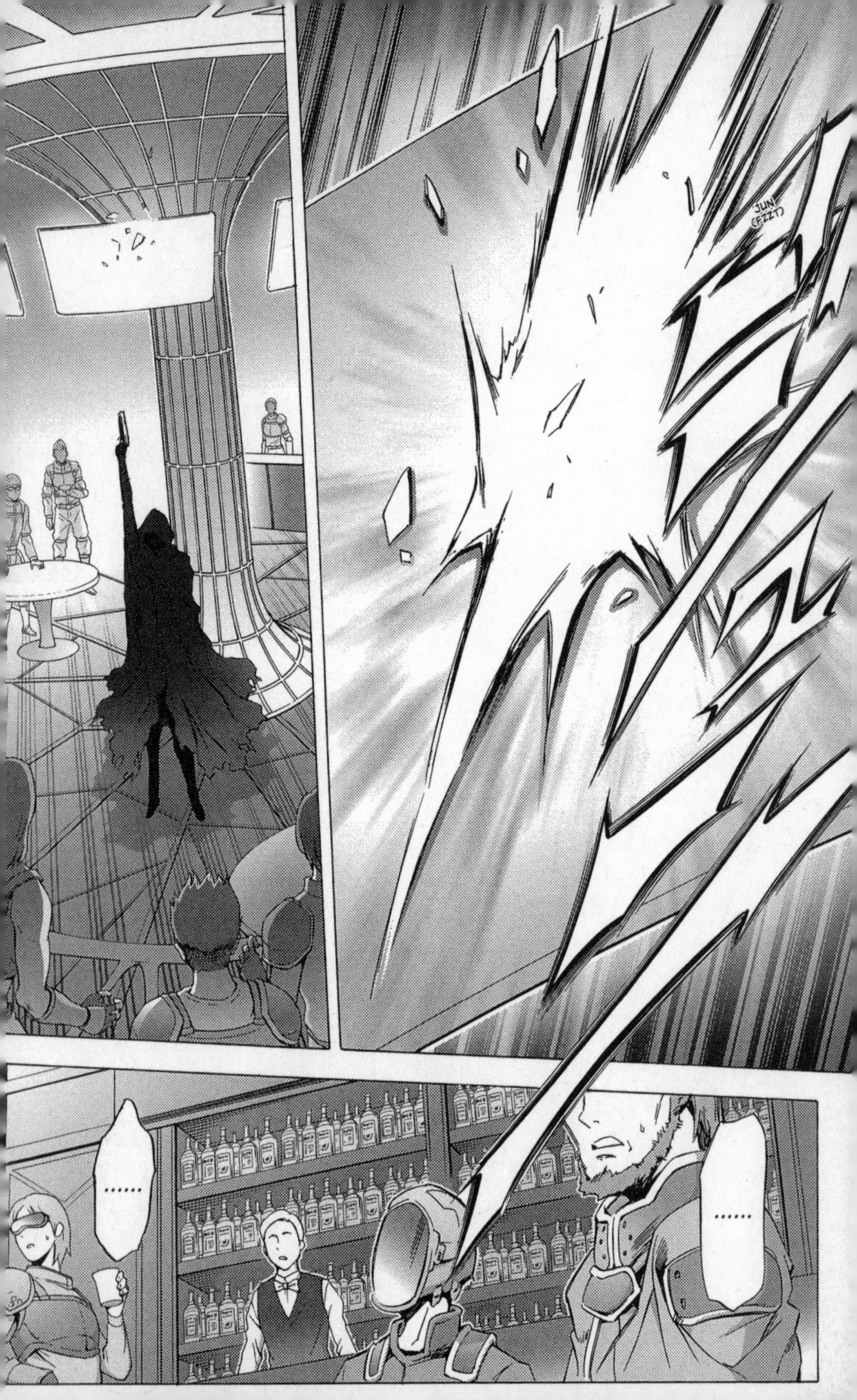
JUN
(FZZT)
......
......

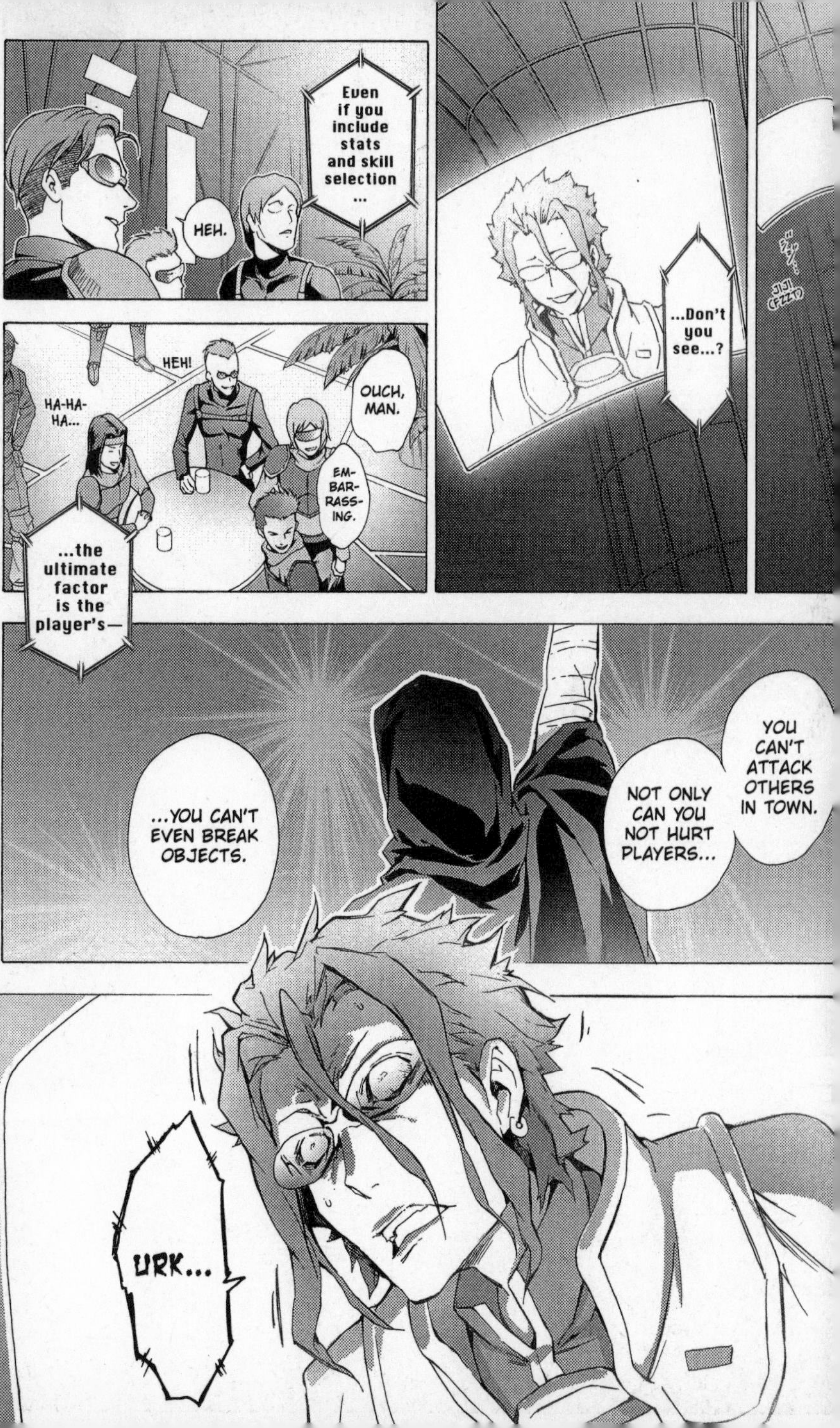
JIJI (FZZT)
...Don't you see...?
Even if you include stats and skill selection ...
HEH.
HEH!
OUCH, MAN.
EM-BAR-RASS-ING.
HA-HA-HA...
...the ultimate factor is the player's—
YOU CAN'T ATTACK OTHERS IN TOWN.
NOT ONLY CAN YOU NOT HURT PLAYERS...
...YOU CAN'T EVEN BREAK OBJECTS.
URK...

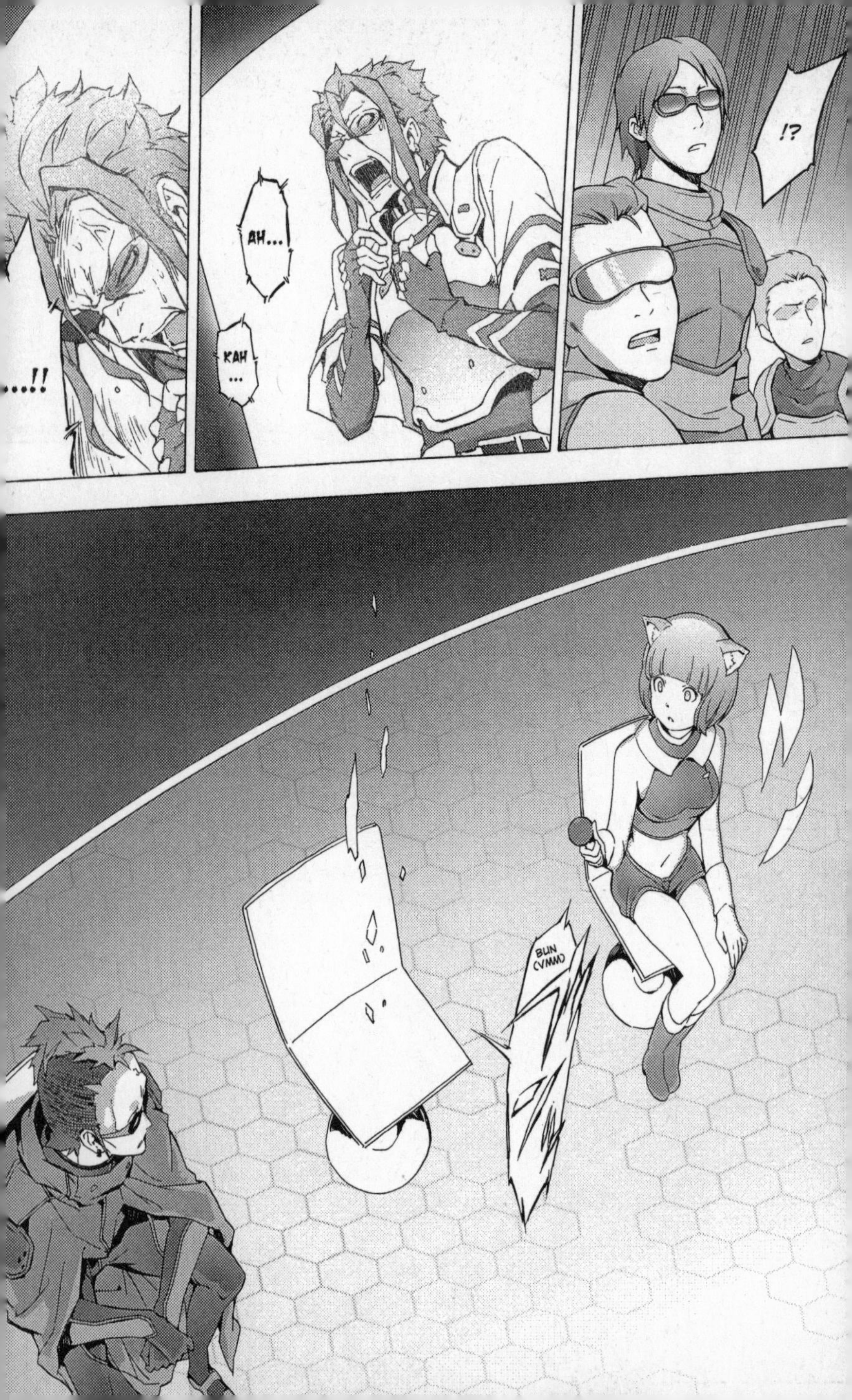
!?
AH...
KAH ...
...!!
BUN (VMM)

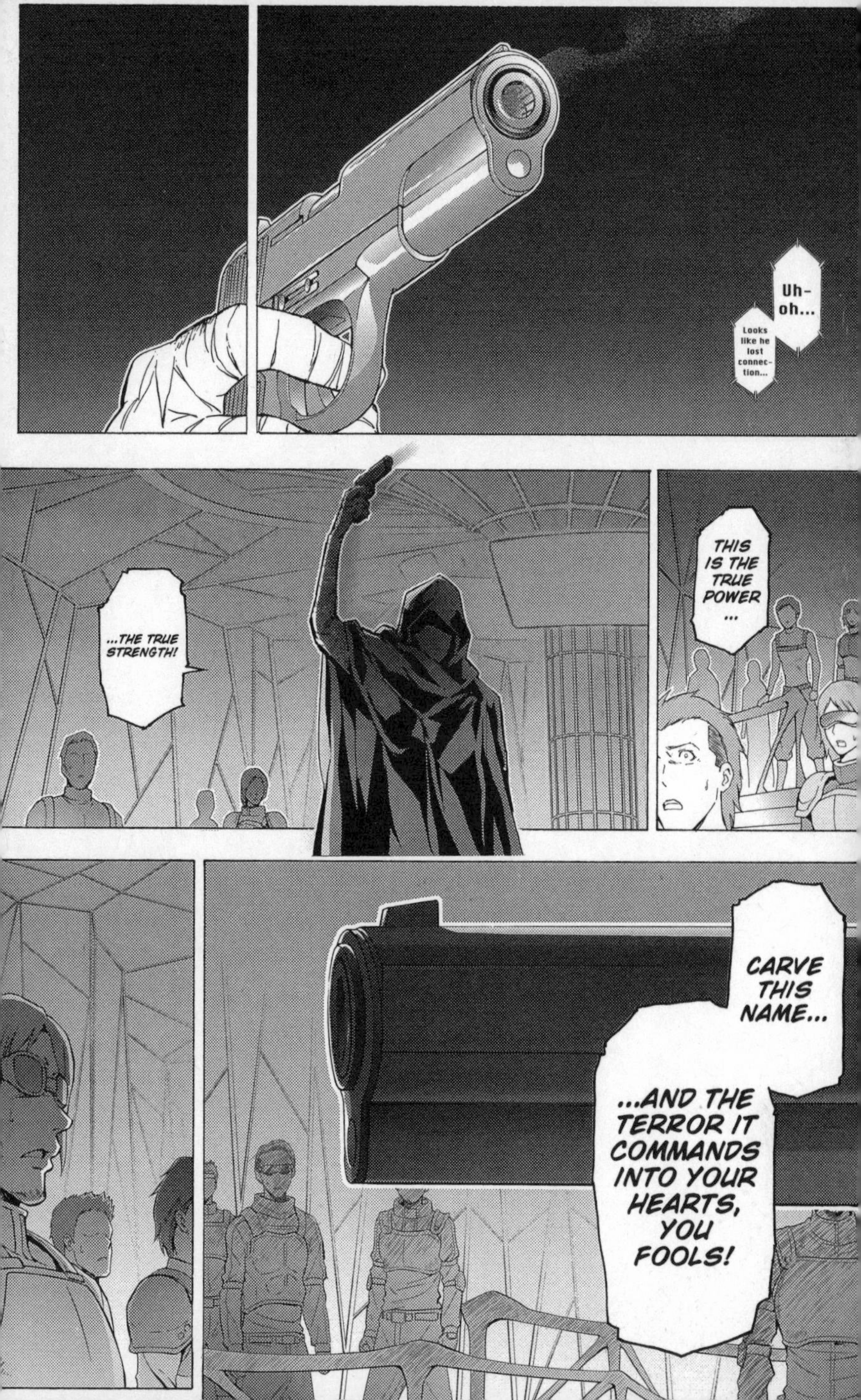
Uh-oh...
Looks like he lost connec-tion...
THIS IS THE TRUE POWER...
...THE TRUE STRENGTH!
CARVE THIS NAME...
...AND THE TERROR IT COMMANDS INTO YOUR HEARTS, YOU FOOLS!

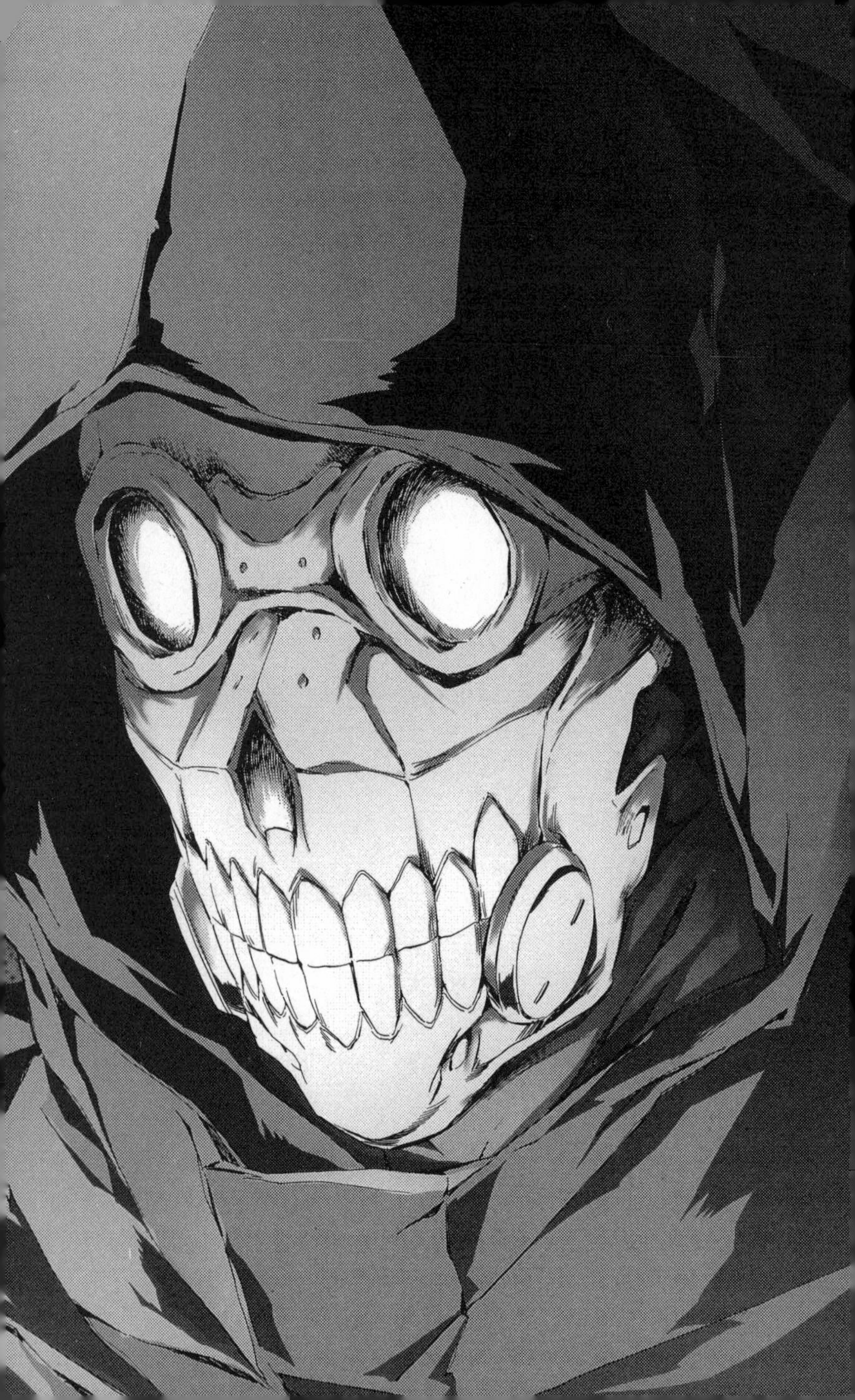

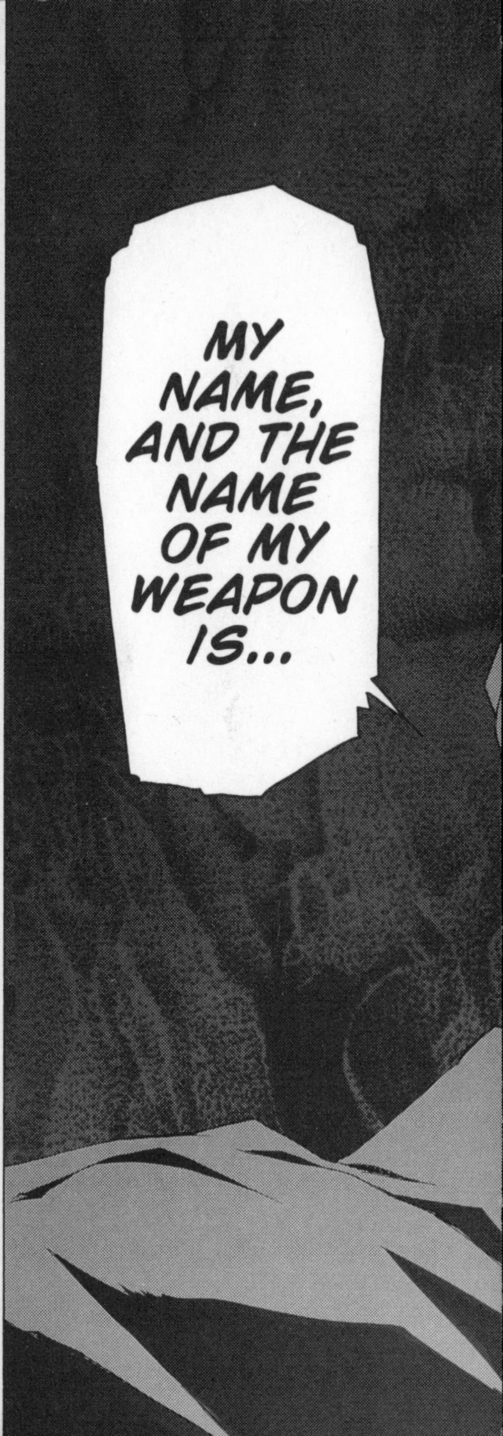
MY NAME, AND THE NAME OF MY WEAPON IS...
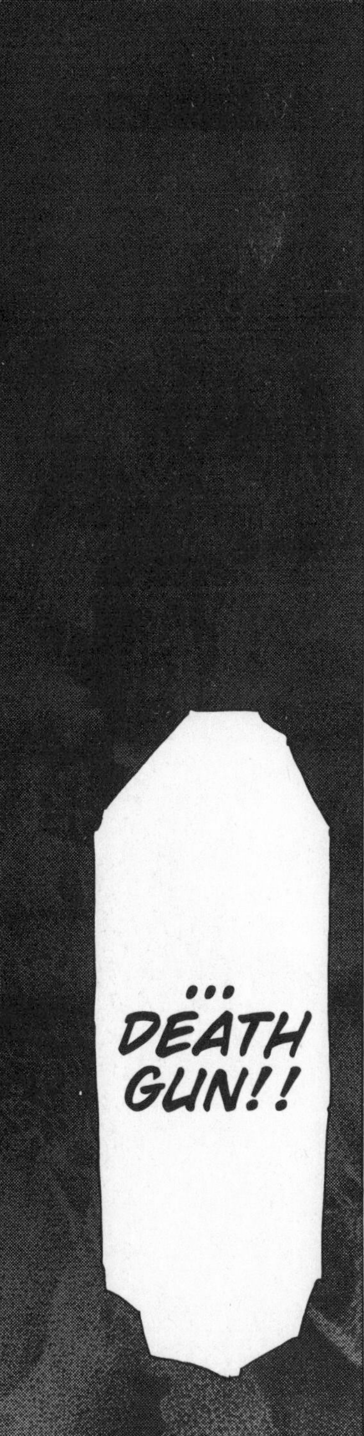
...DEATH GUN!!

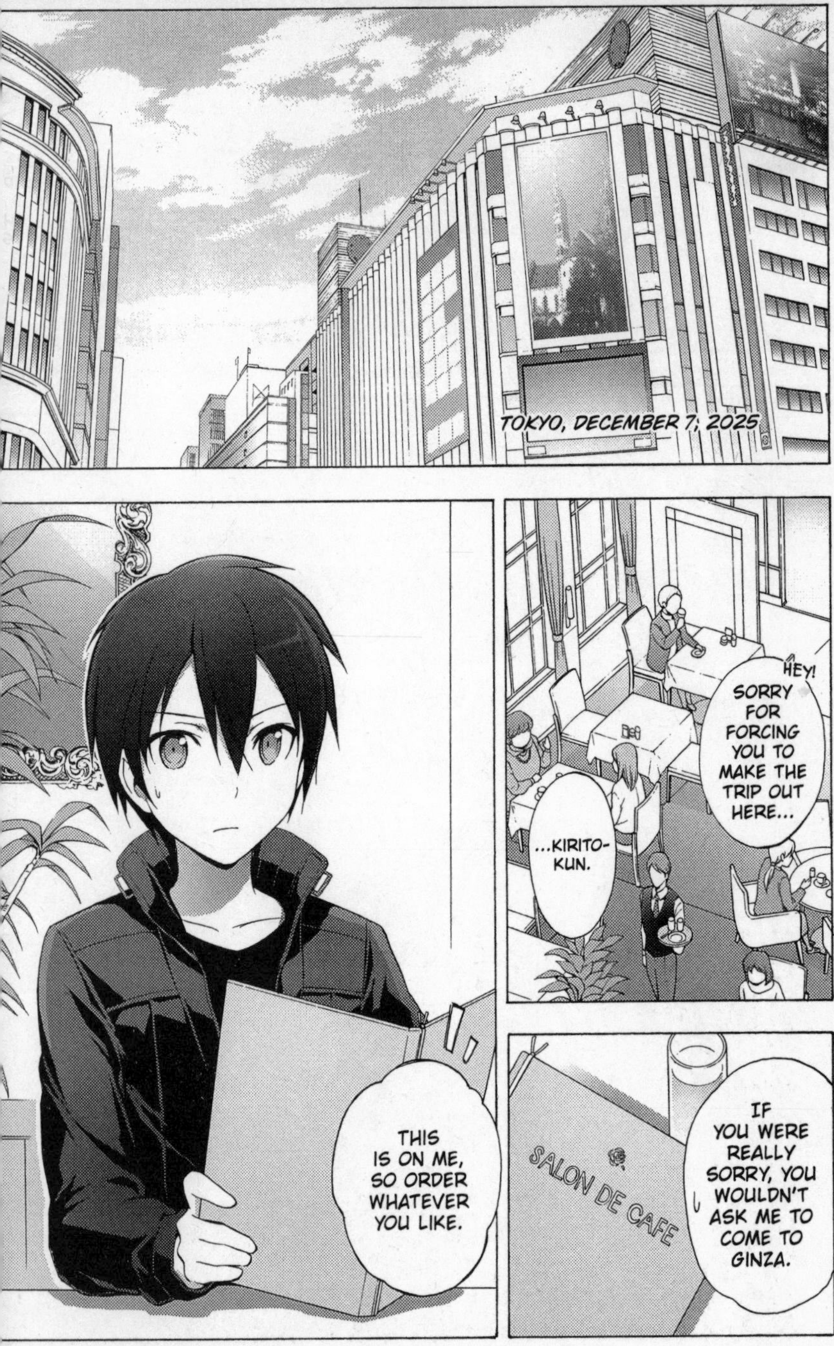
TOKYO, DECEMBER 7, 2025
HEY! SORRY FOR FORCING YOU TO MAKE THE TRIP OUT HERE...
...KIRITO-KUN.
SALON DE CAFE
IF YOU WERE REALLY SORRY, YOU WOULDN'T ASK ME TO COME TO GINZA.
THIS IS ON ME, SO ORDER WHATEVER YOU LIKE.

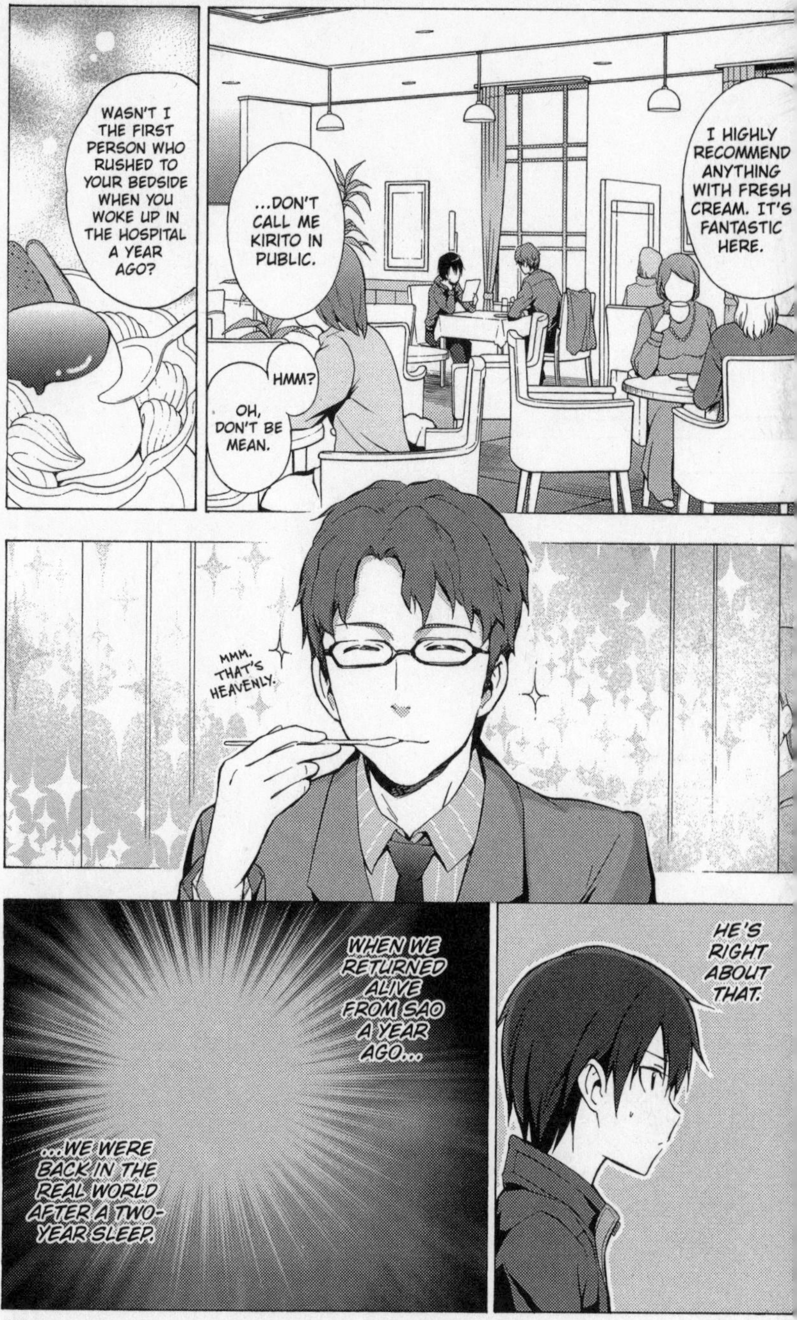
I HIGHLY RECOMMEND ANYTHING WITH FRESH CREAM. IT'S FANTASTIC HERE.
...DON'T CALL ME KIRITO IN PUBLIC.
HMM?
OH, DON'T BE MEAN.
WASN'T I THE FIRST PERSON WHO RUSHED TO YOUR BEDSIDE WHEN YOU WOKE UP IN THE HOSPITAL A YEAR AGO?
MMM. THAT'S HEAVENLY.
HE'S RIGHT ABOUT THAT.
WHEN WE RETURNED ALIVE FROM SAO A YEAR AGO...
...WE WERE BACK IN THE REAL WORLD AFTER A TWO-YEAR SLEEP.

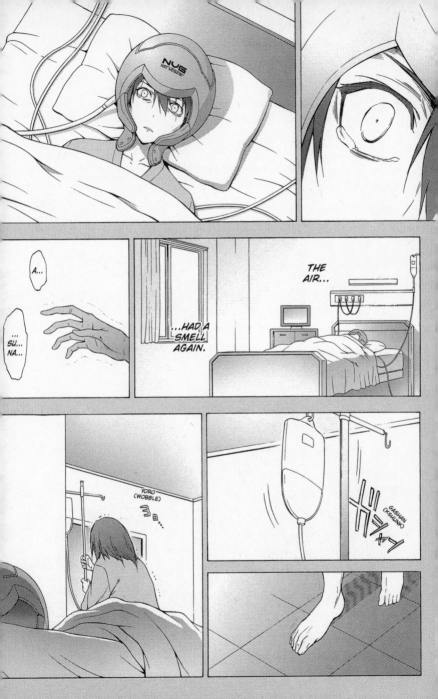

A...

... SU... NA...

THE AIR...

...HAD A SMELL AGAIN.

YORO (WOBBLE)

GASHAN (CRUNCH)

PETERBOROUGH PUBLIC LIBRARY

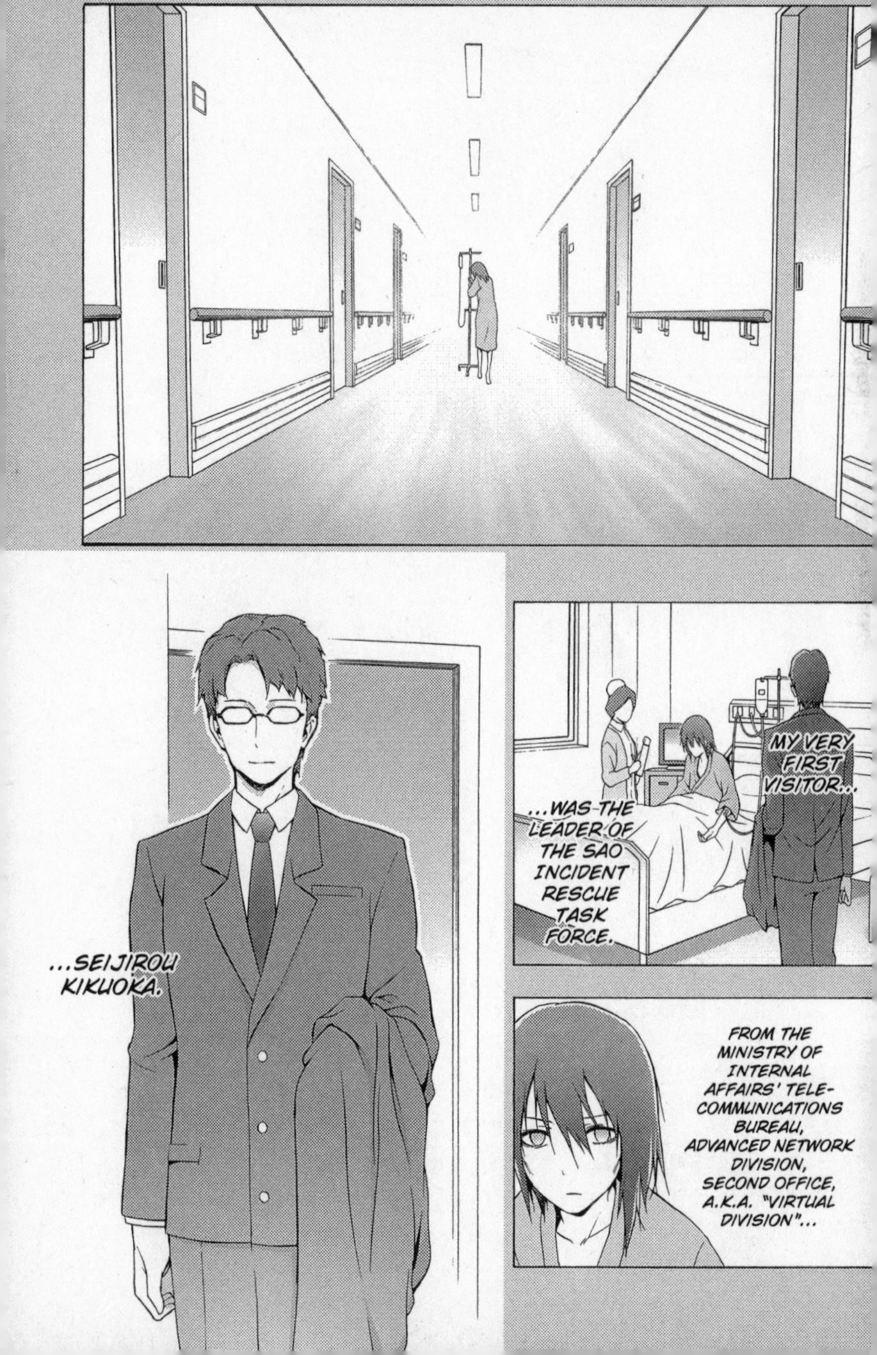
MY VERY FIRST VISITOR...
...WAS THE LEADER OF THE SAO INCIDENT RESCUE TASK FORCE.
FROM THE MINISTRY OF INTERNAL AFFAIRS' TELE-COMMUNICATIONS BUREAU, ADVANCED NETWORK DIVISION, SECOND OFFICE, A.K.A. "VIRTUAL DIVISION"...
...SEIJIROU KIKUOKA.

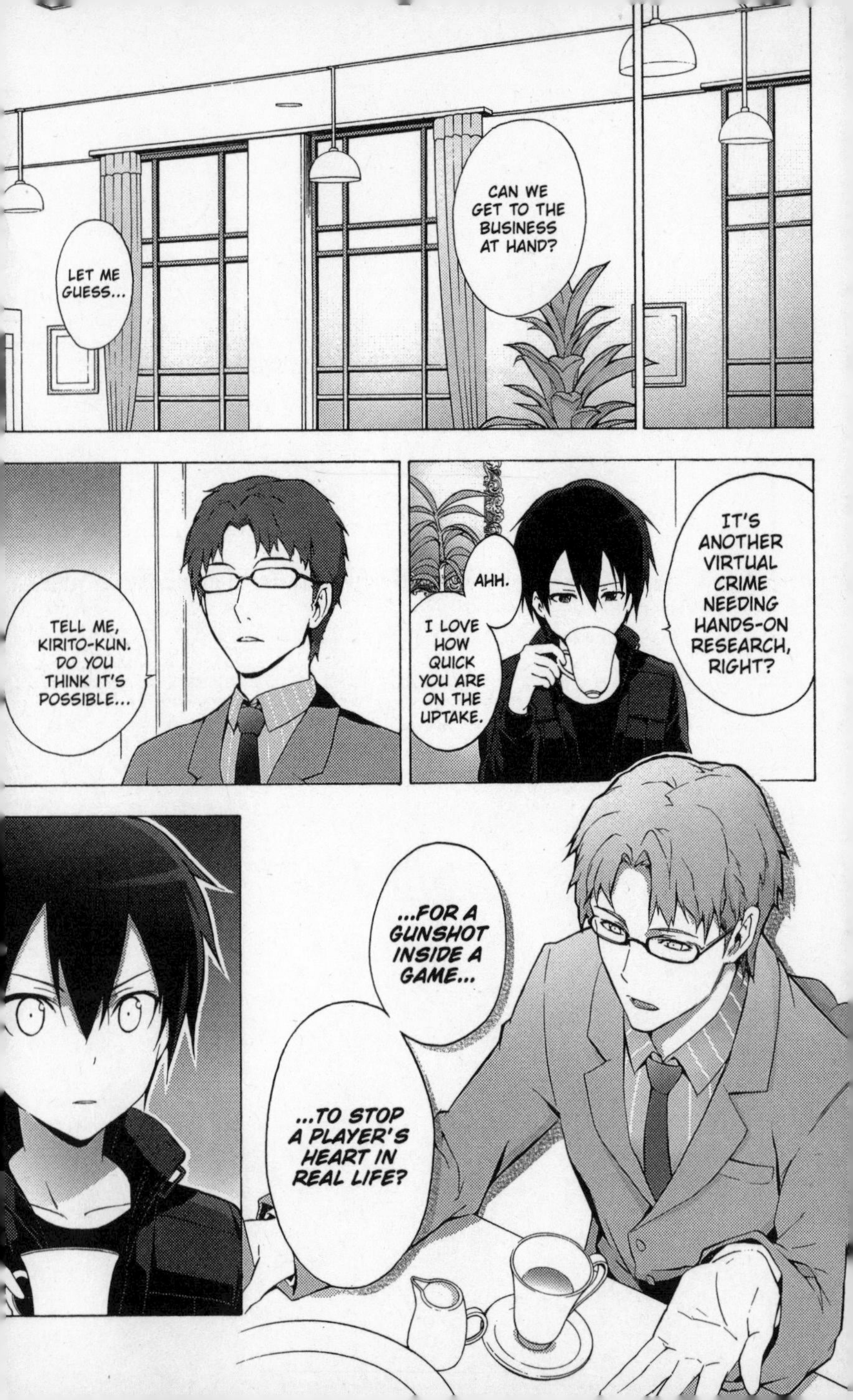
CAN WE GET TO THE BUSINESS AT HAND?
LET ME GUESS...
IT'S ANOTHER VIRTUAL CRIME NEEDING HANDS-ON RESEARCH, RIGHT?
AHH.
I LOVE HOW QUICK YOU ARE ON THE UPTAKE.
TELL ME, KIRITO-KUN. DO YOU THINK IT'S POSSIBLE...
...FOR A GUNSHOT INSIDE A GAME...
...TO STOP A PLAYER'S HEART IN REAL LIFE?

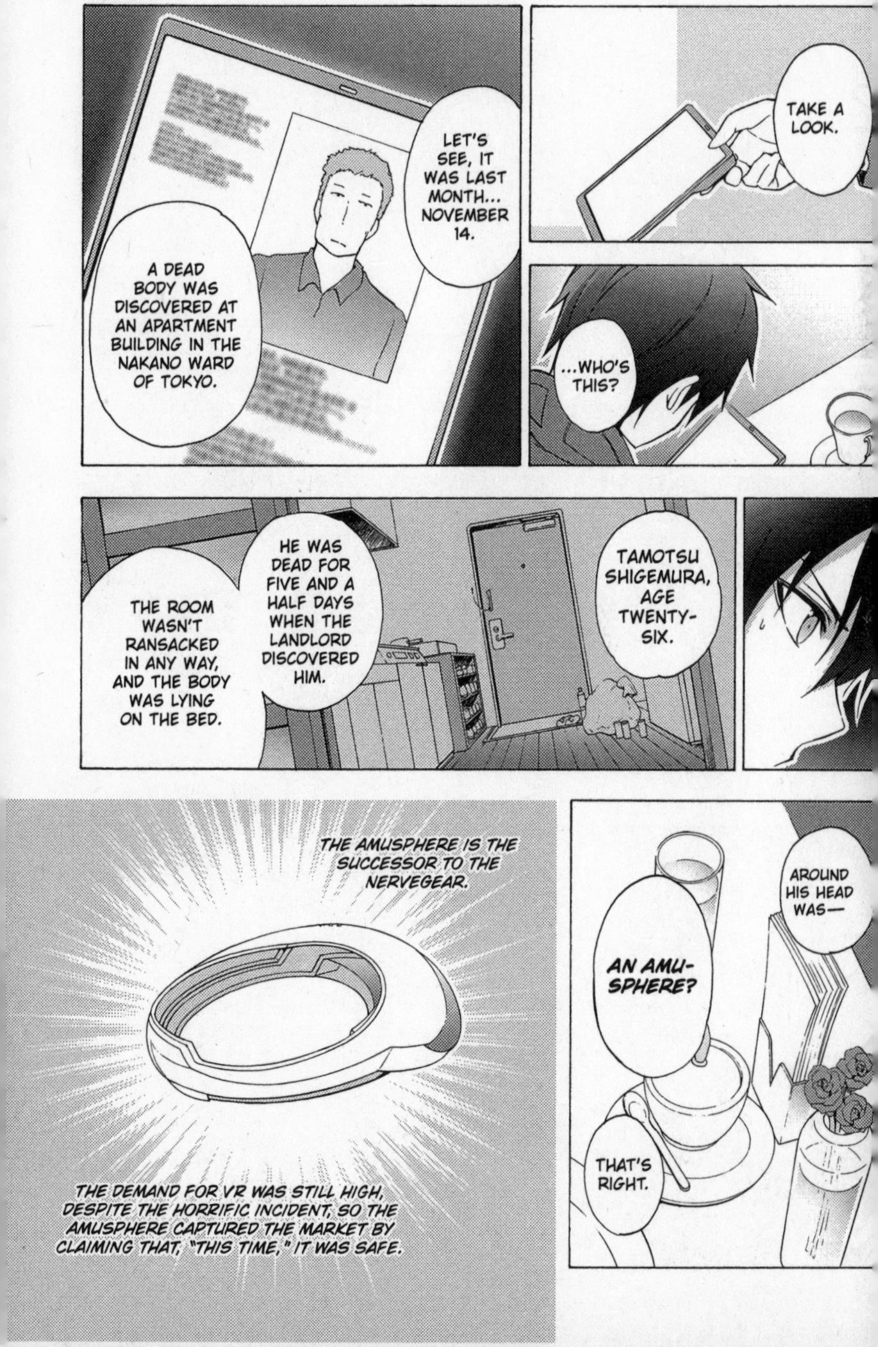
TAKE A LOOK.
...WHO'S THIS?
LET'S SEE, IT WAS LAST MONTH... NOVEMBER 14.
A DEAD BODY WAS DISCOVERED AT AN APARTMENT BUILDING IN THE NAKANO WARD OF TOKYO.
TAMOTSU SHIGEMURA, AGE TWENTY-SIX.
HE WAS DEAD FOR FIVE AND A HALF DAYS WHEN THE LANDLORD DISCOVERED HIM.
THE ROOM WASN'T RANSACKED IN ANY WAY, AND THE BODY WAS LYING ON THE BED.
AROUND HIS HEAD WAS—
AN AMUSPHERE?
THAT'S RIGHT.
THE AMUSPHERE IS THE SUCCESSOR TO THE NERVEGEAR.
THE DEMAND FOR VR WAS STILL HIGH, DESPITE THE HORRIFIC INCIDENT, SO THE AMUSPHERE CAPTURED THE MARKET BY CLAIMING THAT, "THIS TIME," IT WAS SAFE.

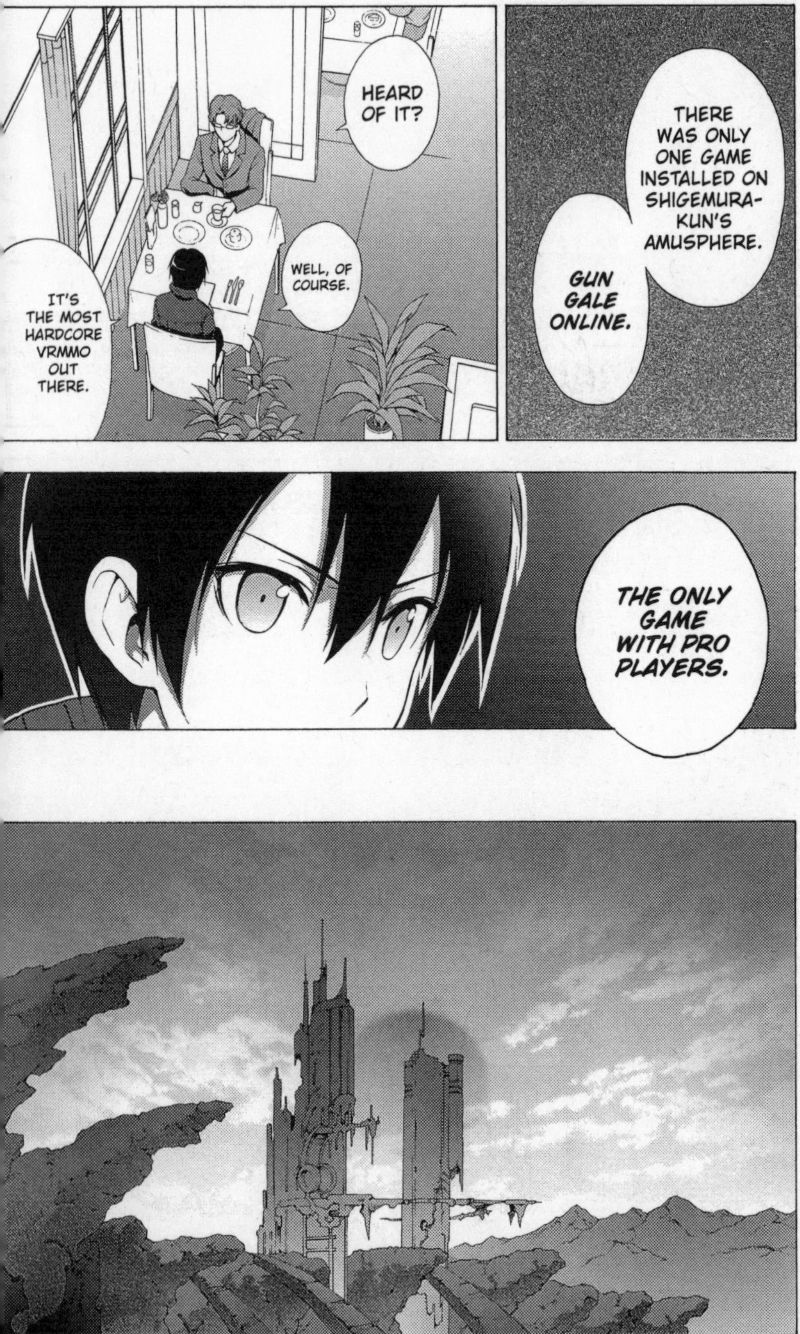
THERE WAS ONLY ONE GAME INSTALLED ON SHIGEMURA-KUN'S AMUSPHERE.
GUN GALE ONLINE.
HEARD OF IT?
WELL, OF COURSE.
IT'S THE MOST HARDCORE VRMMO OUT THERE.
THE ONLY GAME WITH PRO PLAYERS.

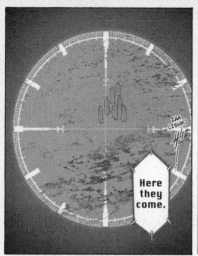

ZAA (ZSHK)
Here they come.
Seven in all.
Course and speed are steady.
Distance to you, 400.
Distance to me, 1,500.
They're still a ways off. Are you ready?
GACHA (CLICK)
JAKO (CHUNK)
Not a problem.

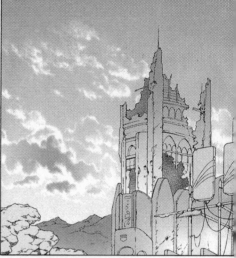

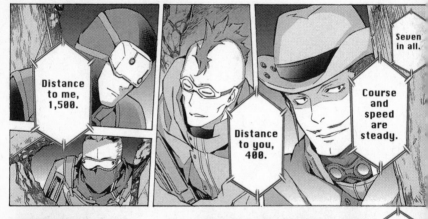

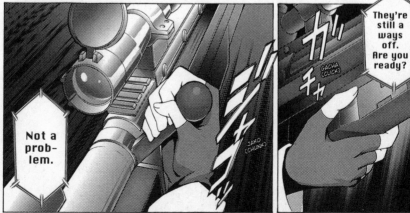

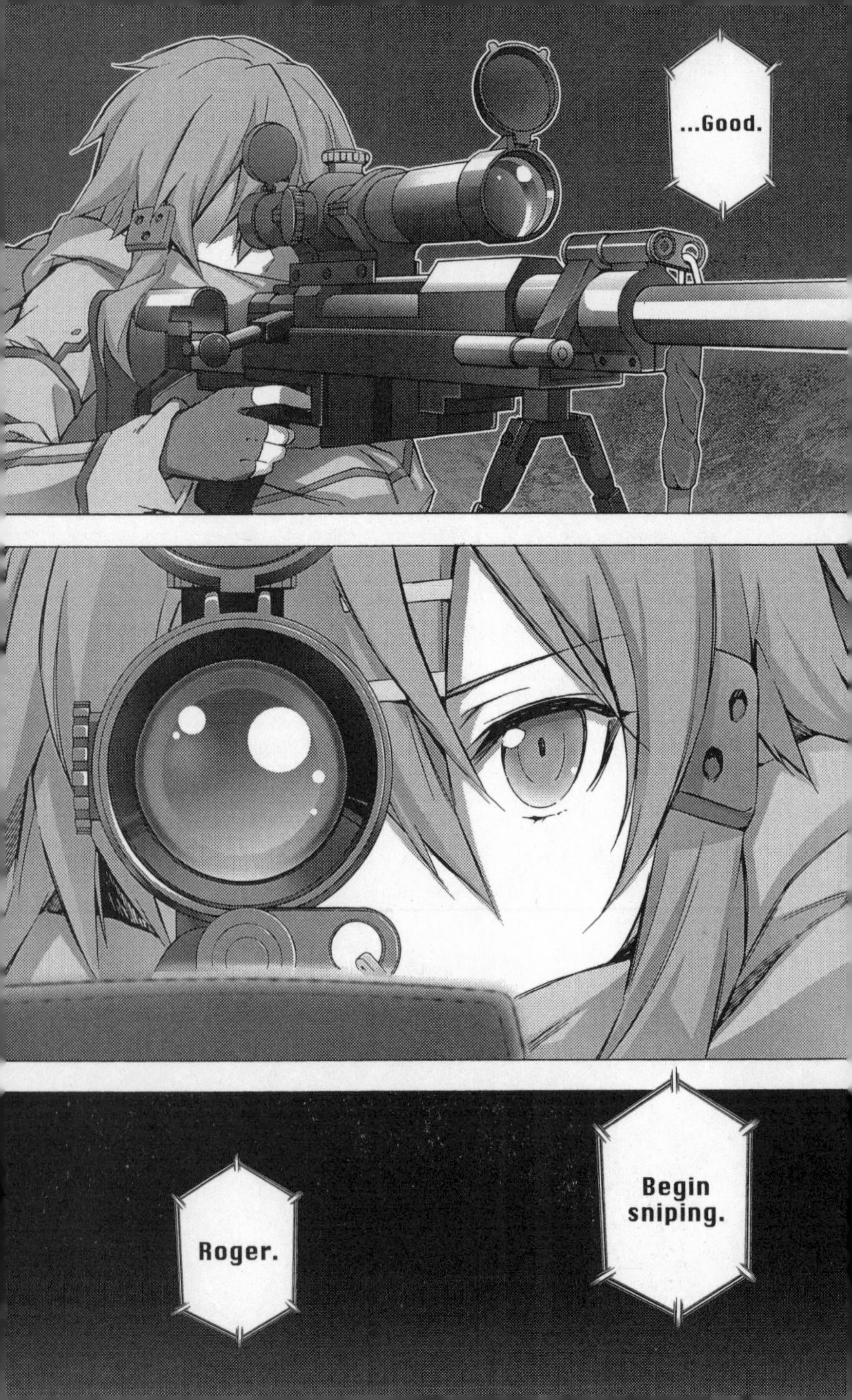
...Good.
Begin sniping.
Roger.

SWORD ART ONLINE
phantom bullet

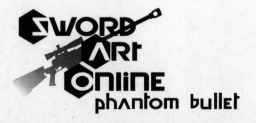

SWORD ART ONLINE
phantom bullet
001

check point!

GGO: WORLD

GUN GALE ONLINE IS A VRMMO RUN BY THE AMERICAN COMPANY ZASKAR. UNLIKE THE FANTASY WORLDS OF SAO AND ALO, IT HAS A HEAVY, GRITTY SETTING BASED AROUND GUNS. WHILE IT DOES HAVE THE MOB HUNTING AND DUNGEON CRAWLING OF ANY OTHER RPG, IT PLACES A MUCH HEAVIER EMPHASIS ON PLAYER-VS-PLAYER ACTION. IT'S ALSO THE ONLY VRMMO WITH A GAME-CURRENCY-TO-CASH PAYOUT SYSTEM, SUPPORTING THE EXISTENCE OF "PRO GAMERS" WHO MAKE A LIVING BY EARNING MONEY THROUGH THE GAME.

ULTIMA RATIO HECATE II: ITEM

AN ANTIMATERIEL SNIPER RIFLE MANU-FACTURED BY PGM PRÉCISION IN FRANCE. IT FIRES ENORMOUS 12.7 X 99 MM ROUNDS THAT CAN EASILY PIERCE CONCRETE WALLS BEHIND TARGETS OR LIGHTLY ARMORED VEHICLES. IT'S SO POWERFUL THAT IT CAN BLOW APART A HUMAN BEING WELL OVER A MILE AWAY. IT CAN BE RECOGNIZED BY ITS LARGE MUZZLE BRAKE (THE APPARATUS THAT EXHAUSTS PROPELLANT GAS TO THE SIDES WHEN THE GUN FIRES, REDUCING RECOIL).

COURTESY OF: A-1 PICTURES
©2014 REKI KAWAHARA/KADOKAWA ASCII MEDIA WORKS/SAO II PROJECT

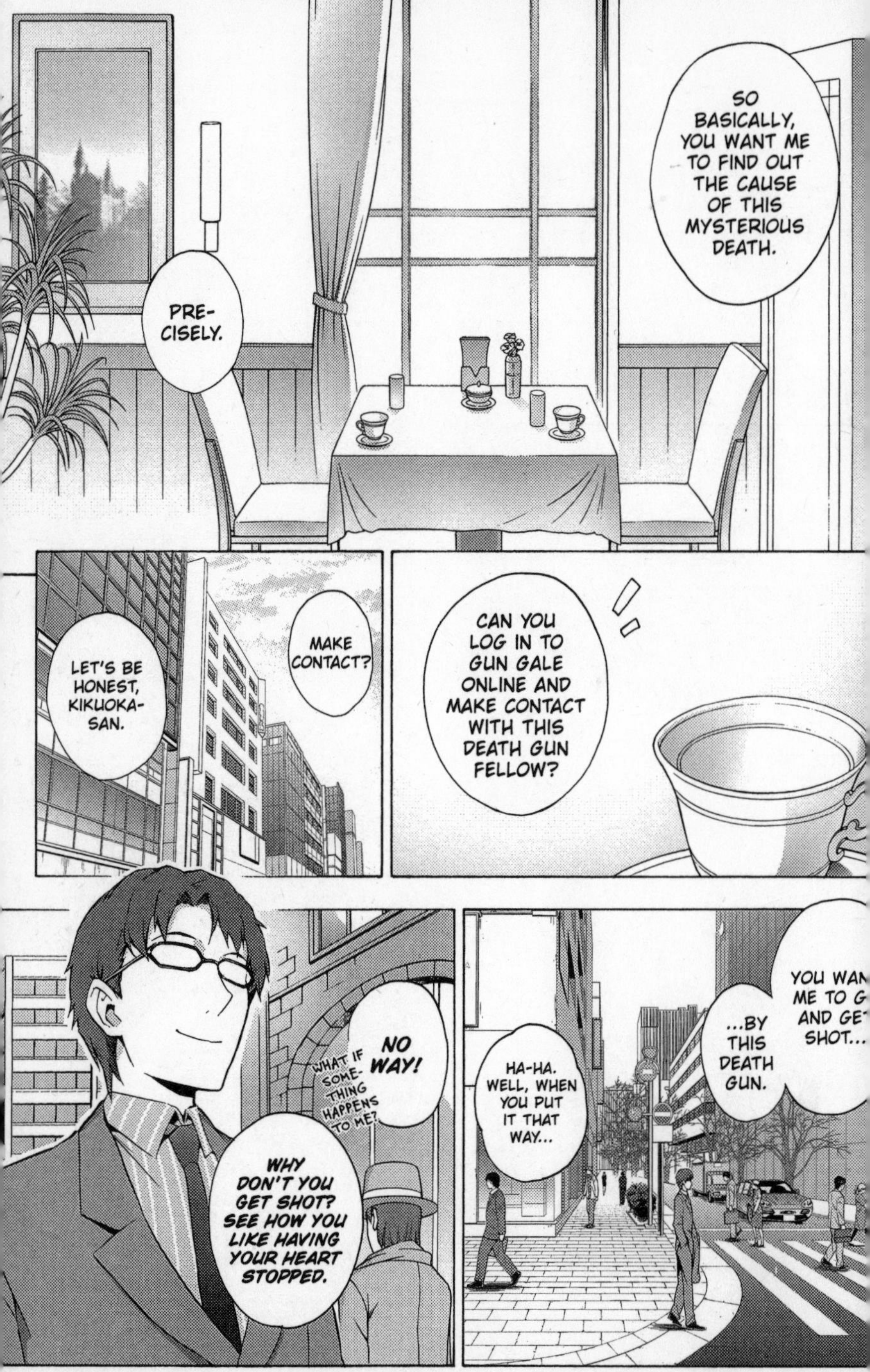
SO BASICALLY, YOU WANT ME TO FIND OUT THE CAUSE OF THIS MYSTERIOUS DEATH.
PRE-CISELY.
CAN YOU LOG IN TO GUN GALE ONLINE AND MAKE CONTACT WITH THIS DEATH GUN FELLOW?
MAKE CONTACT?
LET'S BE HONEST, KIKUOKA-SAN.
YOU WAN ME TO G AND GE SHOT...
...BY THIS DEATH GUN.
HA-HA. WELL, WHEN YOU PUT IT THAT WAY...
NO WAY!
WHAT IF SOME-THING HAPPENS TO ME?
WHY DON'T YOU GET SHOT? SEE HOW YOU LIKE HAVING YOUR HEART STOPPED.

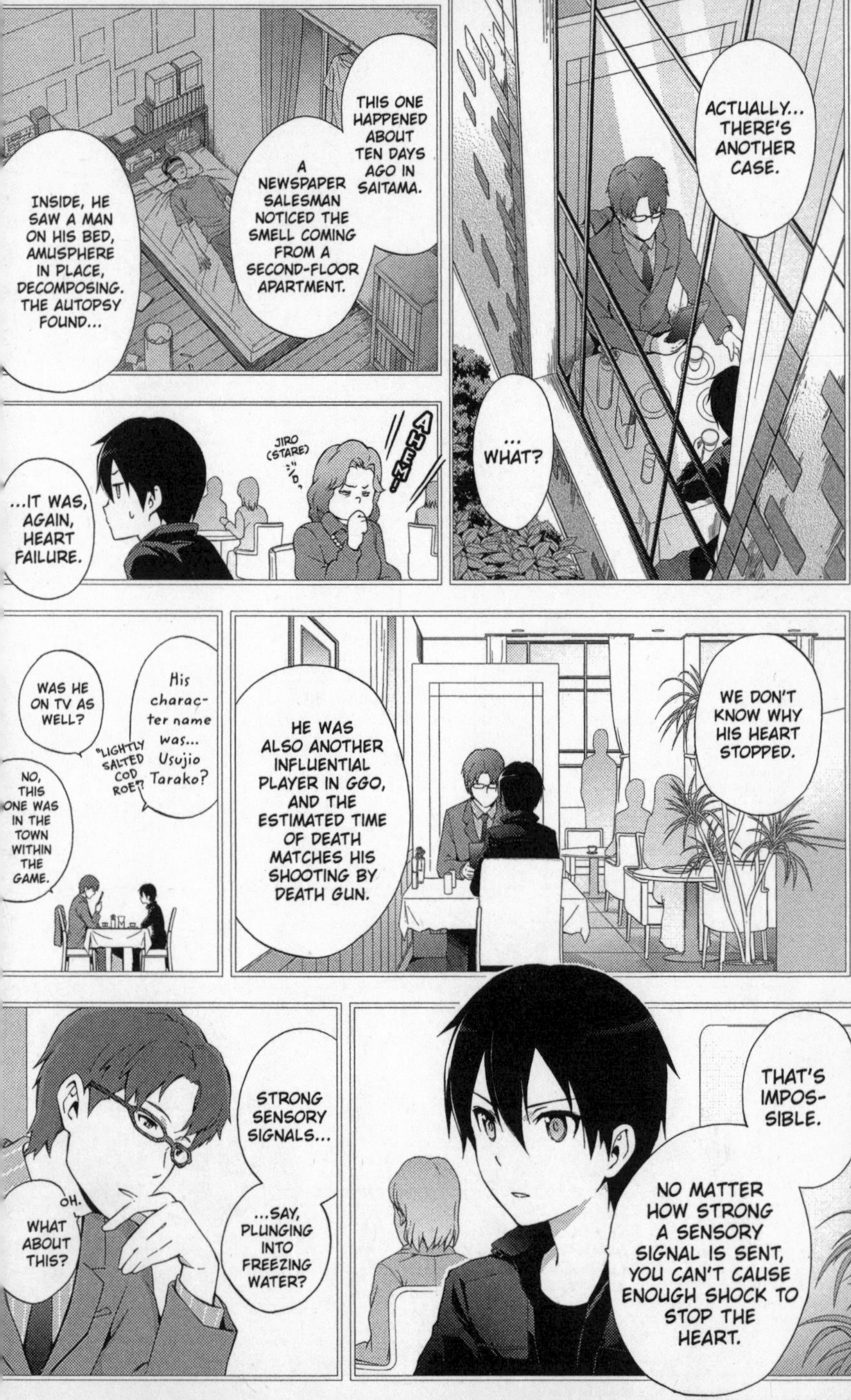
ACTUALLY... THERE'S ANOTHER CASE.
... WHAT?
THIS ONE HAPPENED ABOUT TEN DAYS AGO IN SAITAMA.
A NEWSPAPER SALESMAN NOTICED THE SMELL COMING FROM A SECOND-FLOOR APARTMENT.
INSIDE, HE SAW A MAN ON HIS BED, AMUSPHERE IN PLACE, DECOMPOSING. THE AUTOPSY FOUND...
JIRO (STARE)
...IT WAS, AGAIN, HEART FAILURE.
WE DON'T KNOW WHY HIS HEART STOPPED.
HE WAS ALSO ANOTHER INFLUENTIAL PLAYER IN GGO, AND THE ESTIMATED TIME OF DEATH MATCHES HIS SHOOTING BY DEATH GUN.
His character name was... Usujio Tarako?
"LIGHTLY SALTED COD ROE"
WAS HE ON TV AS WELL?
NO, THIS ONE WAS IN THE TOWN WITHIN THE GAME.
THAT'S IMPOSSIBLE.
NO MATTER HOW STRONG A SENSORY SIGNAL IS SENT, YOU CAN'T CAUSE ENOUGH SHOCK TO STOP THE HEART.
STRONG SENSORY SIGNALS...
...SAY, PLUNGING INTO FREEZING WATER?
OH. WHAT ABOUT THIS?

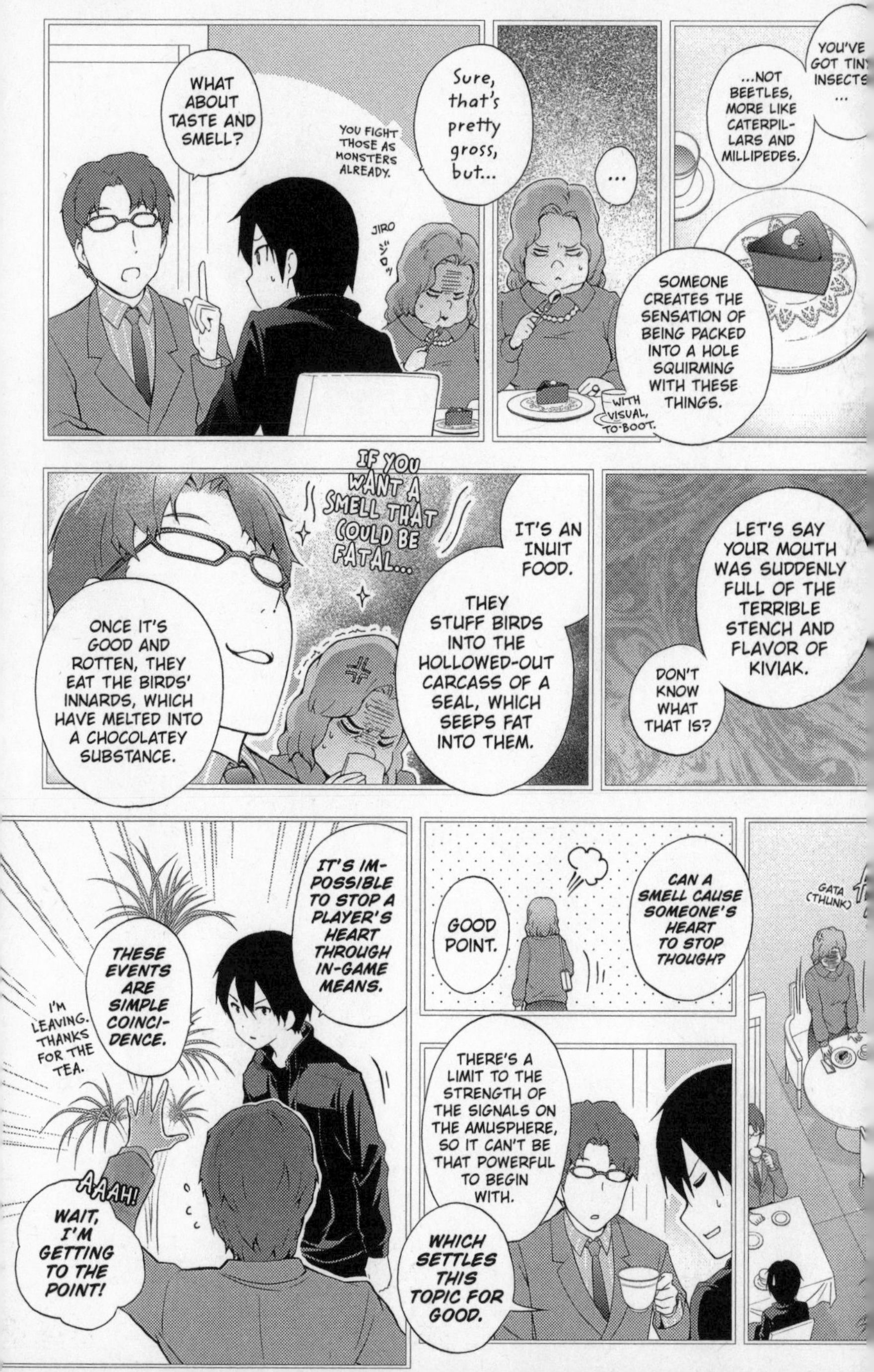
YOU'VE GOT TINY INSECTS...
...NOT BEETLES, MORE LIKE CATERPIL-LARS AND MILLIPEDES.
SOMEONE CREATES THE SENSATION OF BEING PACKED INTO A HOLE SQUIRMING WITH THESE THINGS.
WITH VISUAL, TO-BOOT.
...
Sure, that's pretty gross, but...
YOU FIGHT THOSE AS MONSTERS ALREADY.
JIRO
WHAT ABOUT TASTE AND SMELL?
LET'S SAY YOUR MOUTH WAS SUDDENLY FULL OF THE TERRIBLE STENCH AND FLAVOR OF KIVIAK.
DON'T KNOW WHAT THAT IS?
IT'S AN INUIT FOOD.
THEY STUFF BIRDS INTO THE HOLLOWED-OUT CARCASS OF A SEAL, WHICH SEEPS FAT INTO THEM.
IF YOU WANT A SMELL THAT COULD BE FATAL...
ONCE IT'S GOOD AND ROTTEN, THEY EAT THE BIRDS' INNARDS, WHICH HAVE MELTED INTO A CHOCOLATEY SUBSTANCE.
GATA (THUNK)
CAN A SMELL CAUSE SOMEONE'S HEART TO STOP THOUGH?
GOOD POINT.
THERE'S A LIMIT TO THE STRENGTH OF THE SIGNALS ON THE AMUSPHERE, SO IT CAN'T BE THAT POWERFUL TO BEGIN WITH.
WHICH SETTLES THIS TOPIC FOR GOOD.
IT'S IM-POSSIBLE TO STOP A PLAYER'S HEART THROUGH IN-GAME MEANS.
THESE EVENTS ARE SIMPLE COINCI-DENCE.
I'M LEAVING. THANKS FOR THE TEA.
AAAH!
WAIT, I'M GETTING TO THE POINT!

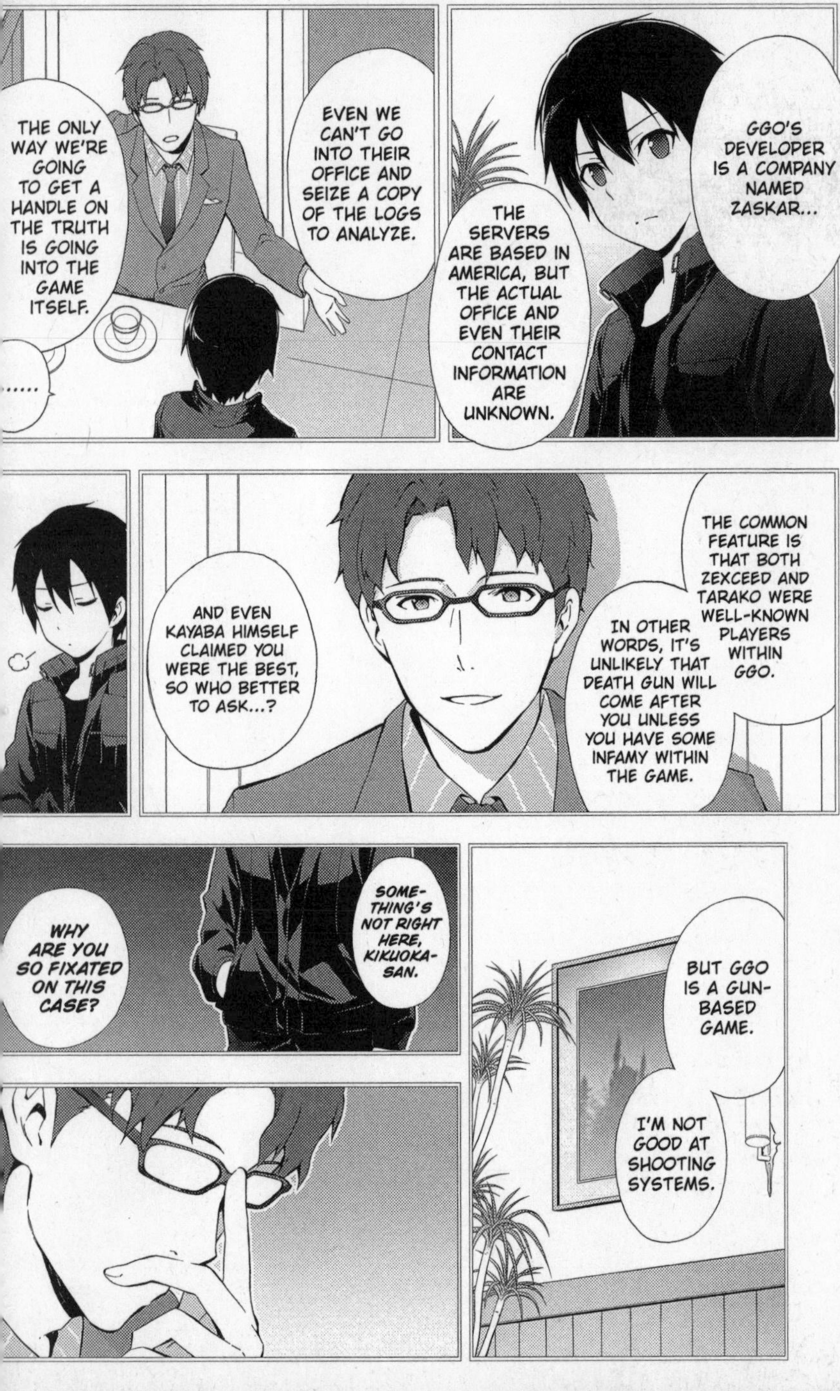
GGO'S DEVELOPER IS A COMPANY NAMED ZASKAR...
THE SERVERS ARE BASED IN AMERICA, BUT THE ACTUAL OFFICE AND EVEN THEIR CONTACT INFORMATION ARE UNKNOWN.
EVEN WE CAN'T GO INTO THEIR OFFICE AND SEIZE A COPY OF THE LOGS TO ANALYZE.
THE ONLY WAY WE'RE GOING TO GET A HANDLE ON THE TRUTH IS GOING INTO THE GAME ITSELF.
......
THE COMMON FEATURE IS THAT BOTH ZEXCEED AND TARAKO WERE WELL-KNOWN PLAYERS WITHIN GGO.
IN OTHER WORDS, IT'S UNLIKELY THAT DEATH GUN WILL COME AFTER YOU UNLESS YOU HAVE SOME INFAMY WITHIN THE GAME.
AND EVEN KAYABA HIMSELF CLAIMED YOU WERE THE BEST, SO WHO BETTER TO ASK...?
BUT GGO IS A GUN-BASED GAME.
I'M NOT GOOD AT SHOOTING SYSTEMS.
SOME-THING'S NOT RIGHT HERE, KIKUOKA-SAN.
WHY ARE YOU SO FIXATED ON THIS CASE?

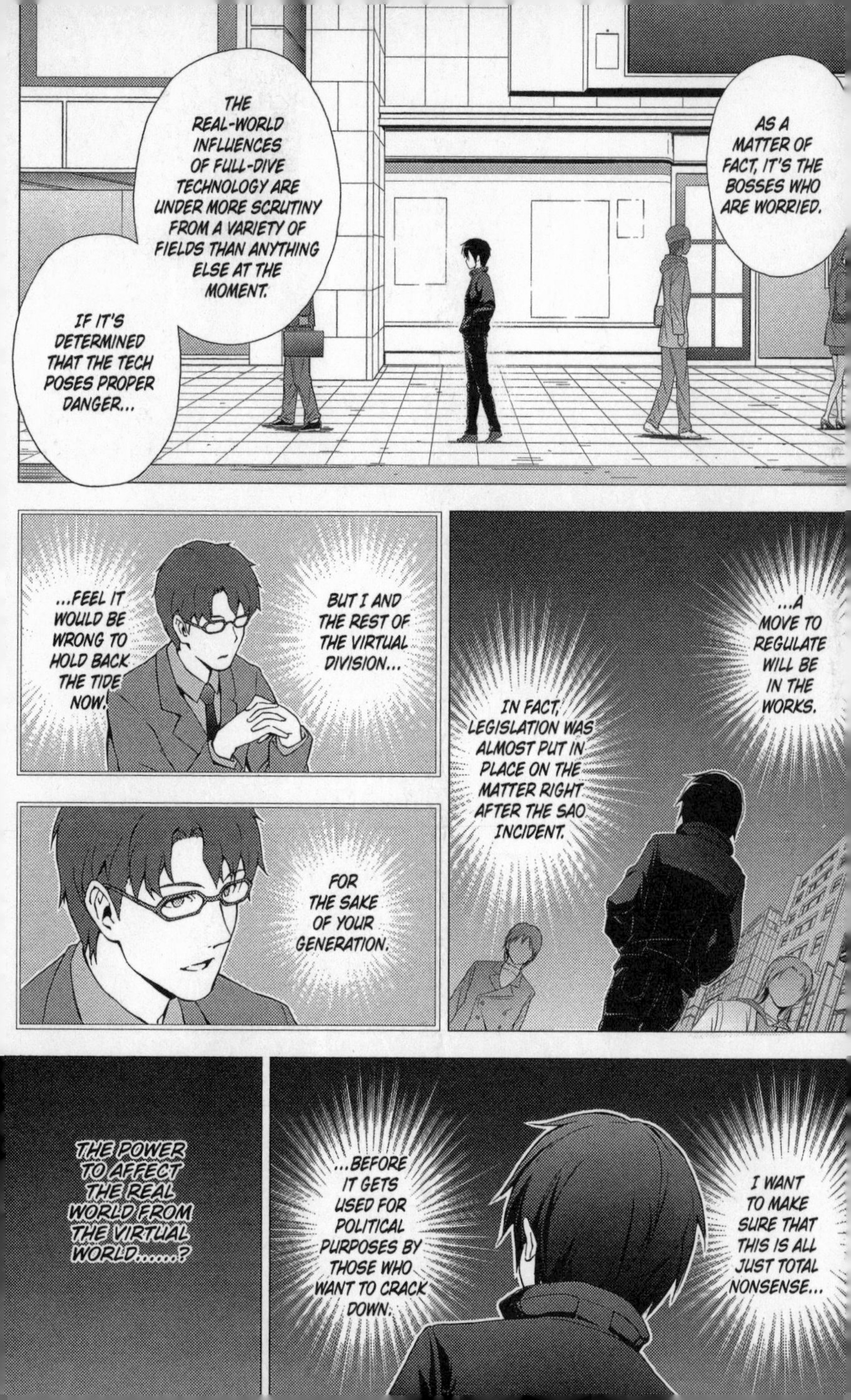
AS A MATTER OF FACT, IT'S THE BOSSES WHO ARE WORRIED.
THE REAL-WORLD INFLUENCES OF FULL-DIVE TECHNOLOGY ARE UNDER MORE SCRUTINY FROM A VARIETY OF FIELDS THAN ANYTHING ELSE AT THE MOMENT.
IF IT'S DETERMINED THAT THE TECH POSES PROPER DANGER...
...A MOVE TO REGULATE WILL BE IN THE WORKS.
IN FACT, LEGISLATION WAS ALMOST PUT IN PLACE ON THE MATTER RIGHT AFTER THE SAO INCIDENT.
BUT I AND THE REST OF THE VIRTUAL DIVISION...
...FEEL IT WOULD BE WRONG TO HOLD BACK THE TIDE NOW!
FOR THE SAKE OF YOUR GENERATION.
I WANT TO MAKE SURE THAT THIS IS ALL JUST TOTAL NONSENSE...
...BEFORE IT GETS USED FOR POLITICAL PURPOSES BY THOSE WHO WANT TO CRACK DOWN.
THE POWER TO AFFECT THE REAL WORLD FROM THE VIRTUAL WORLD......?

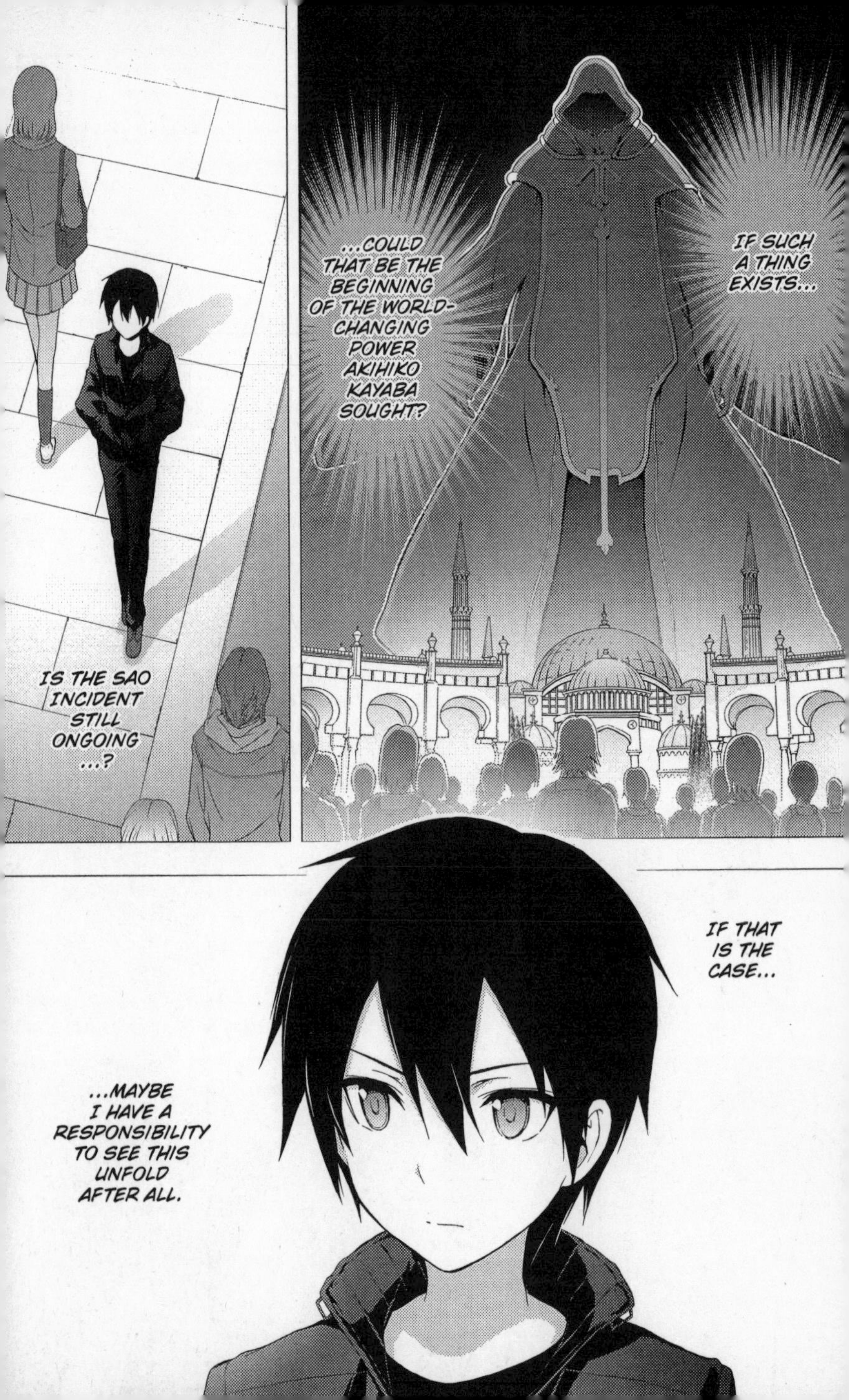
IF SUCH A THING EXISTS...
...COULD THAT BE THE BEGINNING OF THE WORLD-CHANGING POWER AKIHIKO KAYABA SOUGHT?
IS THE SAO INCIDENT STILL ONGOING ...?
IF THAT IS THE CASE...
...MAYBE I HAVE A RESPONSIBILITY TO SEE THIS UNFOLD AFTER ALL.

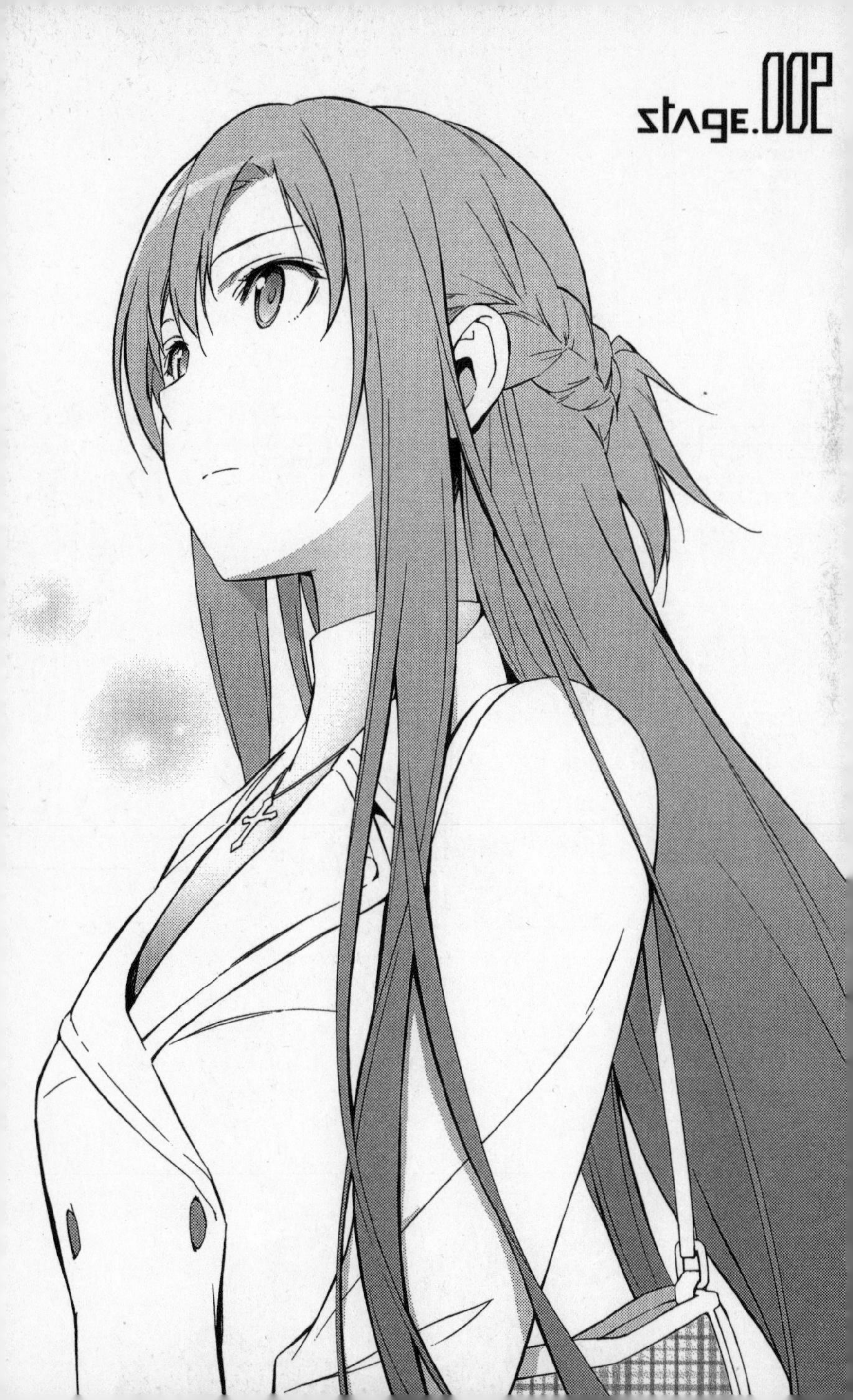
stage.002

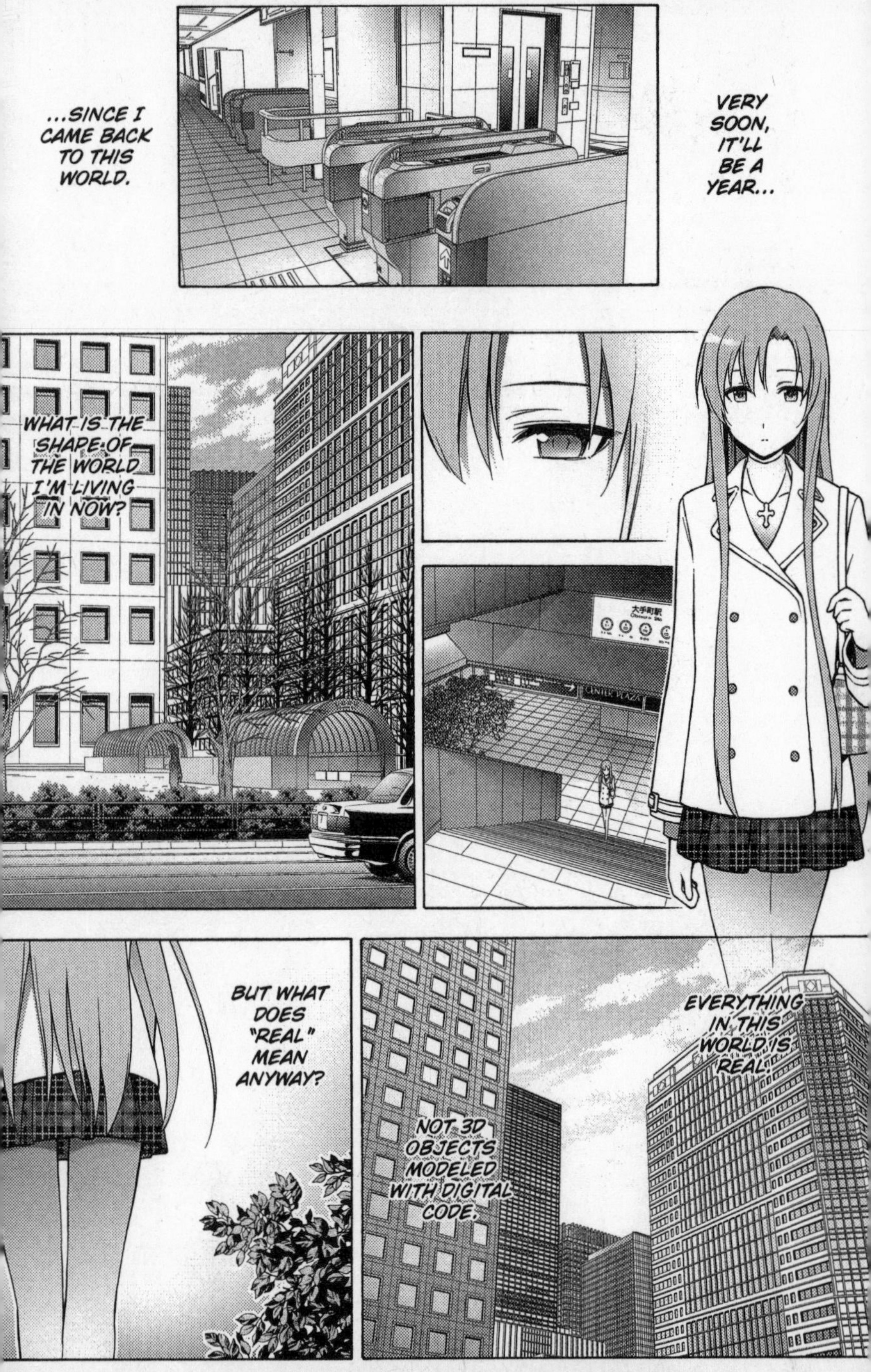
VERY SOON, IT'LL BE A YEAR...
...SINCE I CAME BACK TO THIS WORLD.
大手町駅
CENTER PLAZA
WHAT IS THE SHAPE OF THE WORLD I'M LIVING IN NOW?
EVERYTHING IN THIS WORLD IS REAL.
NOT 3D OBJECTS MODELED WITH DIGITAL CODE.
BUT WHAT DOES "REAL" MEAN ANYWAY?

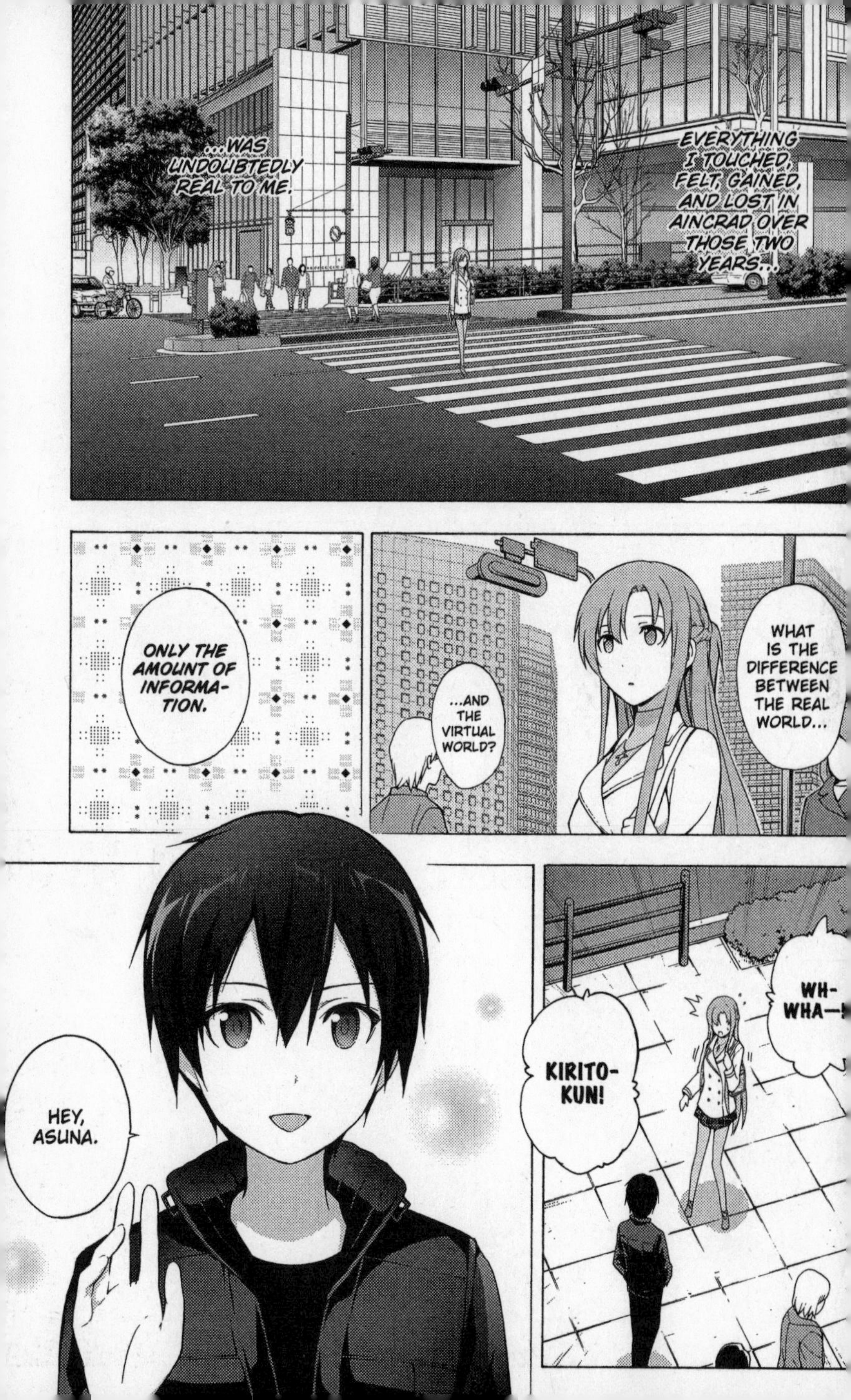
EVERYTHING I TOUCHED, FELT, GAINED, AND LOST IN AINCRAD OVER THOSE TWO YEARS...
...WAS UNDOUBTEDLY REAL TO ME.
WHAT IS THE DIFFERENCE BETWEEN THE REAL WORLD...
...AND THE VIRTUAL WORLD?
ONLY THE AMOUNT OF INFORMA-TION.
WH-WHA—!
KIRITO-KUN!
HEY, ASUNA.

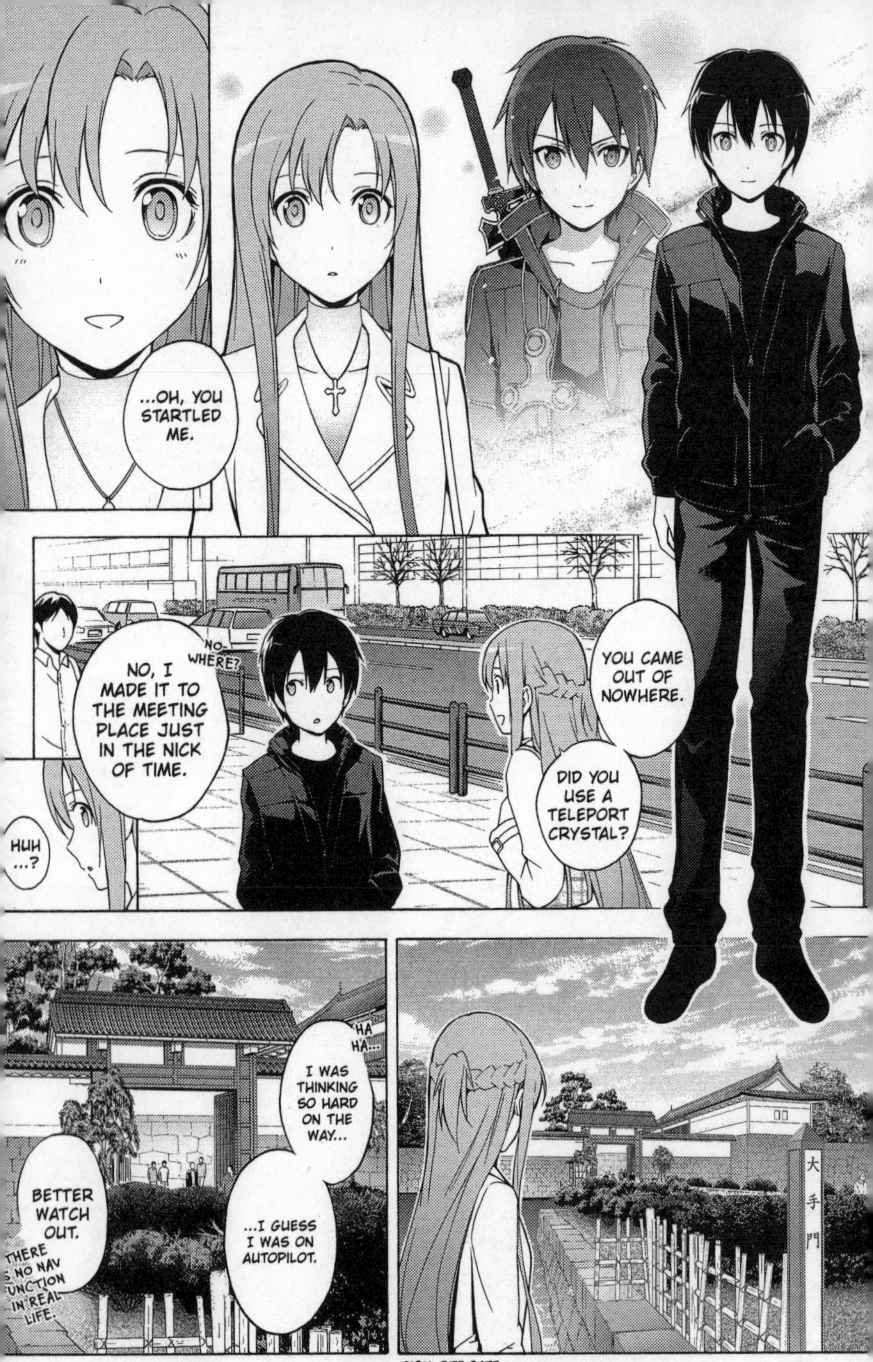
...OH, YOU STARTLED ME.
YOU CAME OUT OF NOWHERE.
DID YOU USE A TELEPORT CRYSTAL?
NO-WHERE?
NO, I MADE IT TO THE MEETING PLACE JUST IN THE NICK OF TIME.
HUH ...?
大手門
HA HA...
I WAS THINKING SO HARD ON THE WAY...
...I GUESS I WAS ON AUTOPILOT.
BETTER WATCH OUT.
THERE'S NO NAV FUNCTION IN REAL LIFE.

SIGN: OTE GATE

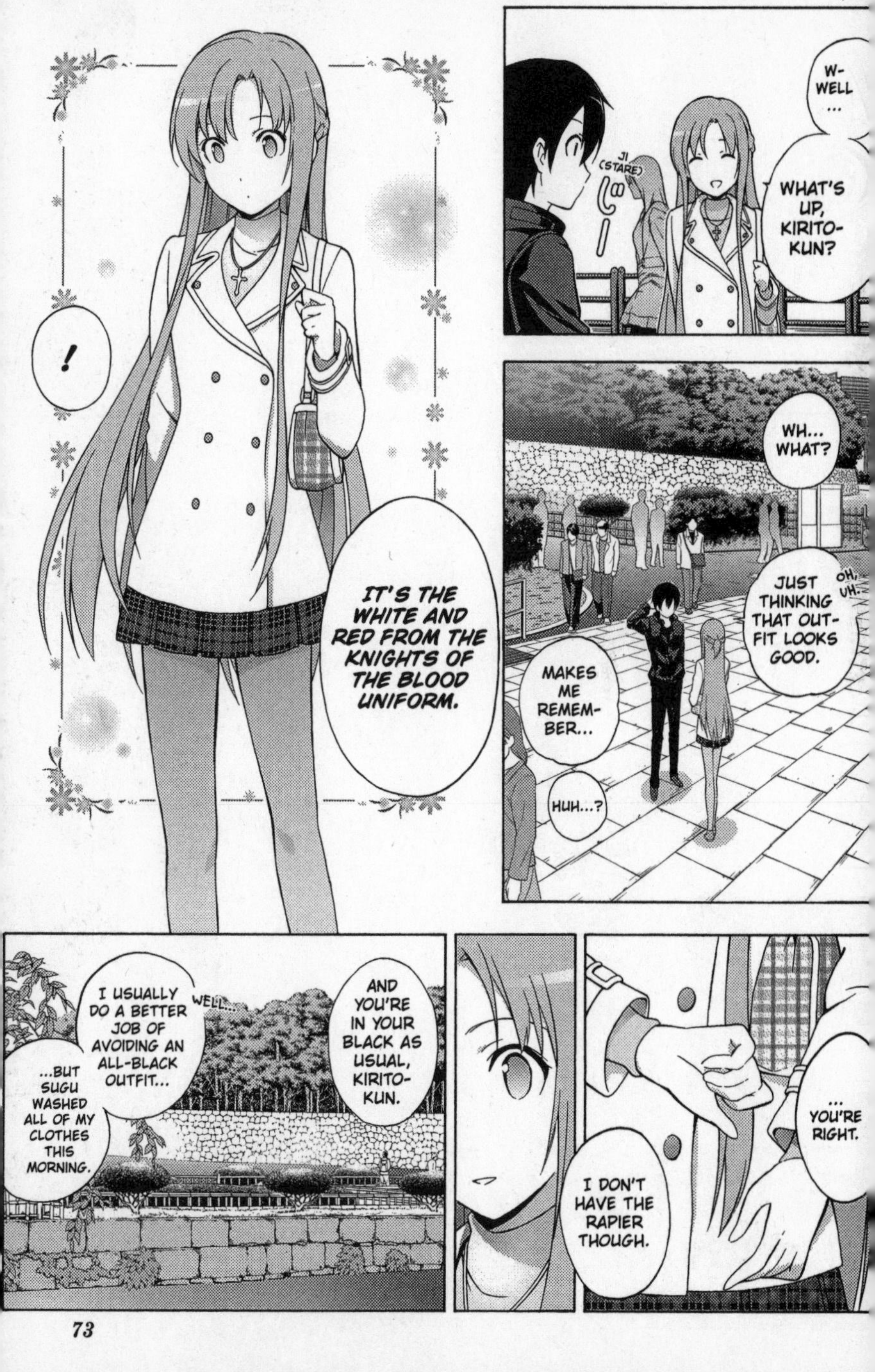
W-WELL...
WHAT'S UP, KIRITO-KUN?
JI (STARE)
WH... WHAT?
OH, UH.
JUST THINKING THAT OUT-FIT LOOKS GOOD.
MAKES ME REMEM-BER...
HUH...?
IT'S THE WHITE AND RED FROM THE KNIGHTS OF THE BLOOD UNIFORM.
!
... YOU'RE RIGHT.
I DON'T HAVE THE RAPIER THOUGH.
AND YOU'RE IN YOUR BLACK AS USUAL, KIRITO-KUN.
WELL...
I USUALLY DO A BETTER JOB OF AVOIDING AN ALL-BLACK OUTFIT...
...BUT SUGU WASHED ALL OF MY CLOTHES THIS MORNING.

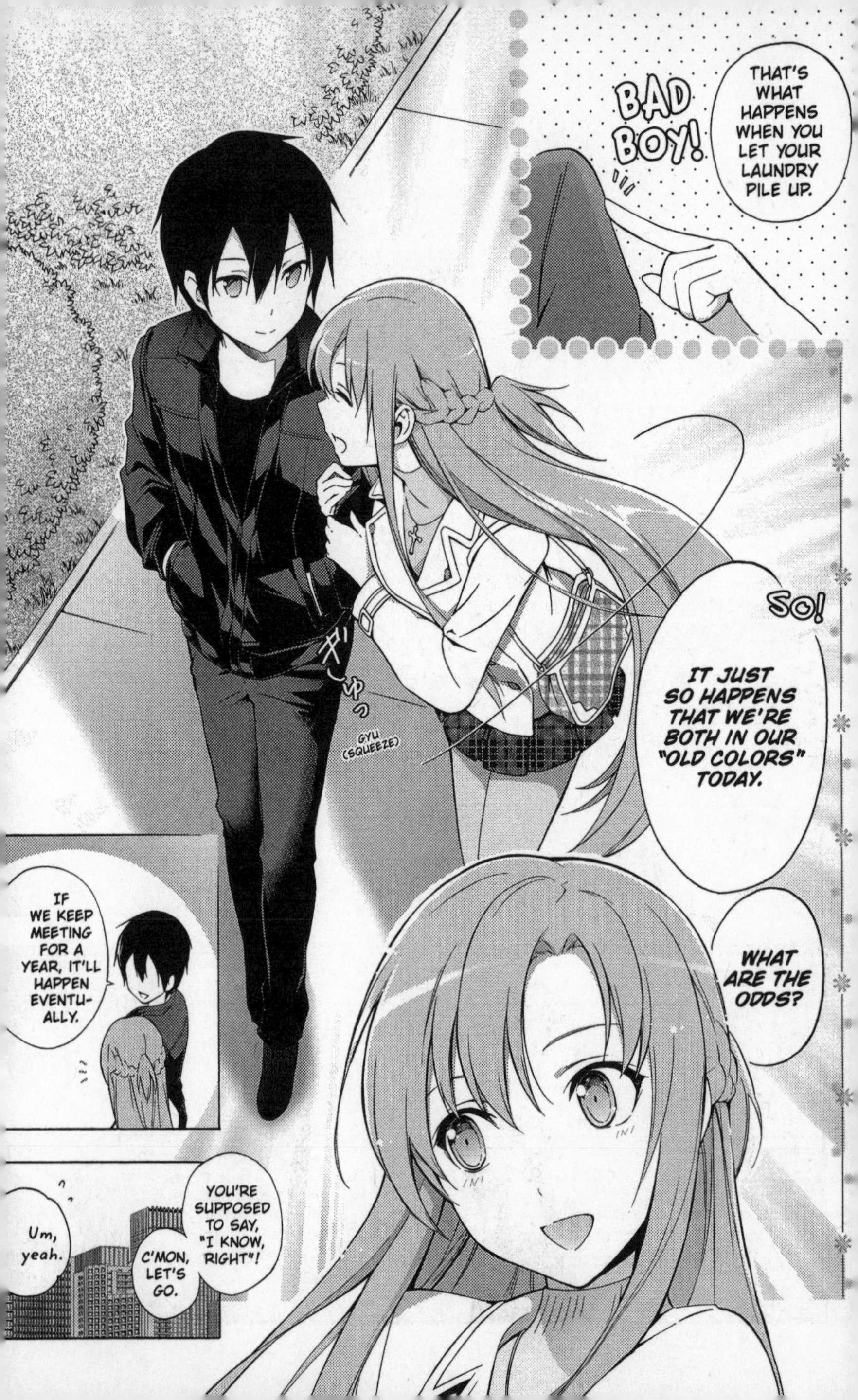
THAT'S WHAT HAPPENS WHEN YOU LET YOUR LAUNDRY PILE UP.
BAD BOY!
SO!
IT JUST SO HAPPENS THAT WE'RE BOTH IN OUR "OLD COLORS" TODAY.
ぎゅっ
GYU (SQUEEZE)
WHAT ARE THE ODDS?
IF WE KEEP MEETING FOR A YEAR, IT'LL HAPPEN EVENTU-ALLY.
YOU'RE SUPPOSED TO SAY, "I KNOW, RIGHT"!
C'MON, LET'S GO.
Um, yeah.

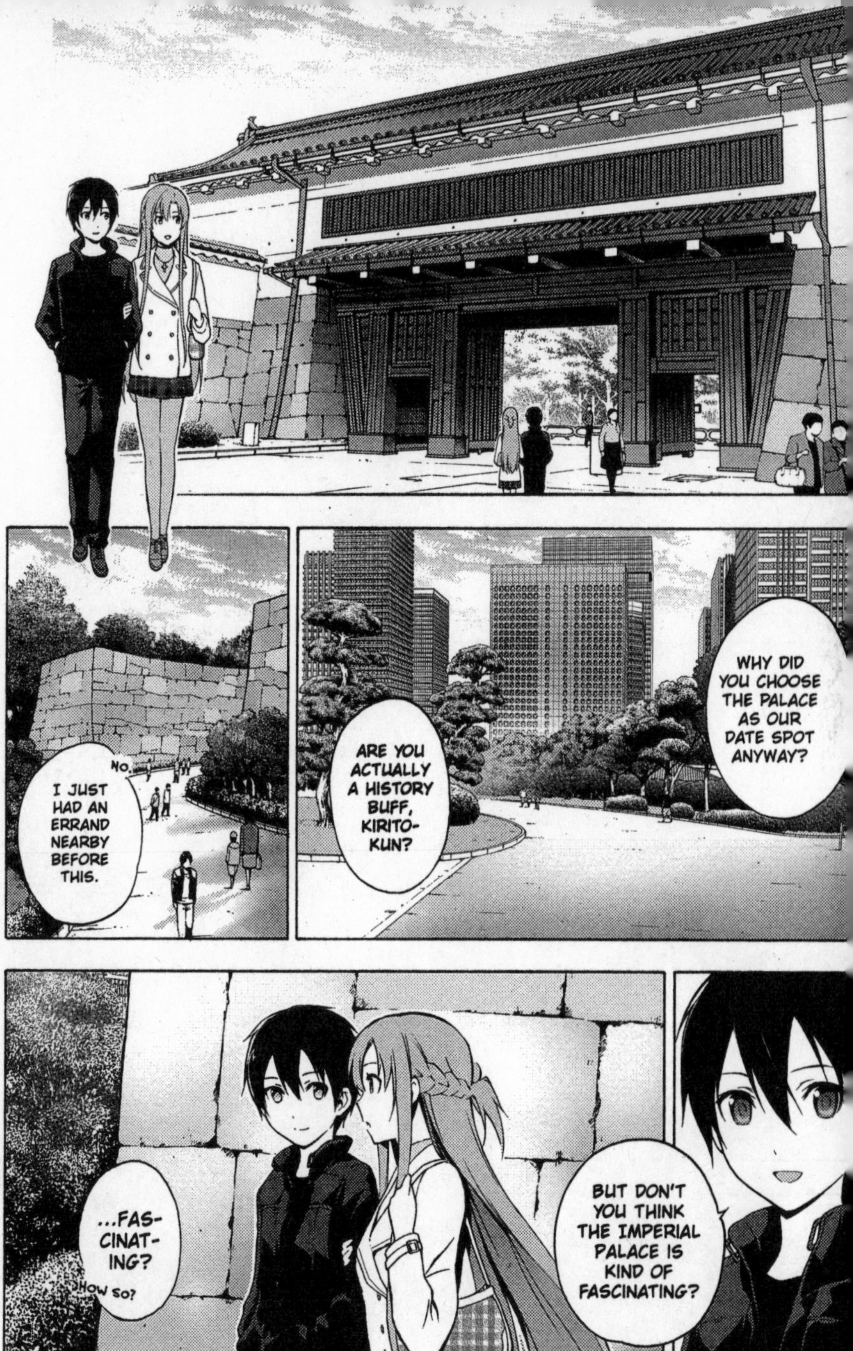
WHY DID YOU CHOOSE THE PALACE AS OUR DATE SPOT ANYWAY?
ARE YOU ACTUALLY A HISTORY BUFF, KIRITO-KUN?
NO.
I JUST HAD AN ERRAND NEARBY BEFORE THIS.
BUT DON'T YOU THINK THE IMPERIAL PALACE IS KIND OF FASCINATING?
...FASCINATING?
HOW SO?

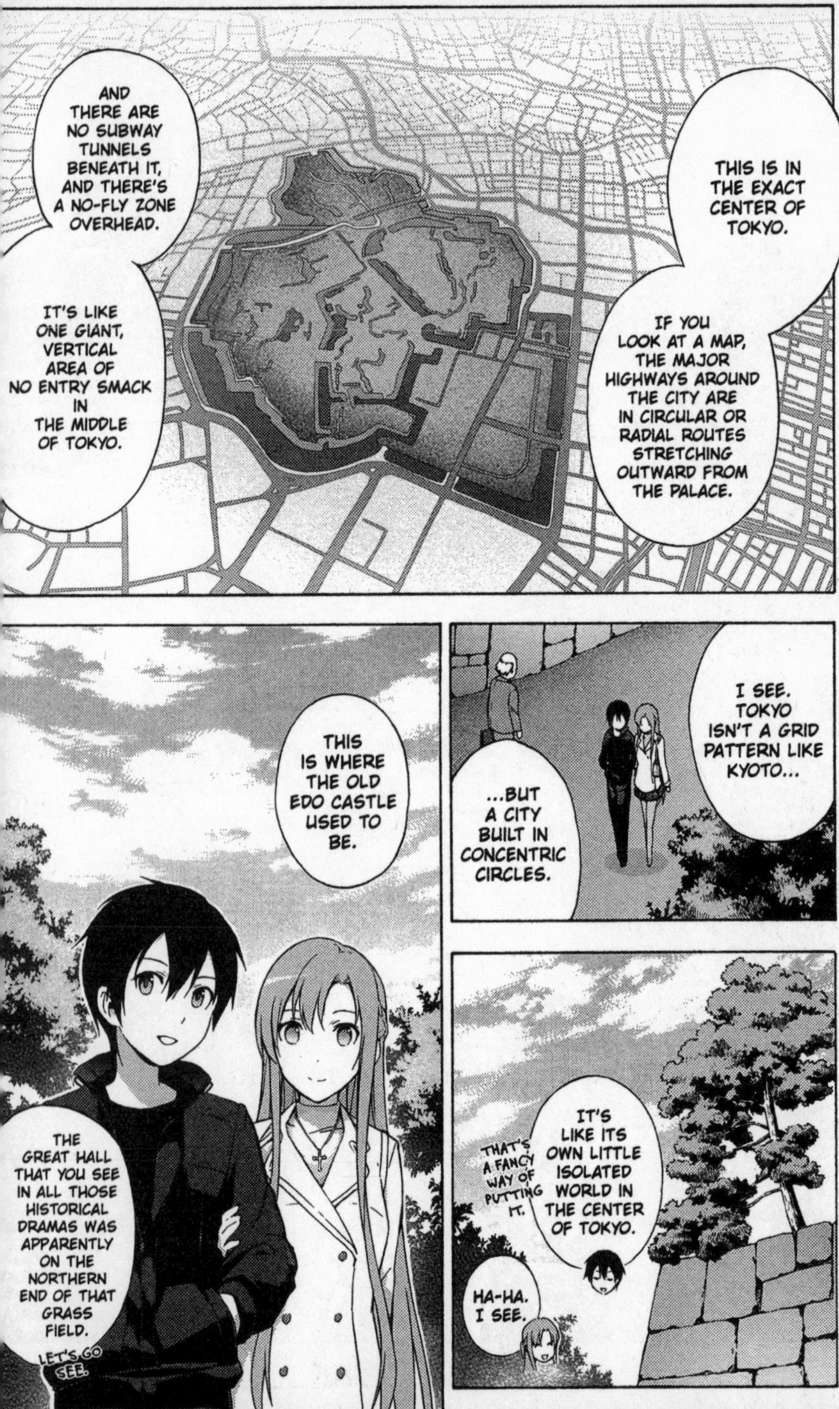
THIS IS IN THE EXACT CENTER OF TOKYO.
IF YOU LOOK AT A MAP, THE MAJOR HIGHWAYS AROUND THE CITY ARE IN CIRCULAR OR RADIAL ROUTES STRETCHING OUTWARD FROM THE PALACE.
AND THERE ARE NO SUBWAY TUNNELS BENEATH IT, AND THERE'S A NO-FLY ZONE OVERHEAD.
IT'S LIKE ONE GIANT, VERTICAL AREA OF NO ENTRY SMACK IN THE MIDDLE OF TOKYO.
I SEE. TOKYO ISN'T A GRID PATTERN LIKE KYOTO...
...BUT A CITY BUILT IN CONCENTRIC CIRCLES.
IT'S LIKE ITS OWN LITTLE ISOLATED WORLD IN THE CENTER OF TOKYO.
THAT'S A FANCY WAY OF PUTTING IT.
HA-HA. I SEE.
THIS IS WHERE THE OLD EDO CASTLE USED TO BE.
THE GREAT HALL THAT YOU SEE IN ALL THOSE HISTORICAL DRAMAS WAS APPARENTLY ON THE NORTHERN END OF THAT GRASS FIELD.
LET'S GO SEE.

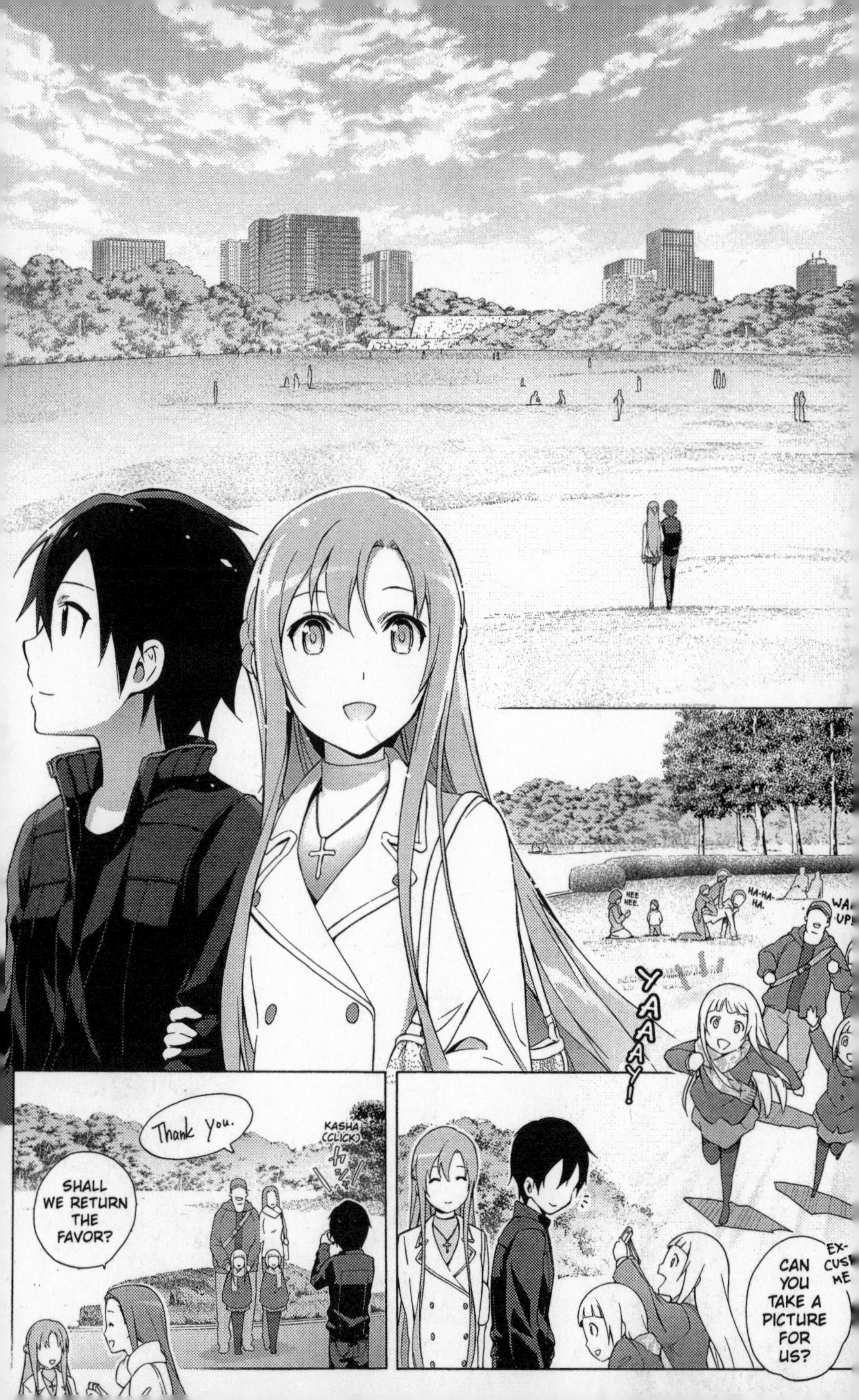
HA-HA-HA.
HEE HEE.
YAAAAY!
EX-CUSE ME
CAN YOU TAKE A PICTURE FOR US?
KASHA (CLICK)
Thank you.
SHALL WE RETURN THE FAVOR?

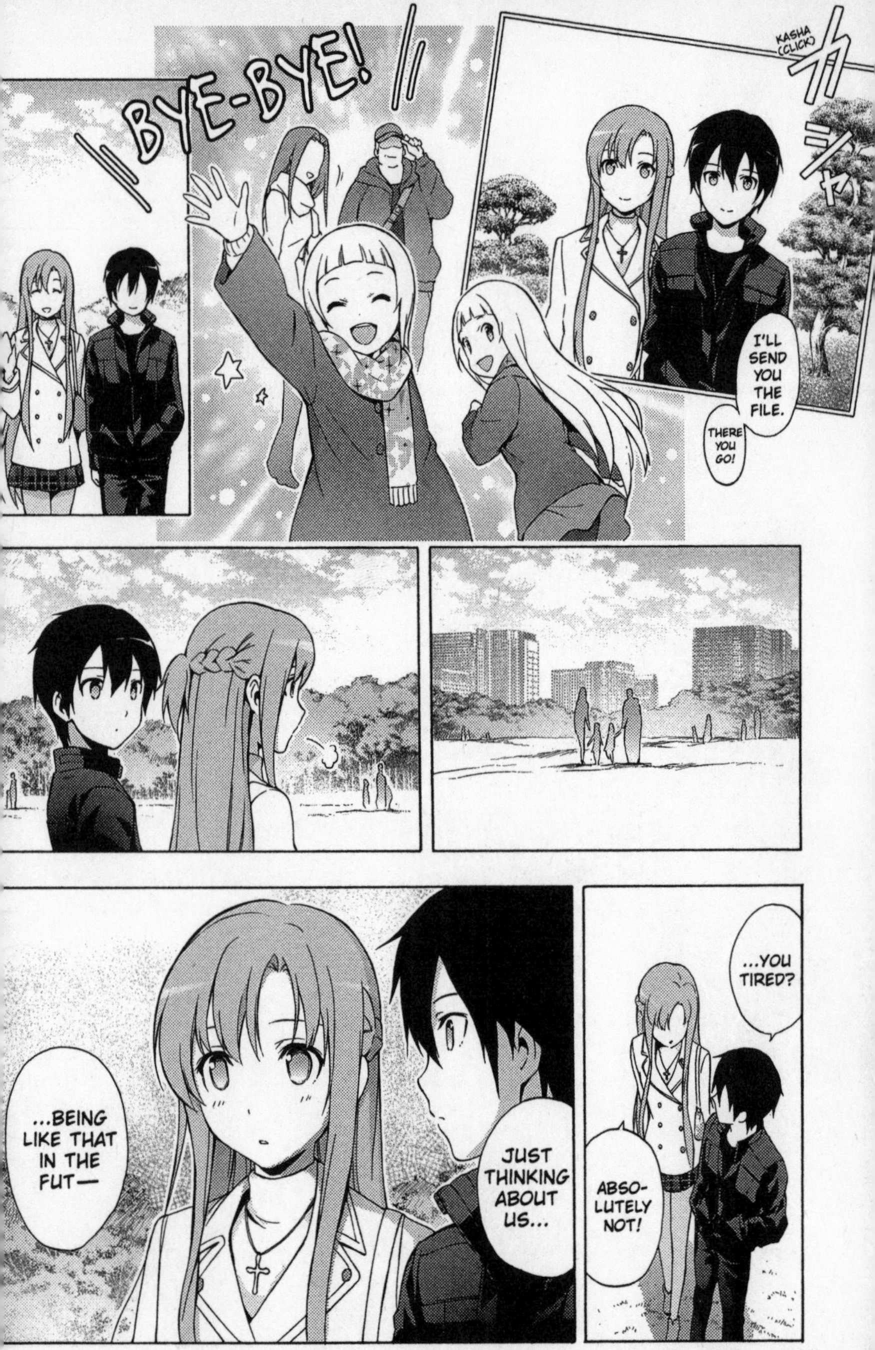
KASHA (CLICK)
カシャ
I'LL SEND YOU THE FILE.
THERE YOU GO!
BYE-BYE!
...YOU TIRED?
ABSO-LUTELY NOT!
JUST THINKING ABOUT US...
...BEING LIKE THAT IN THE FUT—

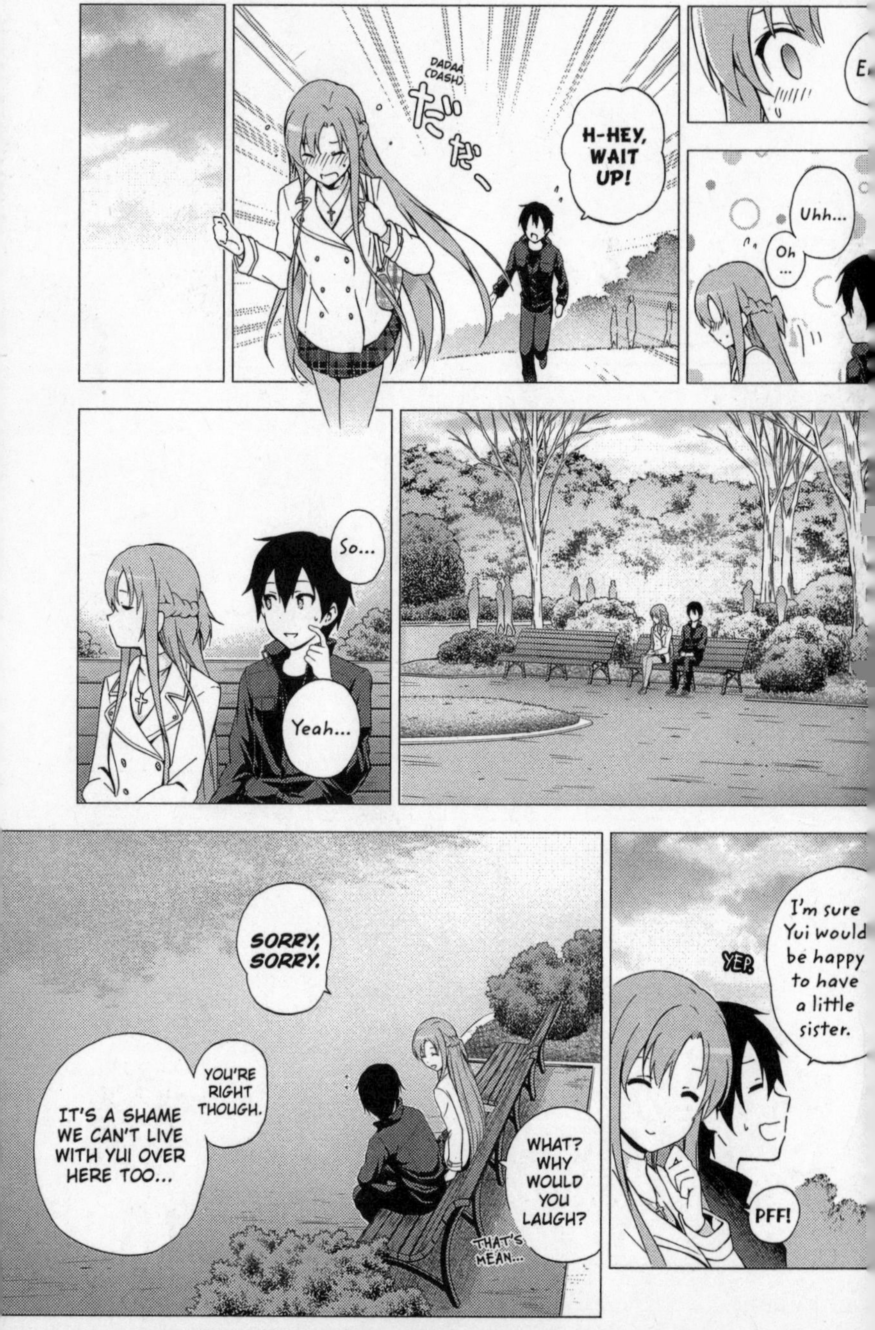
E
Uhh...
Oh ...
H-HEY, WAIT UP!
DADAA (DASH)
だだー
So...
Yeah...
I'm sure Yui would be happy to have a little sister.
YEP.
PFF!
SORRY, SORRY.
WHAT? WHY WOULD YOU LAUGH?
THAT'S MEAN...
YOU'RE RIGHT THOUGH.
IT'S A SHAME WE CAN'T LIVE WITH YUI OVER HERE TOO...

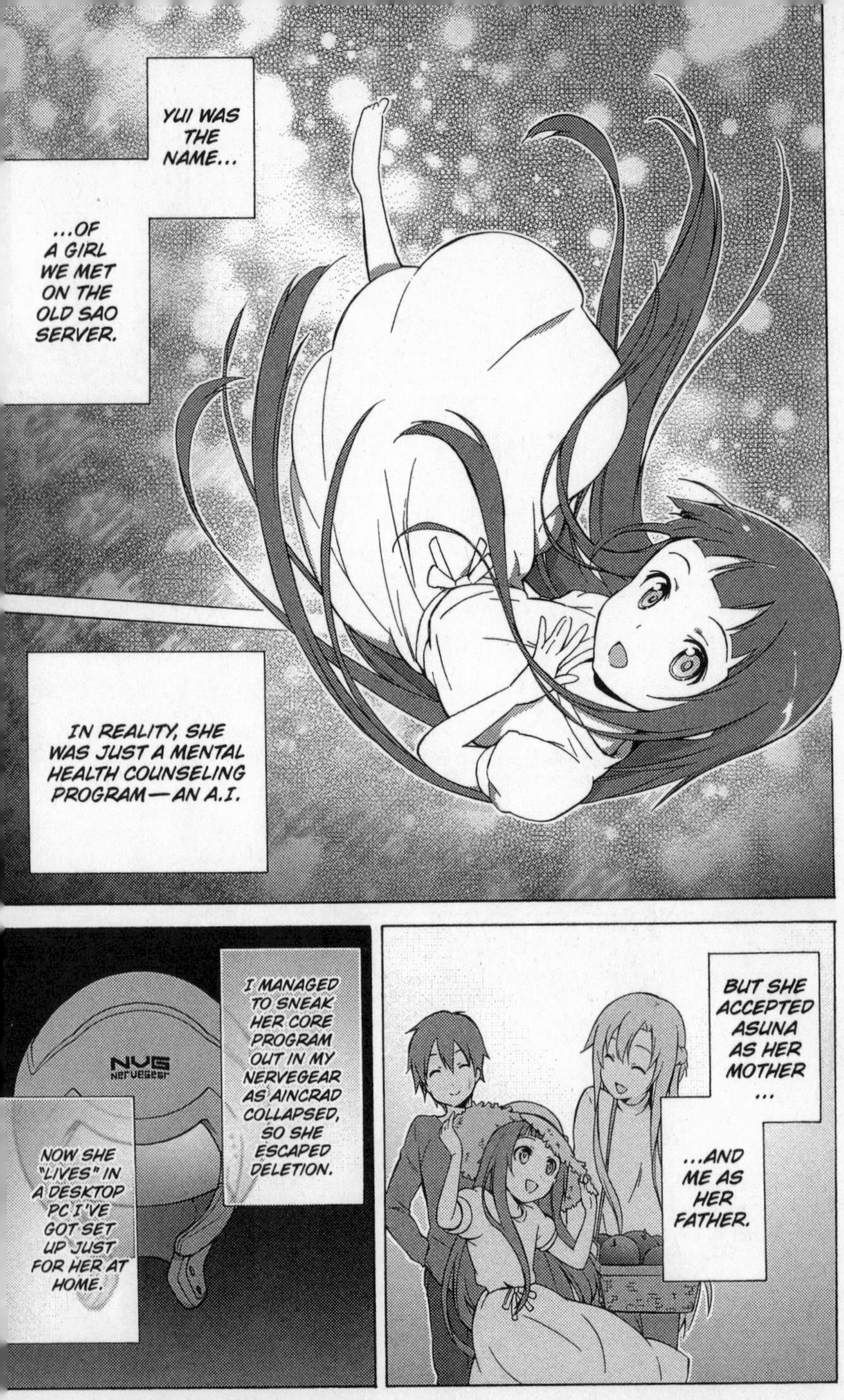
YUI WAS THE NAME...
...OF A GIRL WE MET ON THE OLD SAO SERVER.
IN REALITY, SHE WAS JUST A MENTAL HEALTH COUNSELING PROGRAM—AN A.I.
BUT SHE ACCEPTED ASUNA AS HER MOTHER ...
...AND ME AS HER FATHER.
I MANAGED TO SNEAK HER CORE PROGRAM OUT IN MY NERVEGEAR AS AINCRAD COLLAPSED, SO SHE ESCAPED DELETION.
NOW SHE "LIVES" IN A DESKTOP PC I'VE GOT SET UP JUST FOR HER AT HOME.
NVG
NerveGear

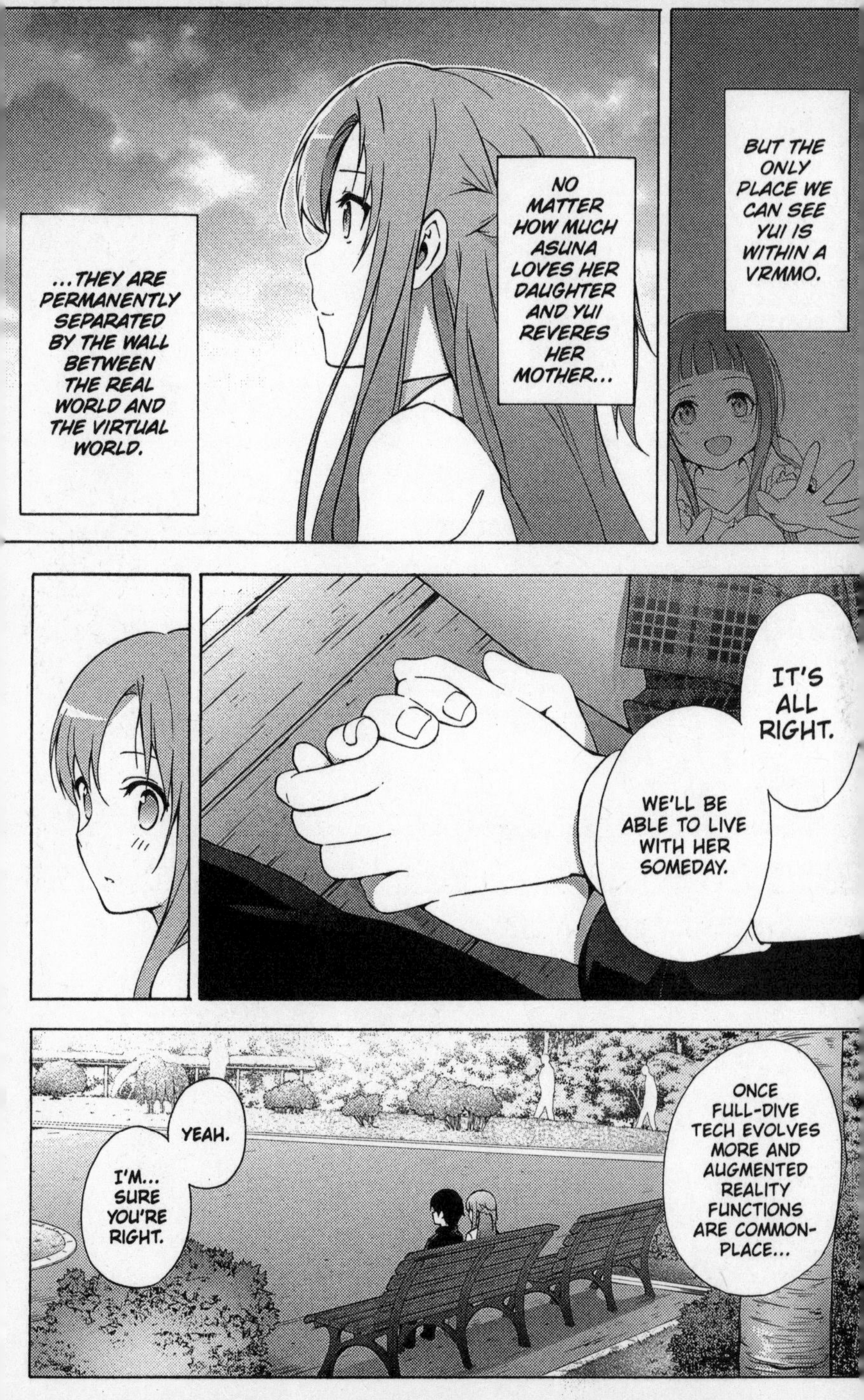
BUT THE ONLY PLACE WE CAN SEE YUI IS WITHIN A VRMMO.
NO MATTER HOW MUCH ASUNA LOVES HER DAUGHTER AND YUI REVERES HER MOTHER...
...THEY ARE PERMANENTLY SEPARATED BY THE WALL BETWEEN THE REAL WORLD AND THE VIRTUAL WORLD.
IT'S ALL RIGHT.
WE'LL BE ABLE TO LIVE WITH HER SOMEDAY.
ONCE FULL-DIVE TECH EVOLVES MORE AND AUGMENTED REALITY FUNCTIONS ARE COMMON-PLACE...
YEAH.
I'M... SURE YOU'RE RIGHT.

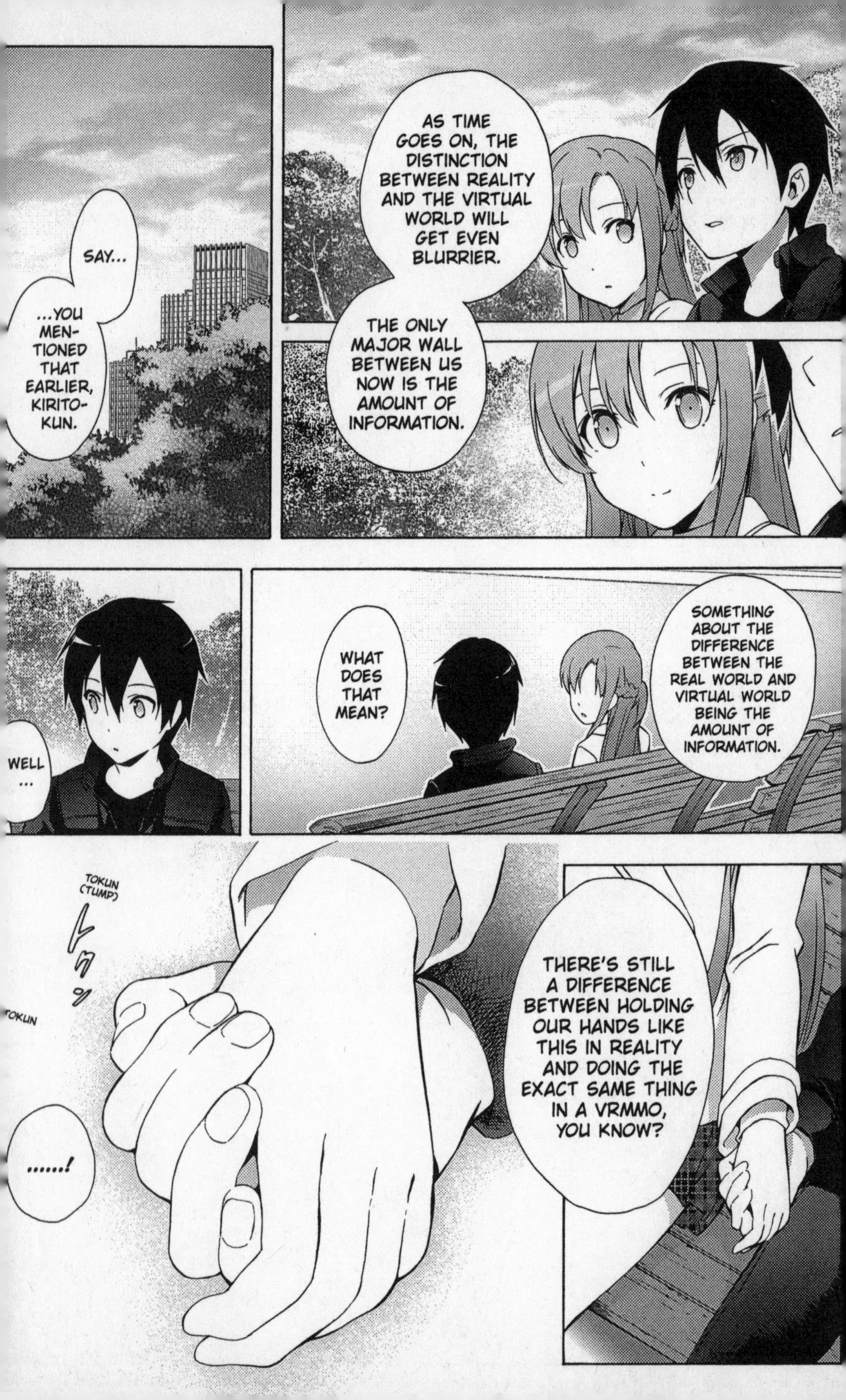
AS TIME GOES ON, THE DISTINCTION BETWEEN REALITY AND THE VIRTUAL WORLD WILL GET EVEN BLURRIER.
THE ONLY MAJOR WALL BETWEEN US NOW IS THE AMOUNT OF INFORMATION.
SAY...
...YOU MENTIONED THAT EARLIER, KIRITO-KUN.
SOMETHING ABOUT THE DIFFERENCE BETWEEN THE REAL WORLD AND VIRTUAL WORLD BEING THE AMOUNT OF INFORMATION.
WHAT DOES THAT MEAN?
WELL...
THERE'S STILL A DIFFERENCE BETWEEN HOLDING OUR HANDS LIKE THIS IN REALITY AND DOING THE EXACT SAME THING IN A VRMMO, YOU KNOW?
TOKUN (TUMP)
TOKUN
......!

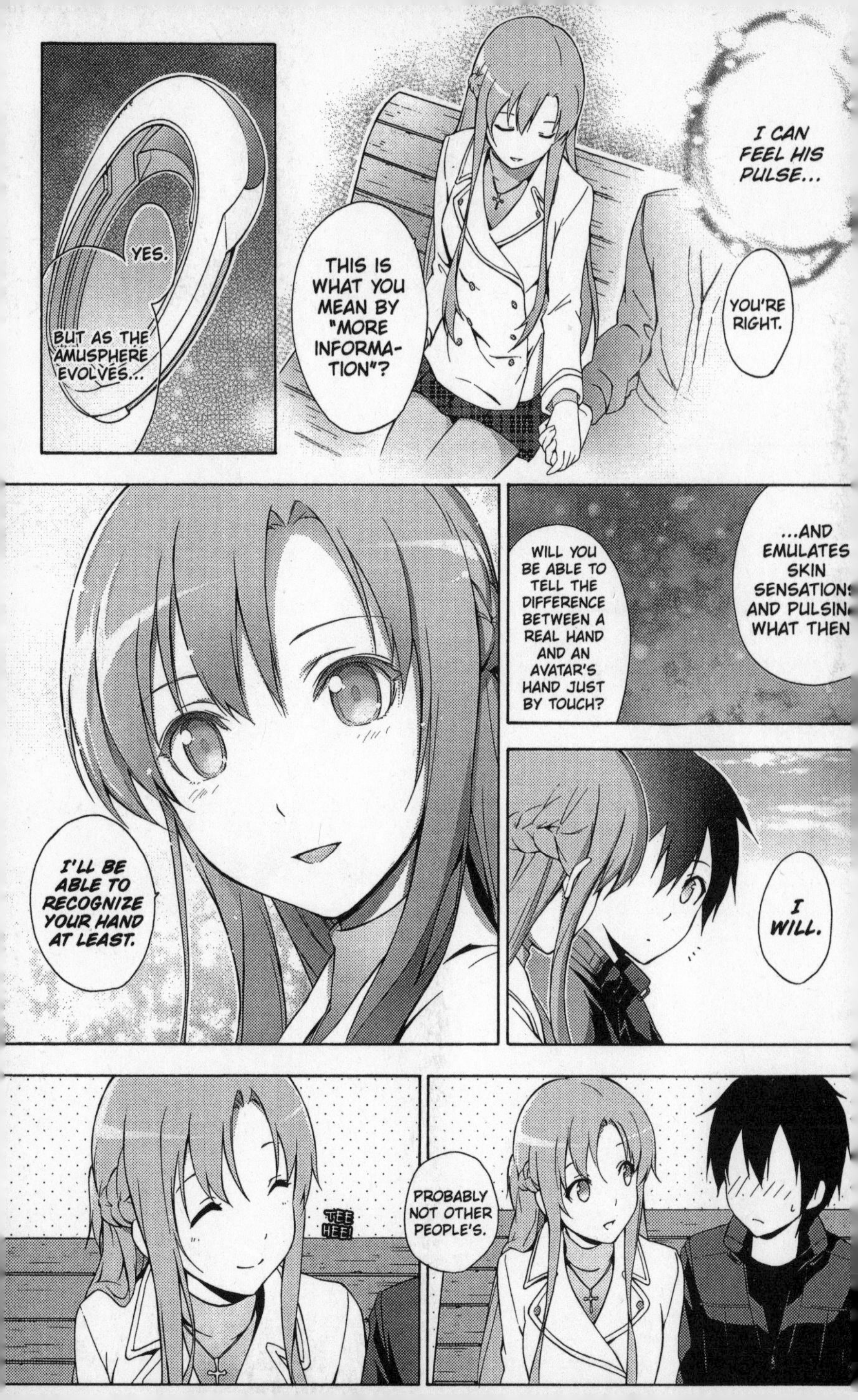
I CAN FEEL HIS PULSE...
YOU'RE RIGHT.
THIS IS WHAT YOU MEAN BY "MORE INFORMATION"?
YES.
BUT AS THE AMUSPHERE EVOLVES...
...AND EMULATES SKIN SENSATION AND PULSIN WHAT THEN
WILL YOU BE ABLE TO TELL THE DIFFERENCE BETWEEN A REAL HAND AND AN AVATAR'S HAND JUST BY TOUCH?
I WILL.
I'LL BE ABLE TO RECOGNIZE YOUR HAND AT LEAST.
PROBABLY NOT OTHER PEOPLE'S.
TEE HEE!

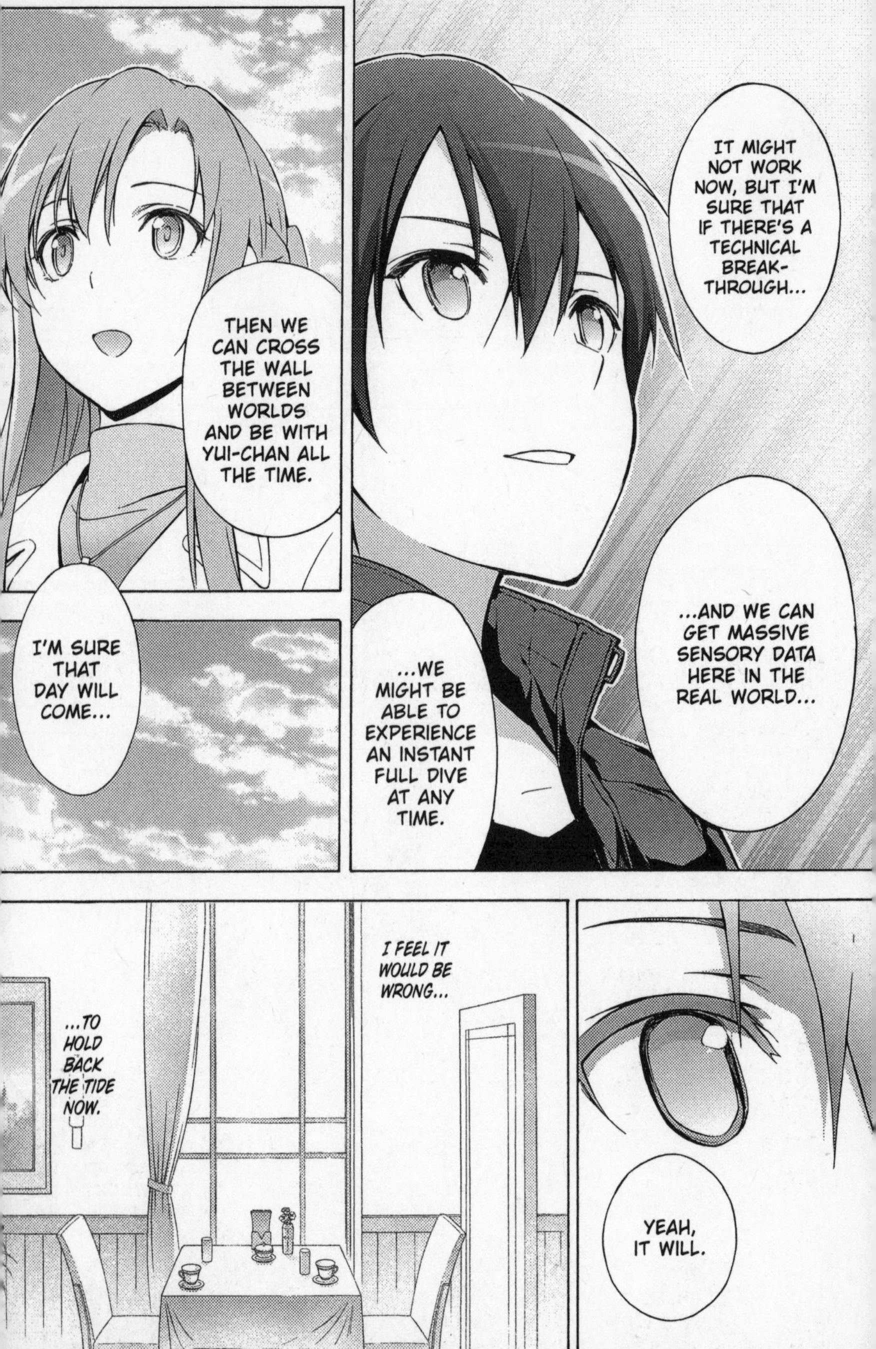
IT MIGHT NOT WORK NOW, BUT I'M SURE THAT IF THERE'S A TECHNICAL BREAK-THROUGH...
...AND WE CAN GET MASSIVE SENSORY DATA HERE IN THE REAL WORLD...
...WE MIGHT BE ABLE TO EXPERIENCE AN INSTANT FULL DIVE AT ANY TIME.
THEN WE CAN CROSS THE WALL BETWEEN WORLDS AND BE WITH YUI-CHAN ALL THE TIME.
I'M SURE THAT DAY WILL COME...
YEAH, IT WILL.
I FEEL IT WOULD BE WRONG...
...TO HOLD BACK THE TIDE NOW.

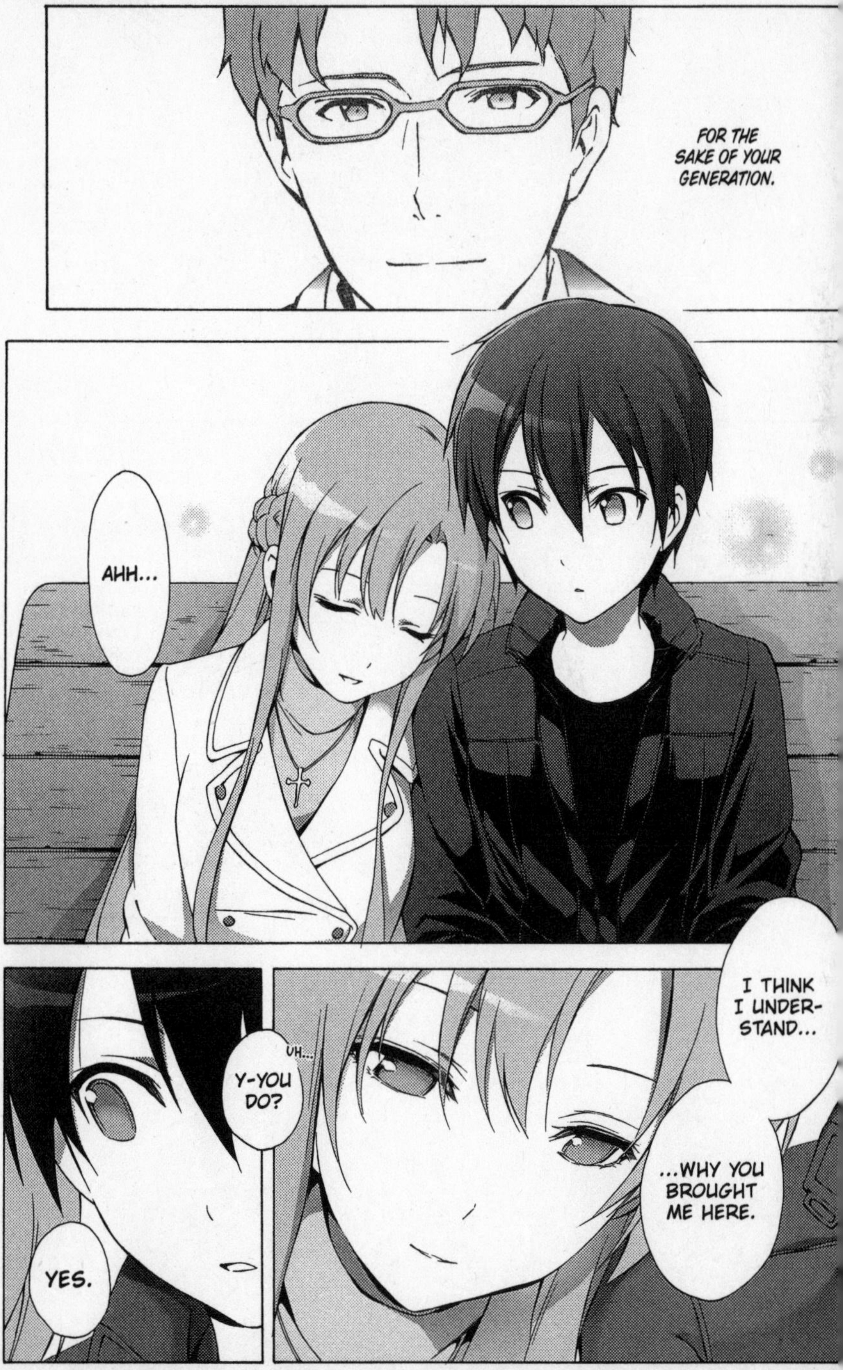
FOR THE SAKE OF YOUR GENERATION.
AHH...
I THINK I UNDER-STAND...
...WHY YOU BROUGHT ME HERE.
UH...
Y-YOU DO?
YES.

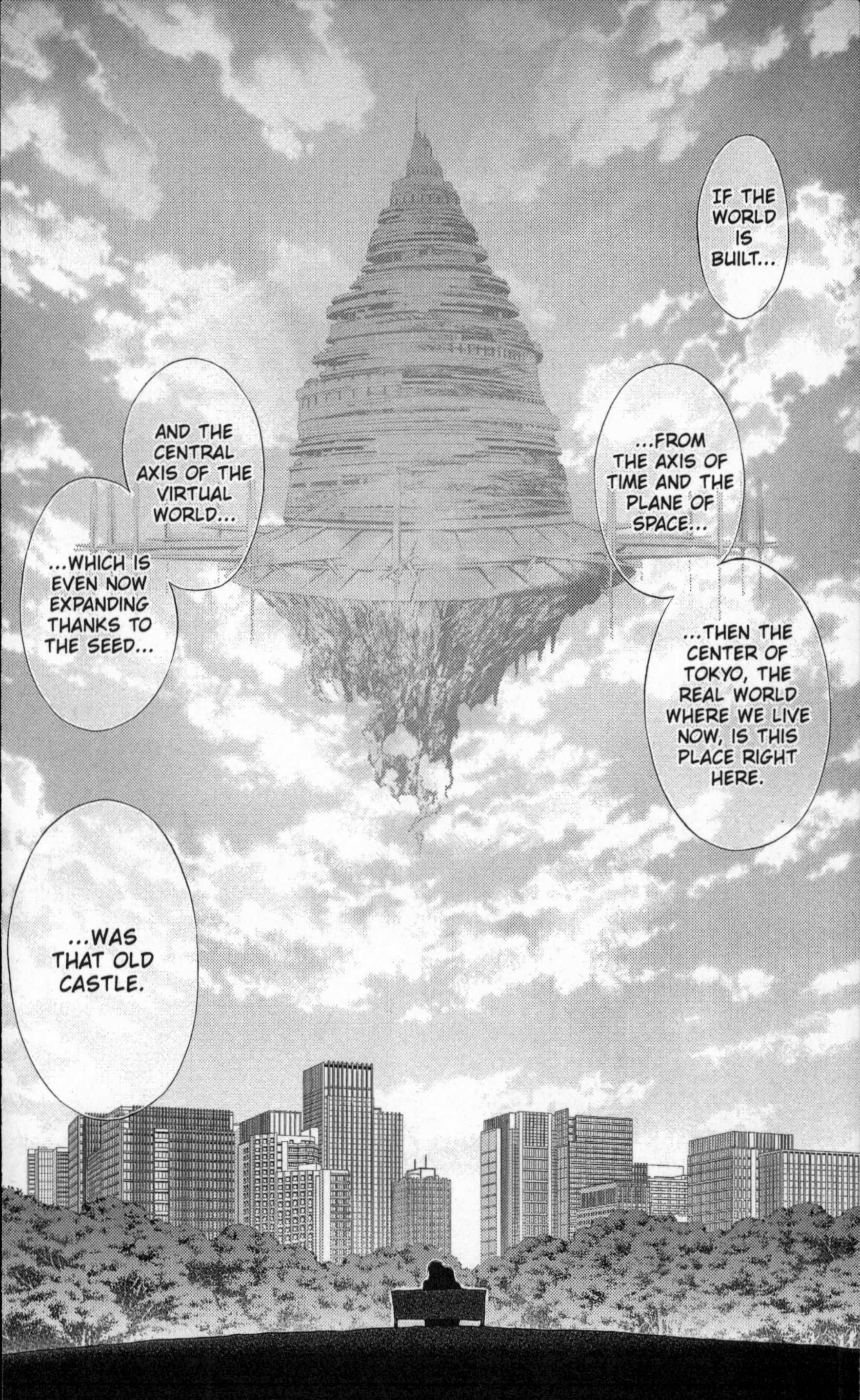
IF THE WORLD IS BUILT...
...FROM THE AXIS OF TIME AND THE PLANE OF SPACE...
...THEN THE CENTER OF TOKYO, THE REAL WORLD WHERE WE LIVE NOW, IS THIS PLACE RIGHT HERE.
AND THE CENTRAL AXIS OF THE VIRTUAL WORLD...
...WHICH IS EVEN NOW EXPANDING THANKS TO THE SEED...
...WAS THAT OLD CASTLE.

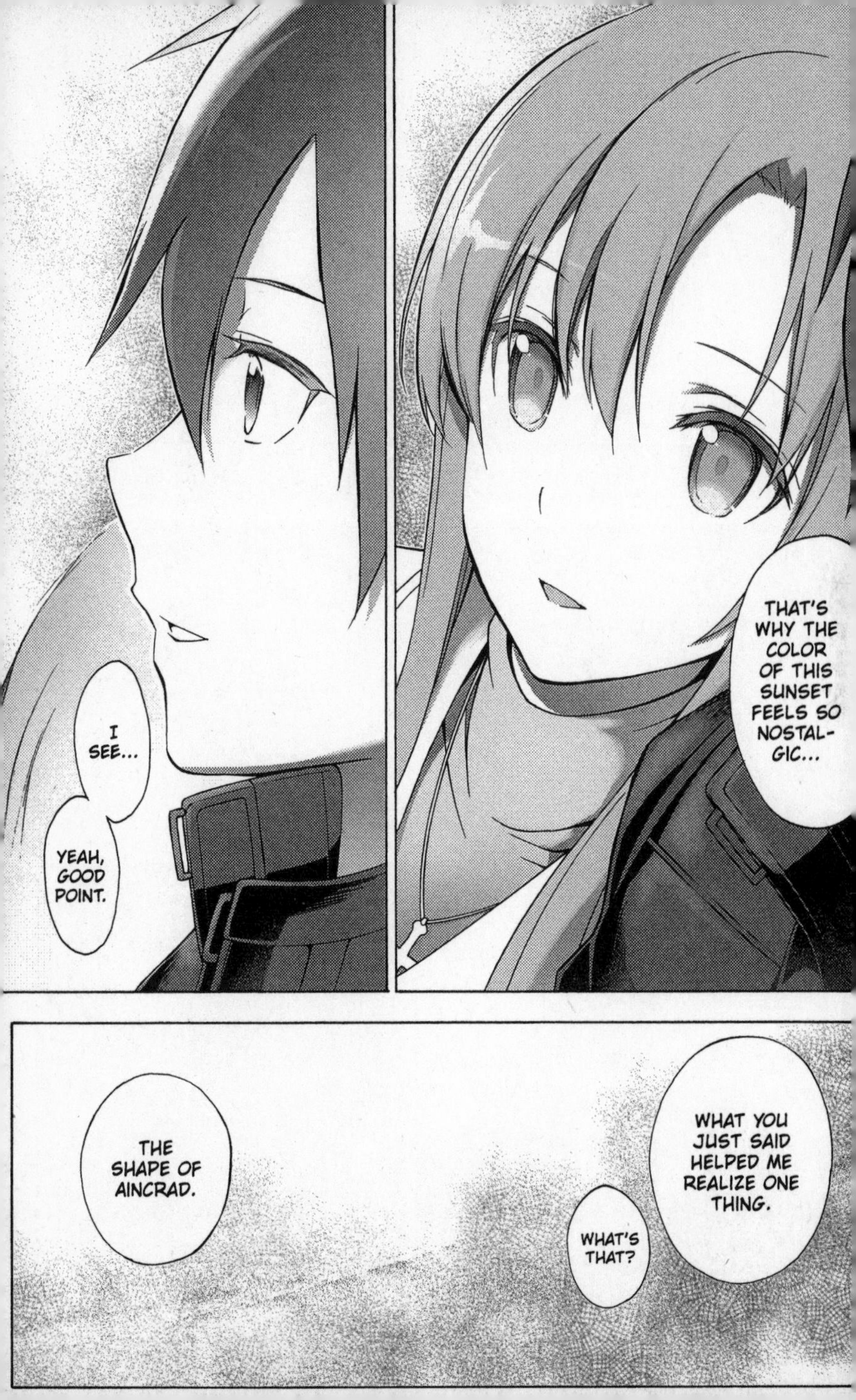
THAT'S WHY THE COLOR OF THIS SUNSET FEELS SO NOSTAL-GIC...
I SEE...
YEAH, GOOD POINT.
WHAT YOU JUST SAID HELPED ME REALIZE ONE THING.
WHAT'S THAT?
THE SHAPE OF AINCRAD.

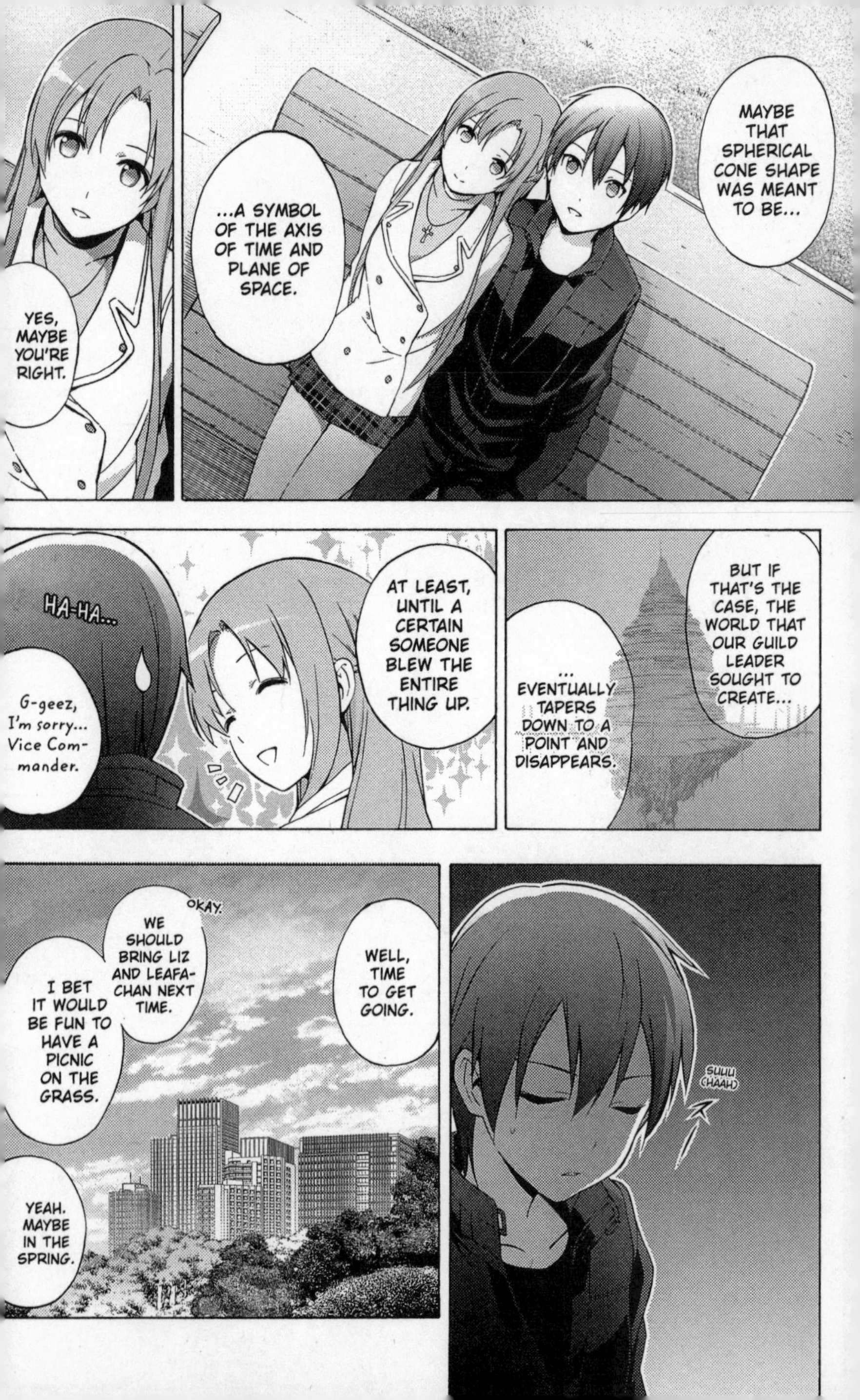
MAYBE THAT SPHERICAL CONE SHAPE WAS MEANT TO BE...
...A SYMBOL OF THE AXIS OF TIME AND PLANE OF SPACE.
YES, MAYBE YOU'RE RIGHT.
BUT IF THAT'S THE CASE, THE WORLD THAT OUR GUILD LEADER SOUGHT TO CREATE...
...EVENTUALLY TAPERS DOWN TO A POINT AND DISAPPEARS.
AT LEAST, UNTIL A CERTAIN SOMEONE BLEW THE ENTIRE THING UP.
HA-HA...
G-geez, I'm sorry... Vice Commander.
SUUU (HAAH)
WELL, TIME TO GET GOING.
OKAY.
WE SHOULD BRING LIZ AND LEAFA-CHAN NEXT TIME.
I BET IT WOULD BE FUN TO HAVE A PICNIC ON THE GRASS.
YEAH. MAYBE IN THE SPRING.

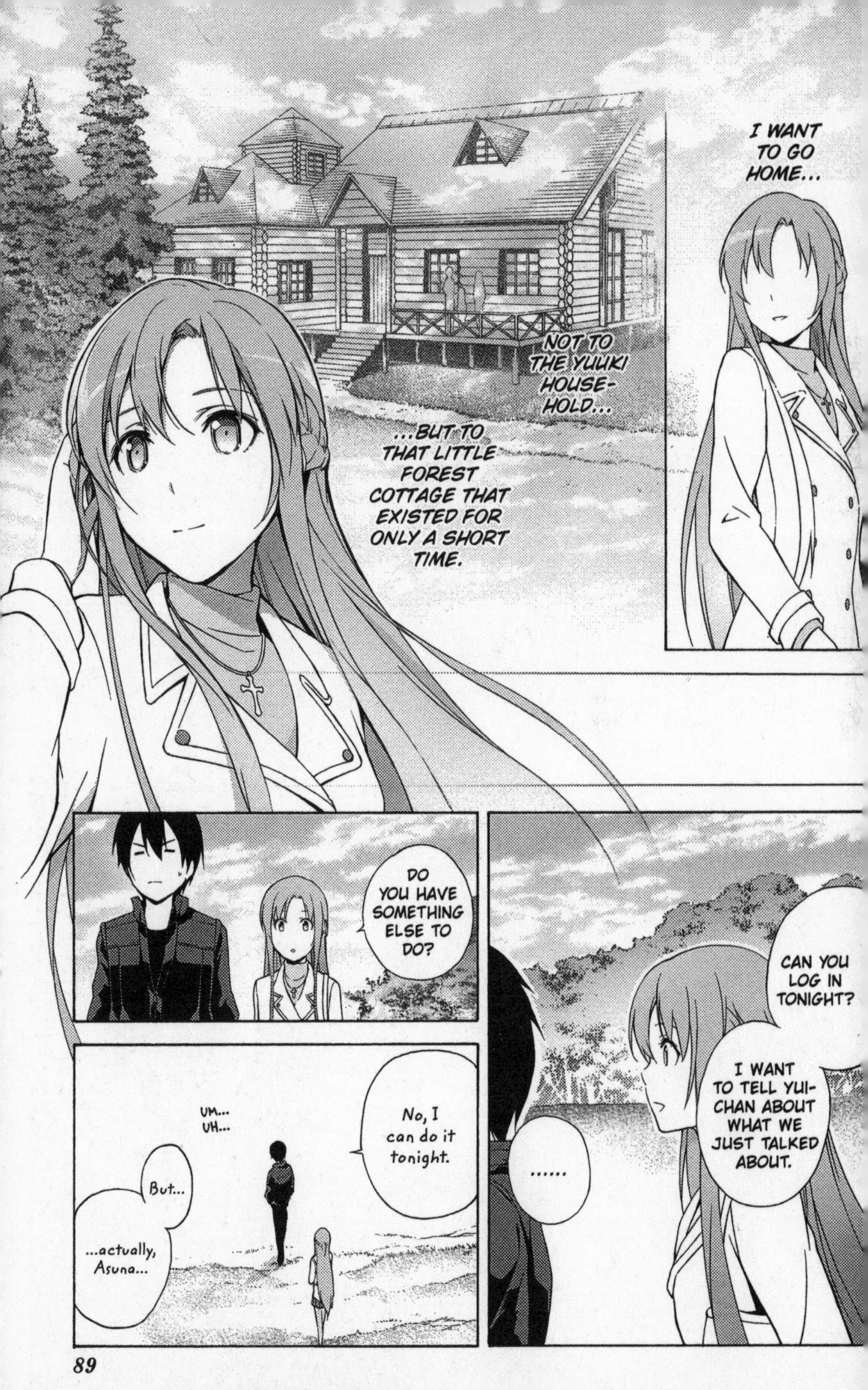
I WANT TO GO HOME...
NOT TO THE YUUKI HOUSE-HOLD...
...BUT TO THAT LITTLE FOREST COTTAGE THAT EXISTED FOR ONLY A SHORT TIME.
CAN YOU LOG IN TONIGHT?
I WANT TO TELL YUI-CHAN ABOUT WHAT WE JUST TALKED ABOUT.
......
DO YOU HAVE SOMETHING ELSE TO DO?
No, I can do it tonight.
UM... UH...
But...
...actually, Asuna...

SWORD ART ONLINE
phantom bullet

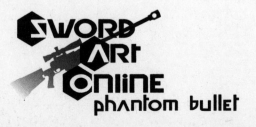

SWORD ART ONLINE
phantom bullet
002
check point!

CHARACTER CONVERSION: WORLD

A SYSTEM FOR MOVING A CHARACTER BETWEEN GAMES BASED ON "THE SEED," THE VRMMO PROGRAM PACKAGE THAT AKIHIKO KAYABA LEFT BEHIND AND KIRITO UPLOADED TO THE INTERNET. BECAUSE LEVELS, STATS, AND SKILLS VARY BETWEEN GAMES, THE SYSTEM PROPERLY BALANCES AND RECONSTRUCTS A CHARACTER'S STRENGTH—ENSURING THAT AN ABOVE AVERAGE WARRIOR IN ONE GAME WILL STILL BE ABOVE AVERAGE AFTER CONVERTING TO A NEW GAME. BECAUSE GEAR, ITEMS, AND MONEY CAN'T BE TRANSFERRED, KIRITO LEFT ALL OF HIS STUFF WITH AGIL'S BUSINESS BEFORE HE CONVERTED TO GGO.

...Pretty soon, I might be converting my ALO Kirito to a different game...

NERVEGEAR AND AMUSPHERE: ITEM

THE NERVEGEAR FULL-DIVE MACHINE THAT CAUSED THE SAO INCIDENT WAS BUILT WITH THE ABILITY TO DESTROY THE USER'S BRAIN WITH MICROWAVES. AS ITS SUCCESSOR, THE AMUSPHERE WAS DESIGNED WITHOUT SUCH A POWERFUL OUTPUT TO PREVENT BRAIN DAMAGE. ON THE OTHER HAND, LIKE ANY COMPUTER, IT CAN STILL BE INFECTED WITH VIRUSES THAT DISPLAY DISGUSTING OR SHOCKING IMAGES. KAZUTO TRIED TO ANALYZE IF THE DEATHS COULD BE CAUSED VIA HACKING SUCH SECURITY HOLES TO ATTACK THE SENSES.

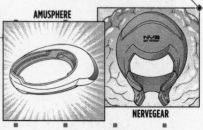

AMUSPHERE

NERVEGEAR

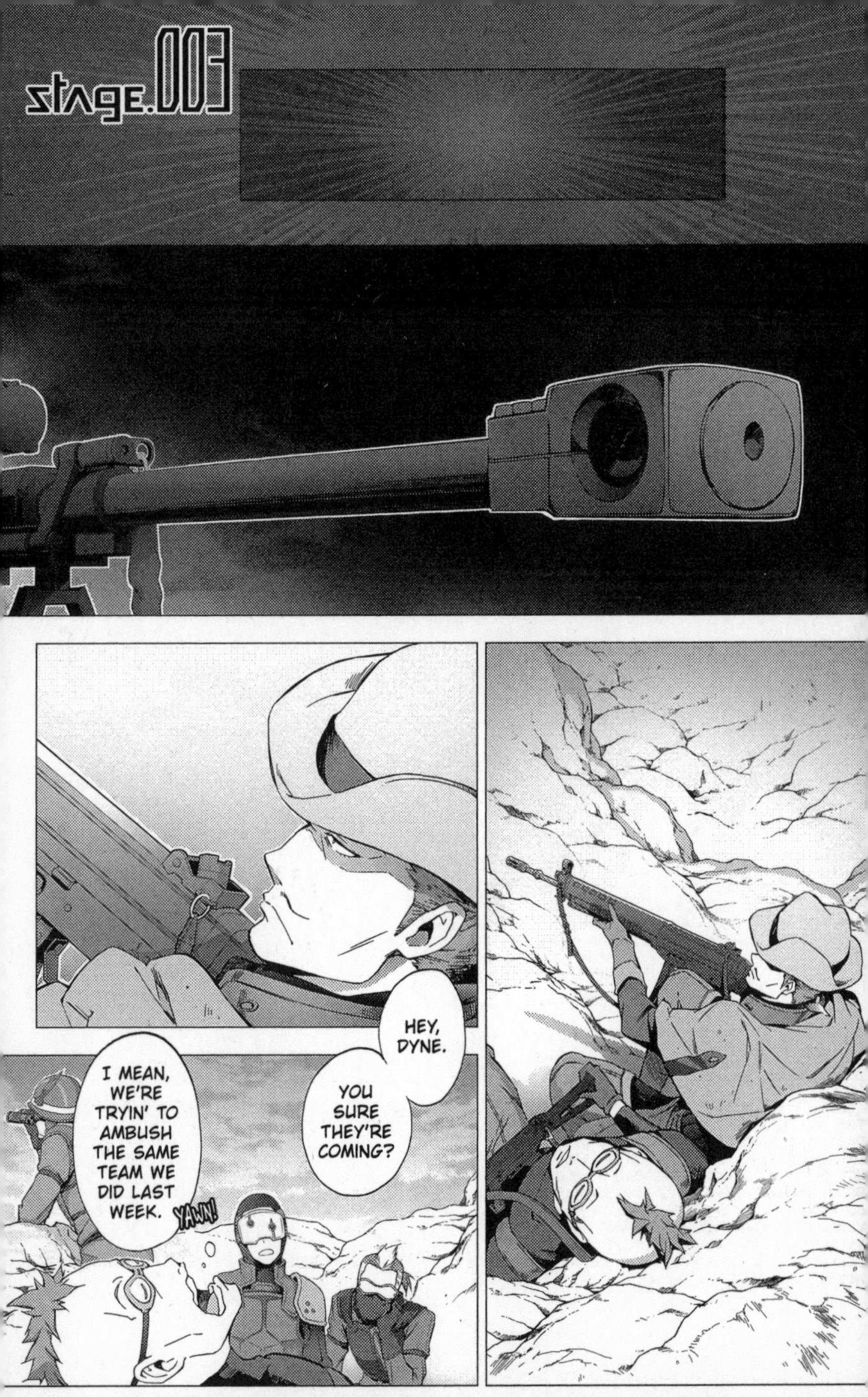
stage.003
HEY, DYNE.
YOU SURE THEY'RE COMING?
I MEAN, WE'RE TRYIN' TO AMBUSH THE SAME TEAM WE DID LAST WEEK.
YAWN!

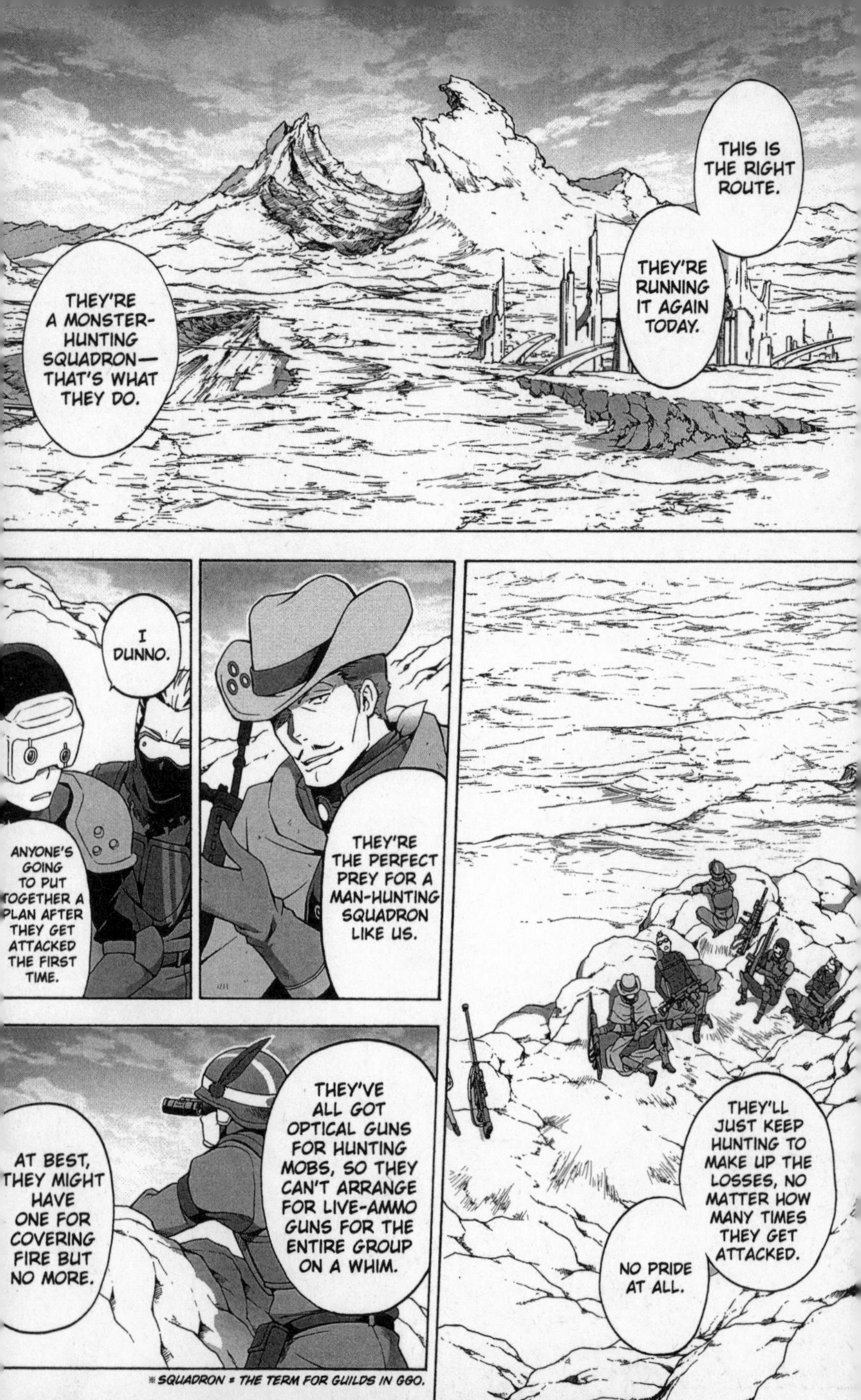
THIS IS THE RIGHT ROUTE.
THEY'RE RUNNING IT AGAIN TODAY.
THEY'RE A MONSTER-HUNTING SQUADRON—THAT'S WHAT THEY DO.
THEY'LL JUST KEEP HUNTING TO MAKE UP THE LOSSES, NO MATTER HOW MANY TIMES THEY GET ATTACKED.
NO PRIDE AT ALL.
THEY'RE THE PERFECT PREY FOR A MAN-HUNTING SQUADRON LIKE US.
I DUNNO.
ANYONE'S GOING TO PUT TOGETHER A PLAN AFTER THEY GET ATTACKED THE FIRST TIME.
THEY'VE ALL GOT OPTICAL GUNS FOR HUNTING MOBS, SO THEY CAN'T ARRANGE FOR LIVE-AMMO GUNS FOR THE ENTIRE GROUP ON A WHIM.
AT BEST, THEY MIGHT HAVE ONE FOR COVERING FIRE BUT NO MORE.

※ SQUADRON = THE TERM FOR GUILDS IN GGO.

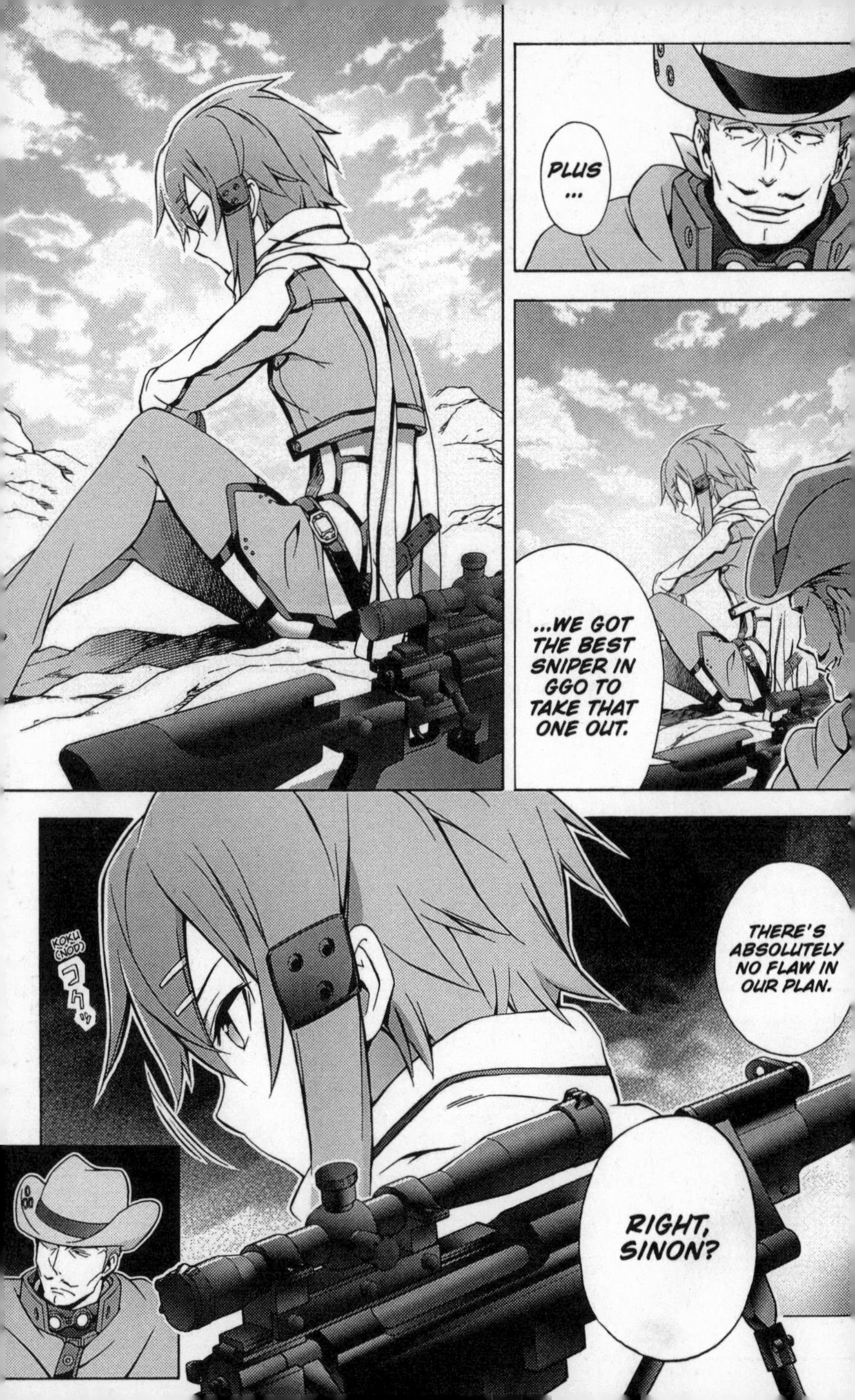
PLUS ...
...WE GOT THE BEST SNIPER IN GGO TO TAKE THAT ONE OUT.
THERE'S ABSOLUTELY NO FLAW IN OUR PLAN.
RIGHT, SINON?
KOKU (NOD)
コクッ

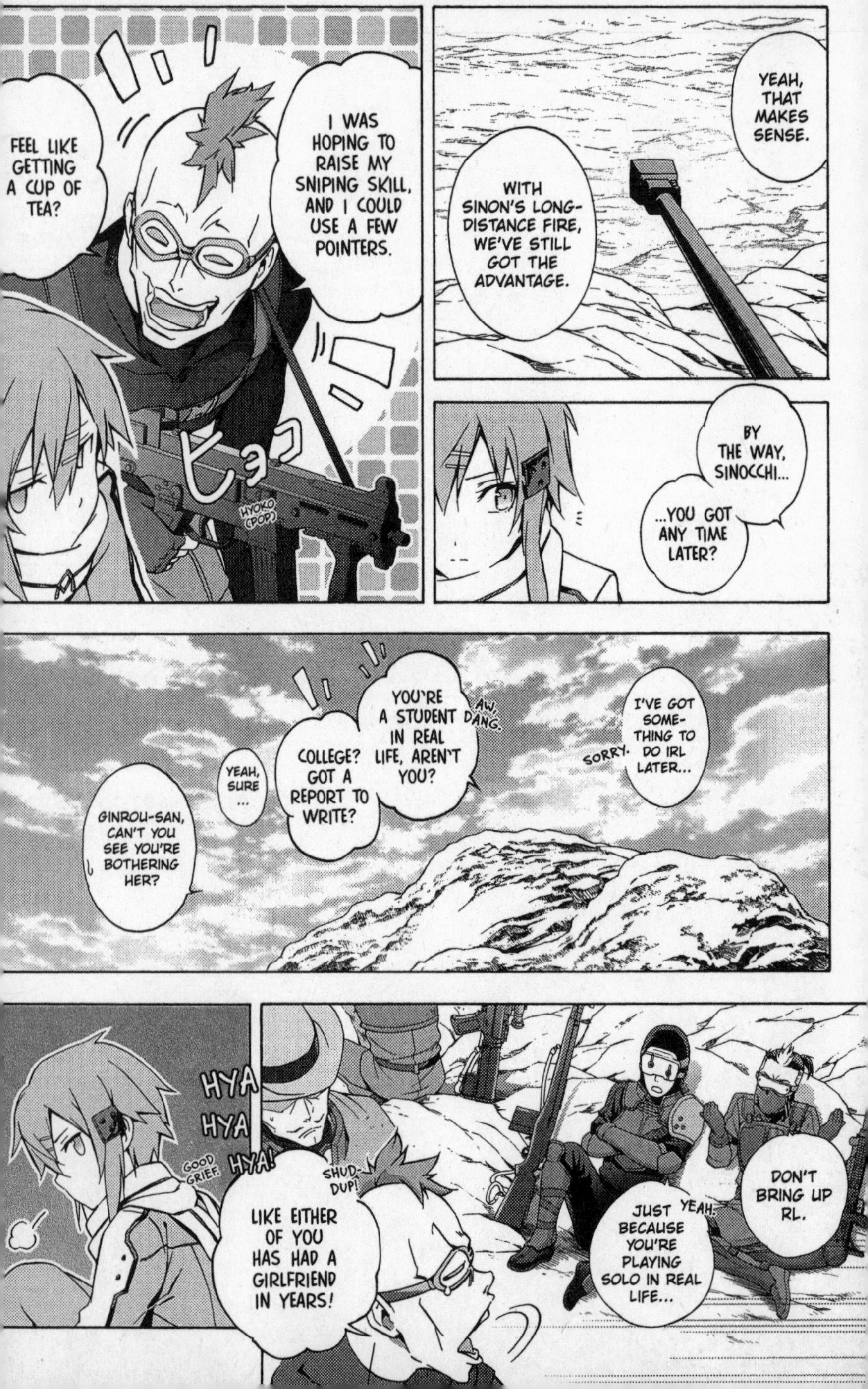
YEAH, THAT MAKES SENSE.
WITH SINON'S LONG-DISTANCE FIRE, WE'VE STILL GOT THE ADVANTAGE.
BY THE WAY, SINOCCHI...
...YOU GOT ANY TIME LATER?
I WAS HOPING TO RAISE MY SNIPING SKILL, AND I COULD USE A FEW POINTERS.
FEEL LIKE GETTING A CUP OF TEA?
HYOKO (POP)
I'VE GOT SOME-THING TO DO IRL LATER...
SORRY.
AW, DANG.
YOU'RE A STUDENT IN REAL LIFE, AREN'T YOU?
COLLEGE? GOT A REPORT TO WRITE?
YEAH, SURE...
GINROU-SAN, CAN'T YOU SEE YOU'RE BOTHERING HER?
DON'T BRING UP RL.
YEAH.
JUST BECAUSE YOU'RE PLAYING SOLO IN REAL LIFE...
SHUD-DUP!
LIKE EITHER OF YOU HAS HAD A GIRLFRIEND IN YEARS!
HYA HYA HYA!
GOOD GRIEF.

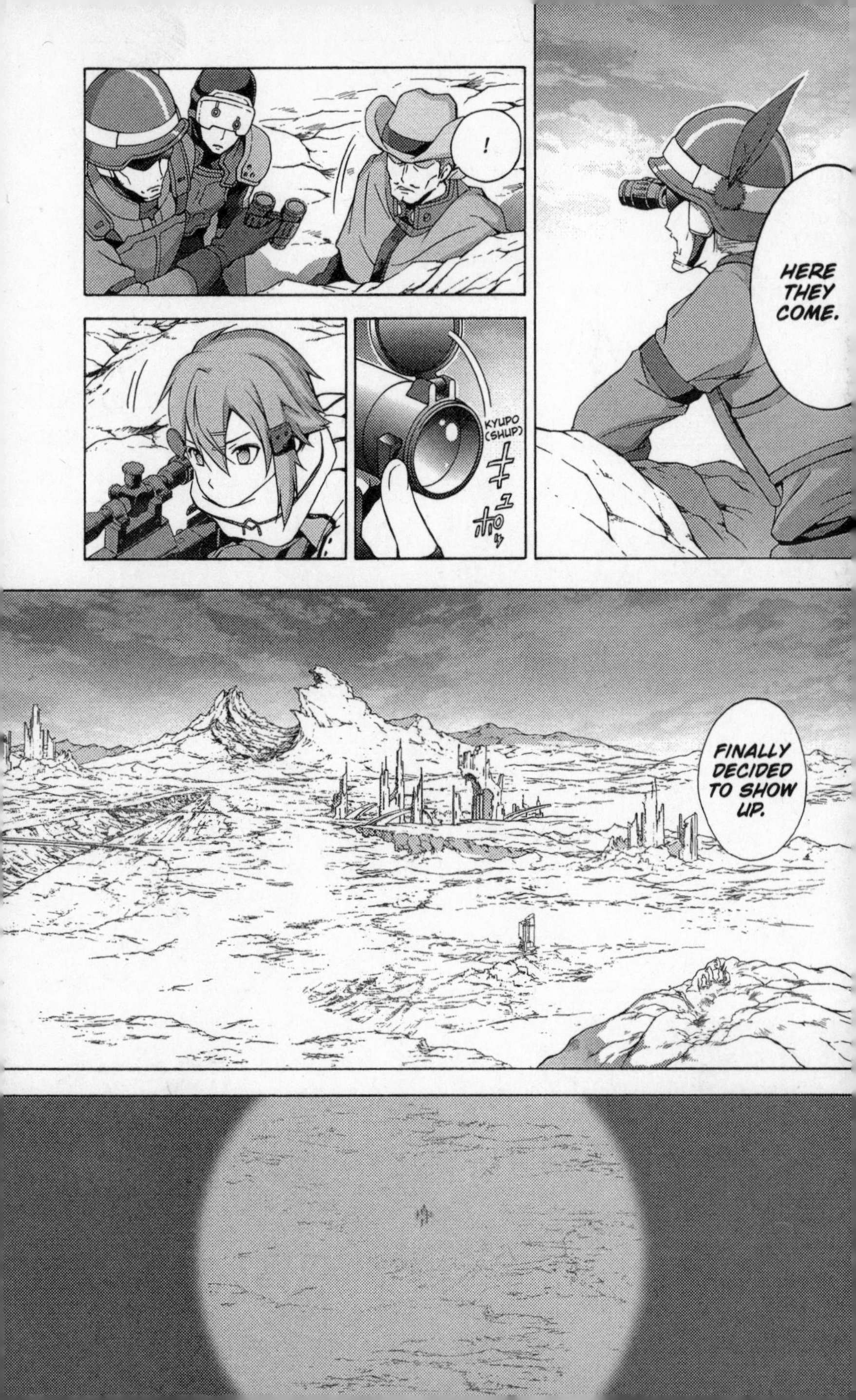
HERE THEY COME.
!
KYUPO (SHUP)
FINALLY DECIDED TO SHOW UP.

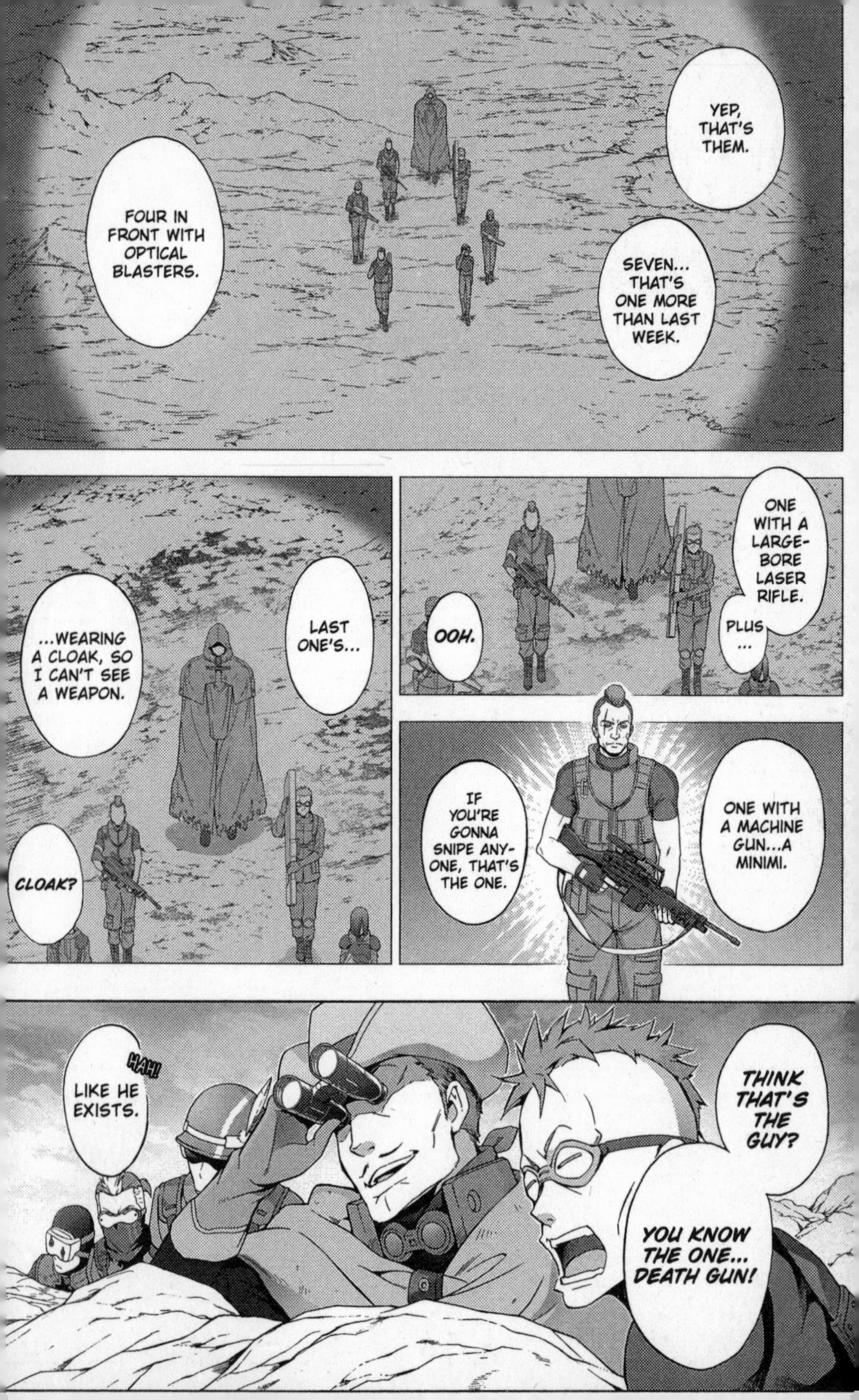
YEP, THAT'S THEM.
SEVEN... THAT'S ONE MORE THAN LAST WEEK.
FOUR IN FRONT WITH OPTICAL BLASTERS.
ONE WITH A LARGE-BORE LASER RIFLE.
PLUS...
OOH.
ONE WITH A MACHINE GUN...A MINIMI.
IF YOU'RE GONNA SNIPE ANY-ONE, THAT'S THE ONE.
LAST ONE'S...
...WEARING A CLOAK, SO I CAN'T SEE A WEAPON.
CLOAK?
THINK THAT'S THE GUY?
YOU KNOW THE ONE... DEATH GUN!
HAH!
LIKE HE EXISTS.

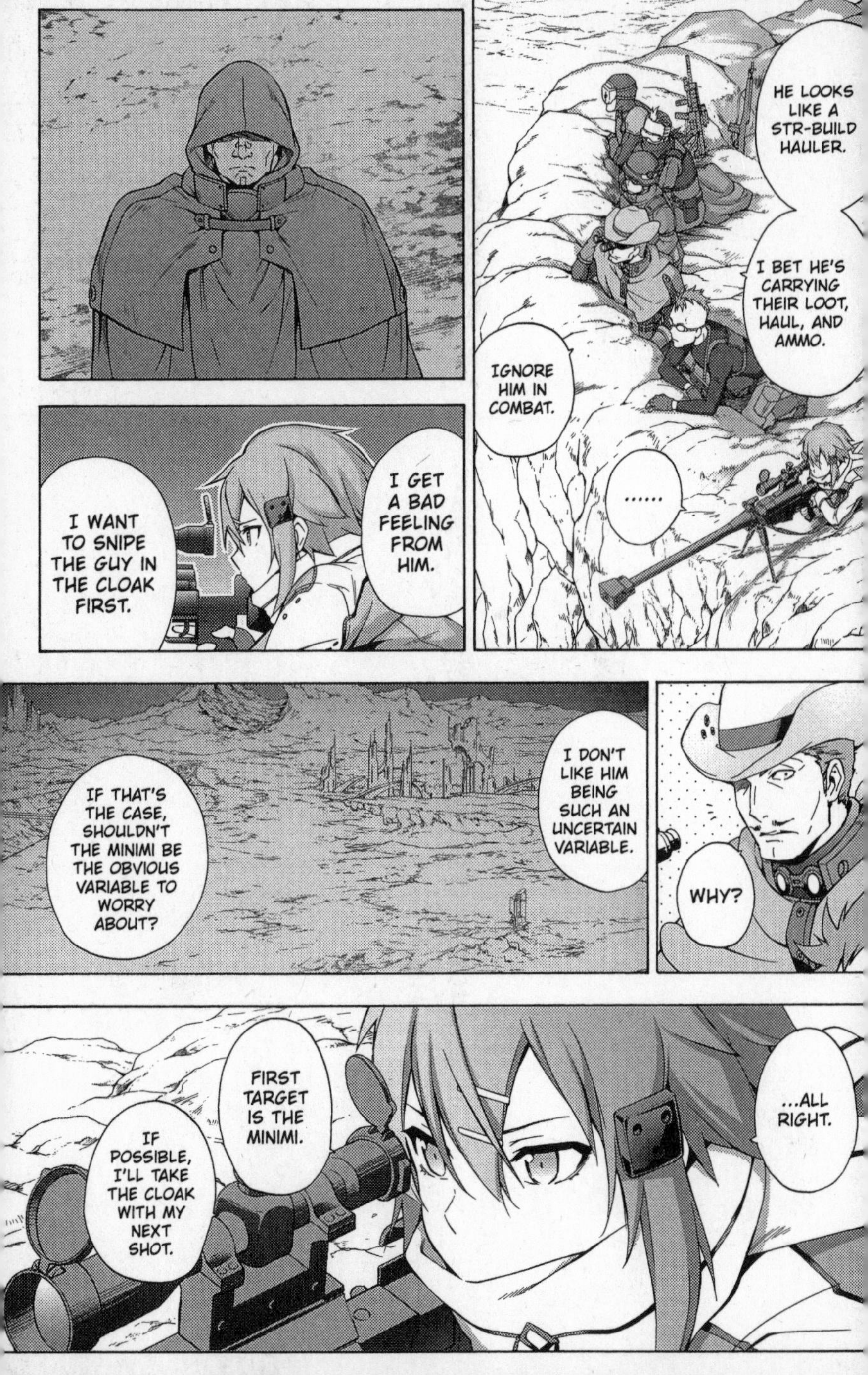
HE LOOKS LIKE A STR-BUILD HAULER.
I BET HE'S CARRYING THEIR LOOT, HAUL, AND AMMO.
IGNORE HIM IN COMBAT.
......
I GET A BAD FEELING FROM HIM.
I WANT TO SNIPE THE GUY IN THE CLOAK FIRST.
WHY?
I DON'T LIKE HIM BEING SUCH AN UNCERTAIN VARIABLE.
IF THAT'S THE CASE, SHOULDN'T THE MINIMI BE THE OBVIOUS VARIABLE TO WORRY ABOUT?
...ALL RIGHT.
FIRST TARGET IS THE MINIMI.
IF POSSIBLE, I'LL TAKE THE CLOAK WITH MY NEXT SHOT.

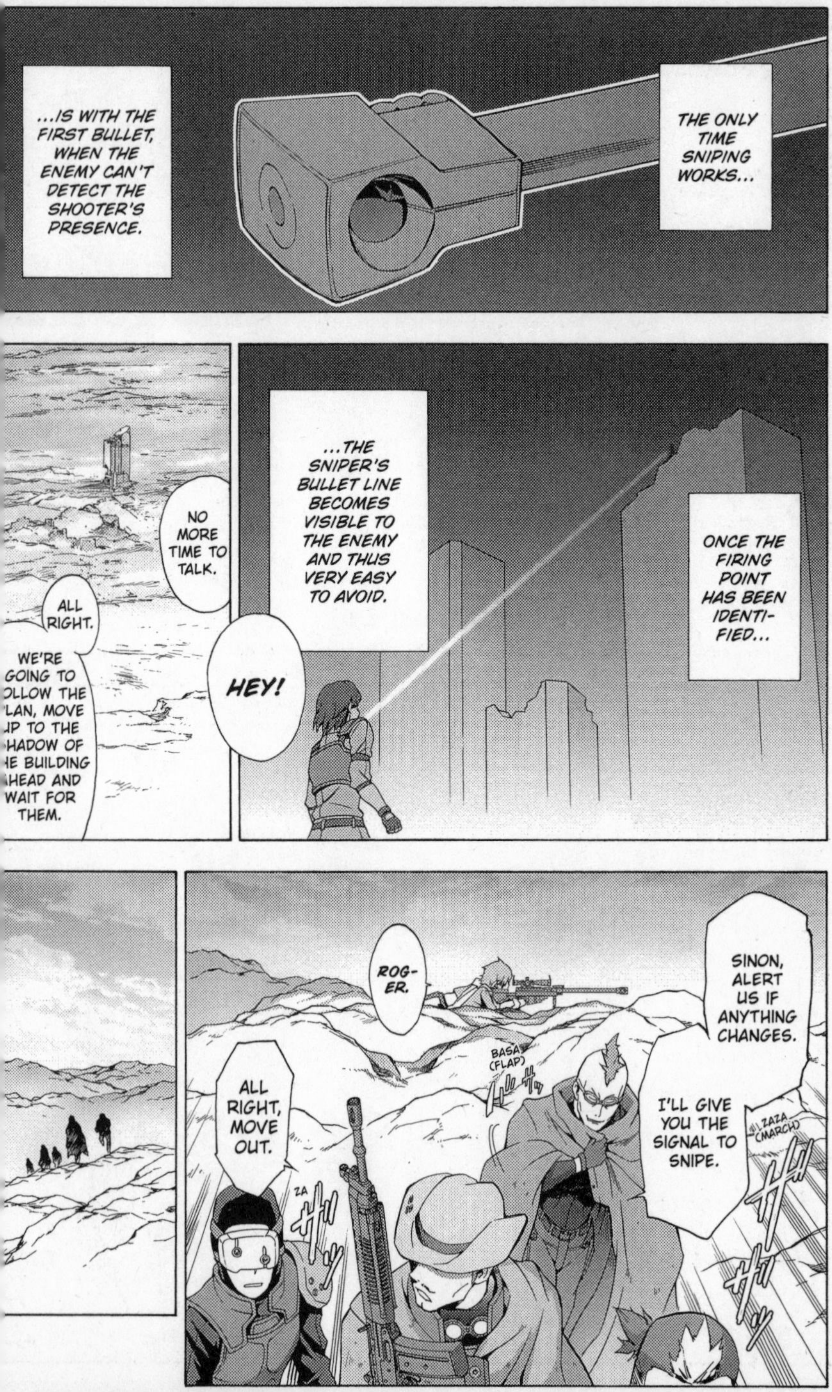
THE ONLY TIME SNIPING WORKS...
...IS WITH THE FIRST BULLET, WHEN THE ENEMY CAN'T DETECT THE SHOOTER'S PRESENCE.
ONCE THE FIRING POINT HAS BEEN IDENTI-FIED...
...THE SNIPER'S BULLET LINE BECOMES VISIBLE TO THE ENEMY AND THUS VERY EASY TO AVOID.
HEY!
NO MORE TIME TO TALK.
ALL RIGHT.
WE'RE GOING TO OLLOW THE LAN, MOVE P TO THE HADOW OF HE BUILDING HEAD AND WAIT FOR THEM.
SINON, ALERT US IF ANYTHING CHANGES.
ROG-ER.
I'LL GIVE YOU THE SIGNAL TO SNIPE.
ZAZA (MARCH)
BASA (FLAP)
ALL RIGHT, MOVE OUT.
ZA

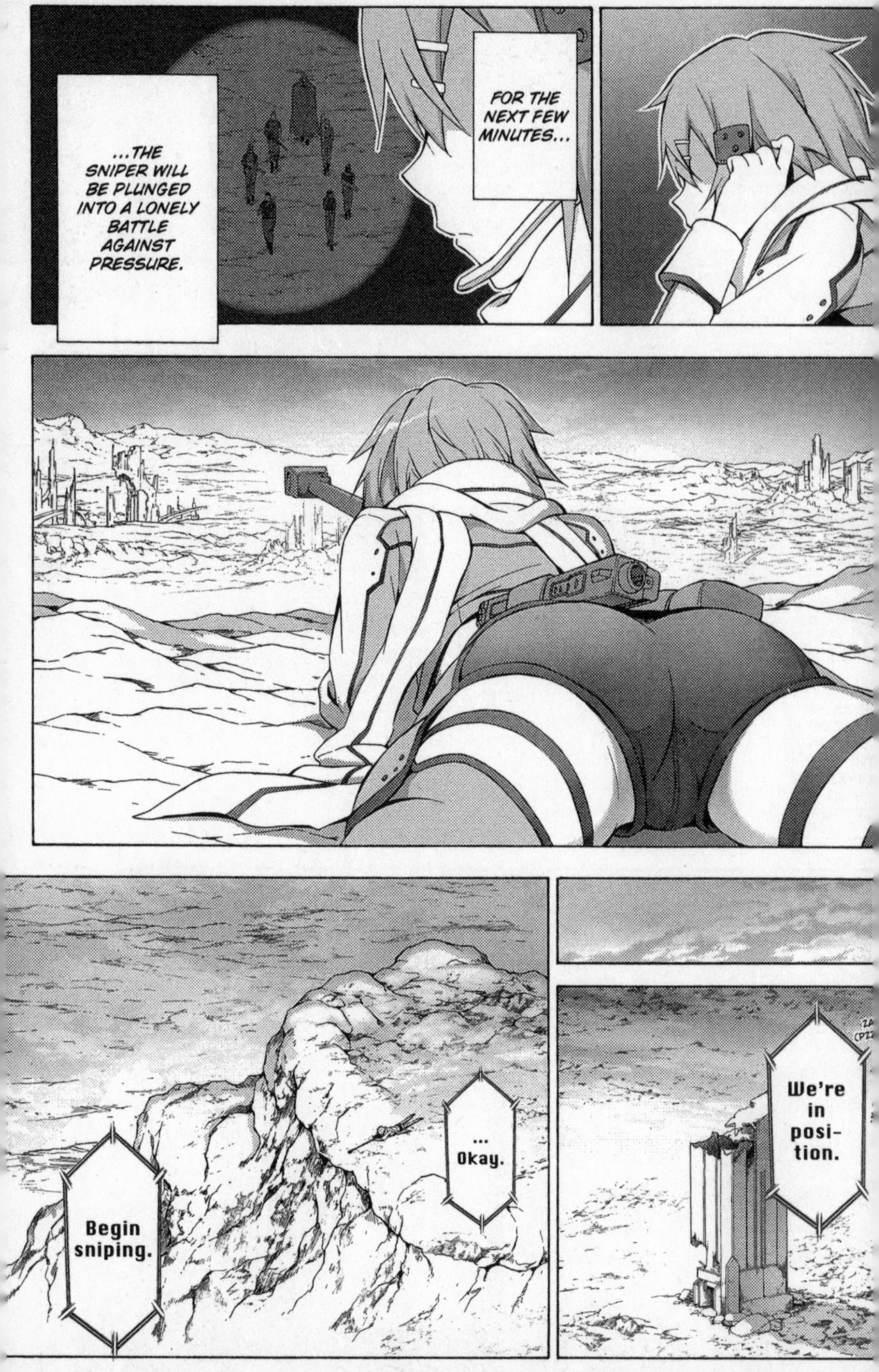
FOR THE NEXT FEW MINUTES...
...THE SNIPER WILL BE PLUNGED INTO A LONELY BATTLE AGAINST PRESSURE.
We're in posi-tion.
...Okay.
Begin sniping.

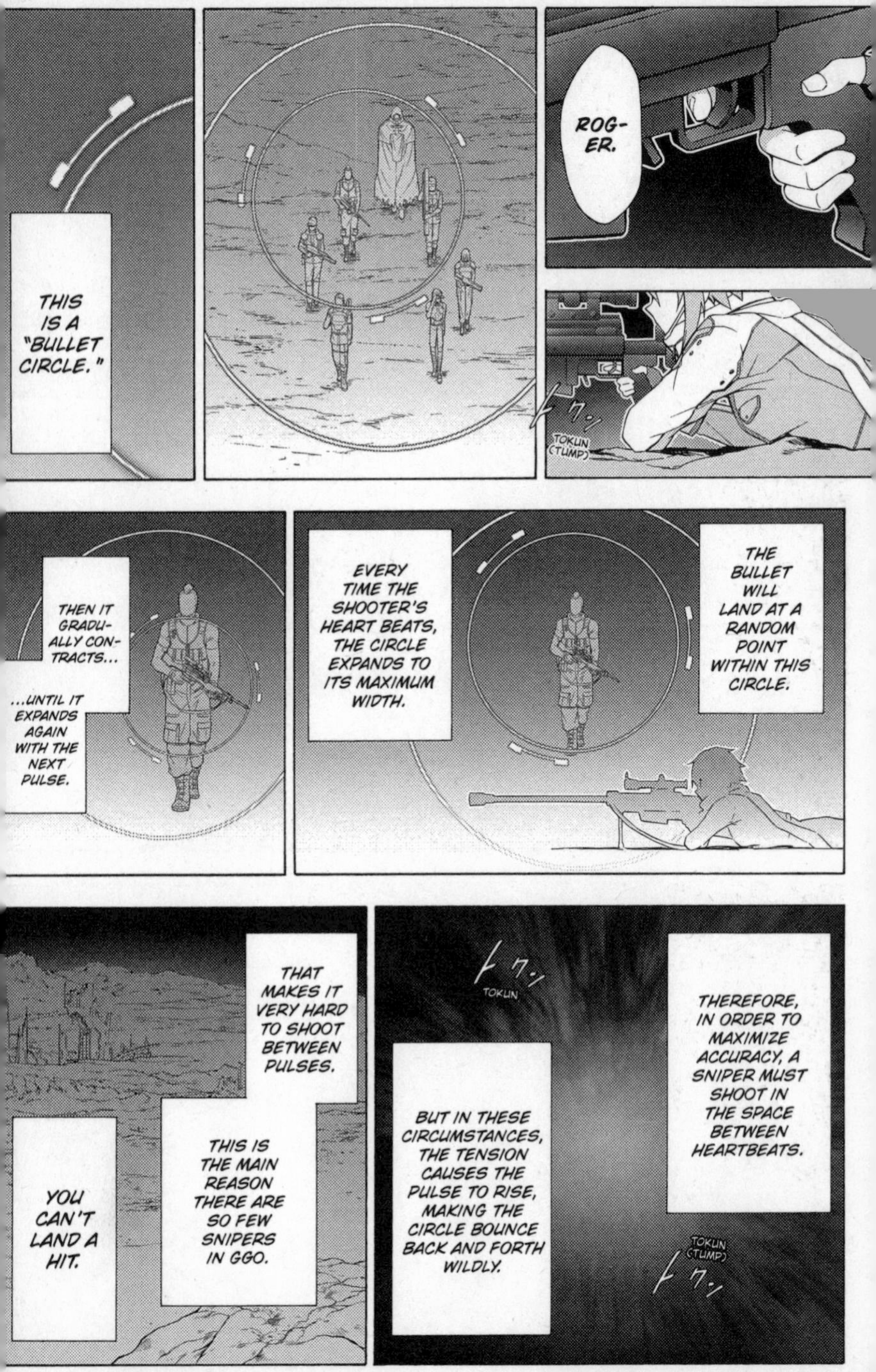
ROG-ER.
トクン
TOKUN (TUMP)
THIS IS A "BULLET CIRCLE."
THE BULLET WILL LAND AT A RANDOM POINT WITHIN THIS CIRCLE.
EVERY TIME THE SHOOTER'S HEART BEATS, THE CIRCLE EXPANDS TO ITS MAXIMUM WIDTH.
THEN IT GRADUALLY CONTRACTS...
...UNTIL IT EXPANDS AGAIN WITH THE NEXT PULSE.
トクン
TOKUN
THEREFORE, IN ORDER TO MAXIMIZE ACCURACY, A SNIPER MUST SHOOT IN THE SPACE BETWEEN HEARTBEATS.
BUT IN THESE CIRCUMSTANCES, THE TENSION CAUSES THE PULSE TO RISE, MAKING THE CIRCLE BOUNCE BACK AND FORTH WILDLY.
TOKUN (TUMP)
トクン
THAT MAKES IT VERY HARD TO SHOOT BETWEEN PULSES.
THIS IS THE MAIN REASON THERE ARE SO FEW SNIPERS IN GGO.
YOU CAN'T LAND A HIT.

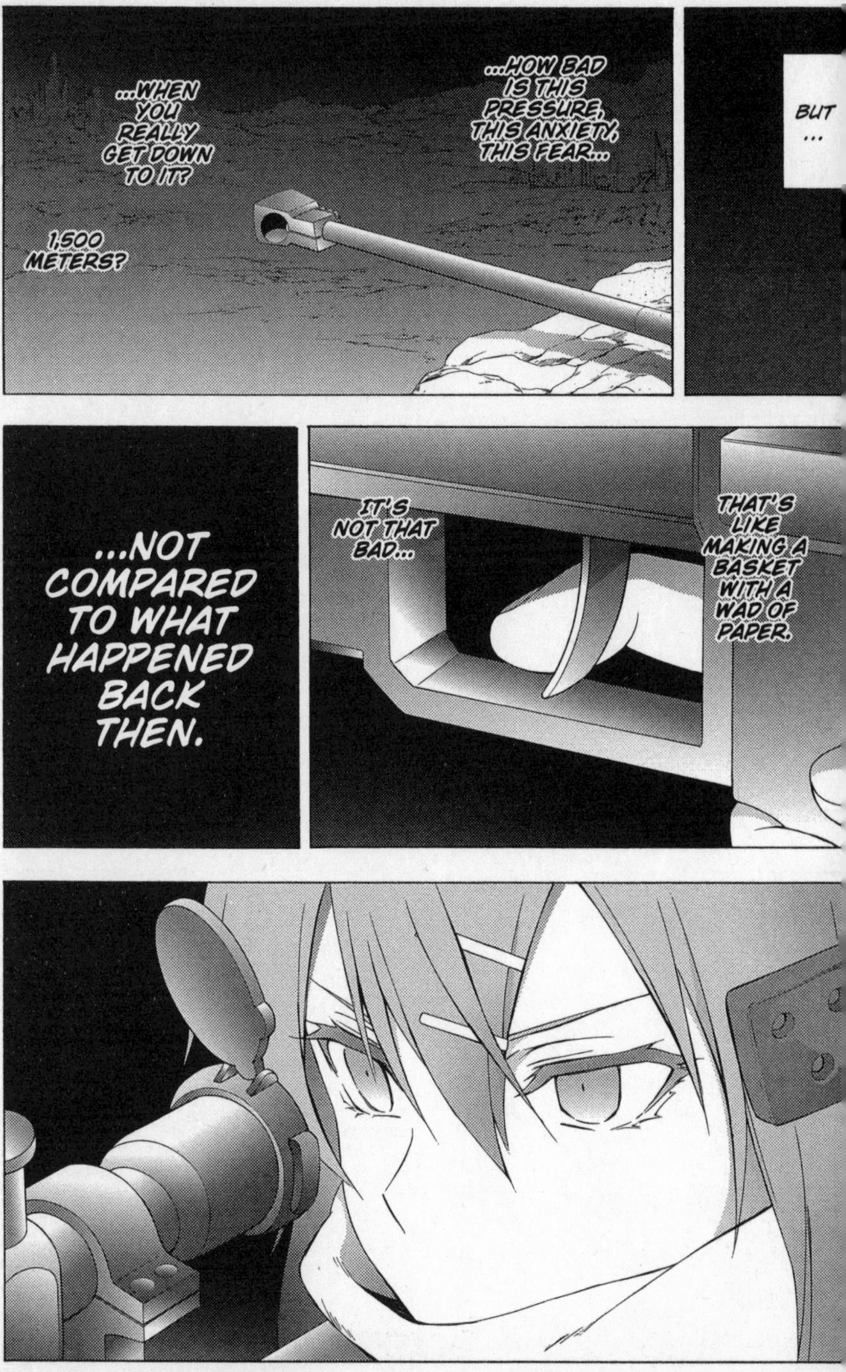
BUT ...
...HOW BAD IS THIS PRESSURE, THIS ANXIETY, THIS FEAR...
...WHEN YOU REALLY GET DOWN TO IT?
1,500 METERS?
THAT'S LIKE MAKING A BASKET WITH A WAD OF PAPER.
IT'S NOT THAT BAD...
...NOT COMPARED TO WHAT HAPPENED BACK THEN.

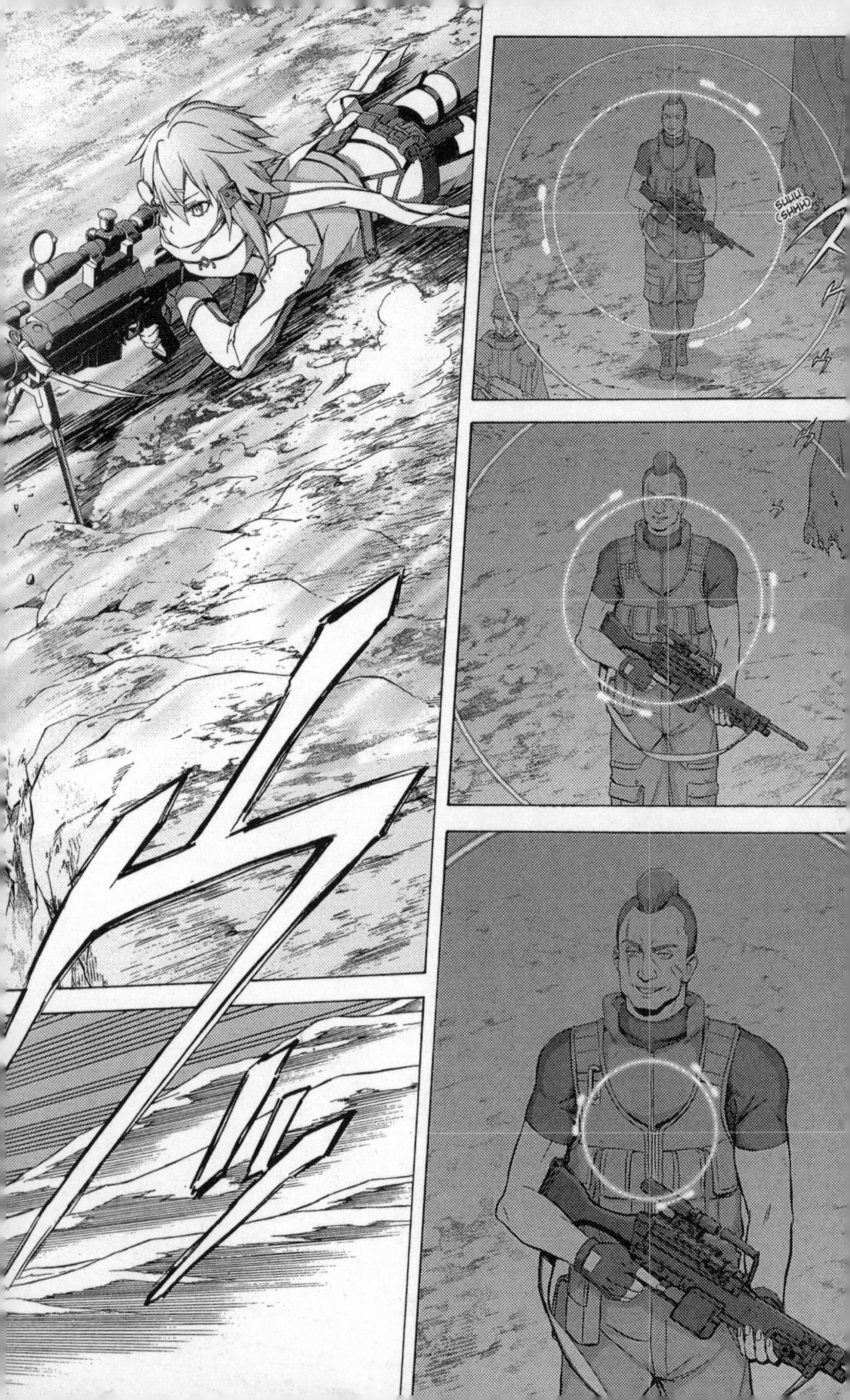
SUUU (SHHH)

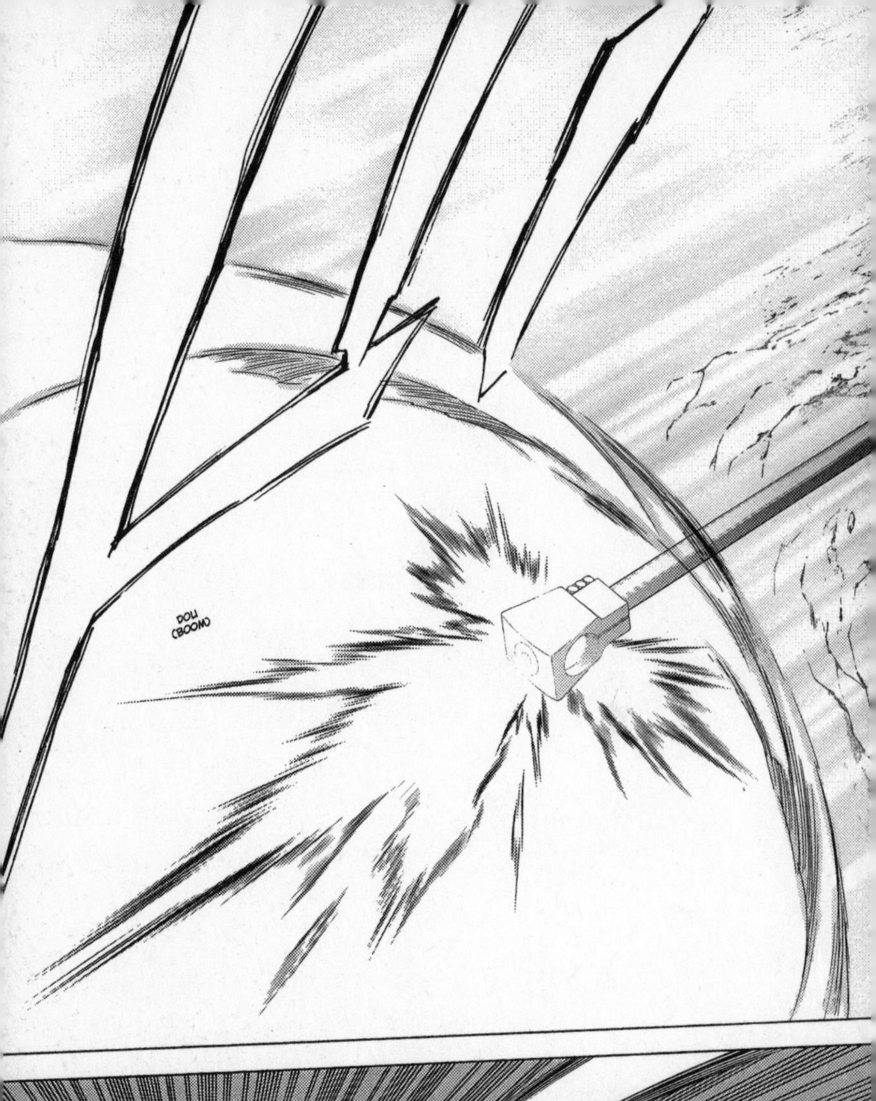
DOU
(BOOM)
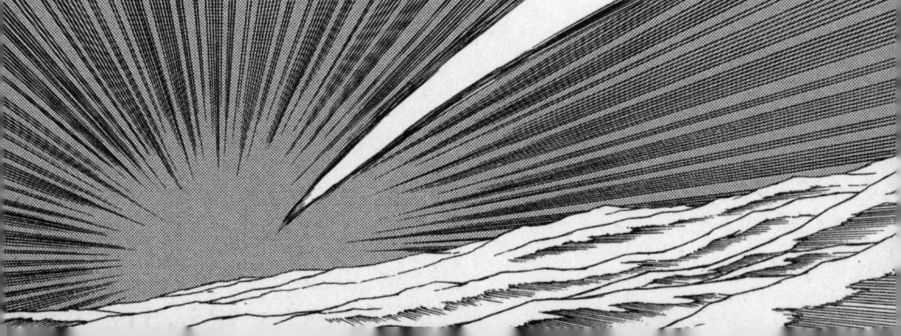

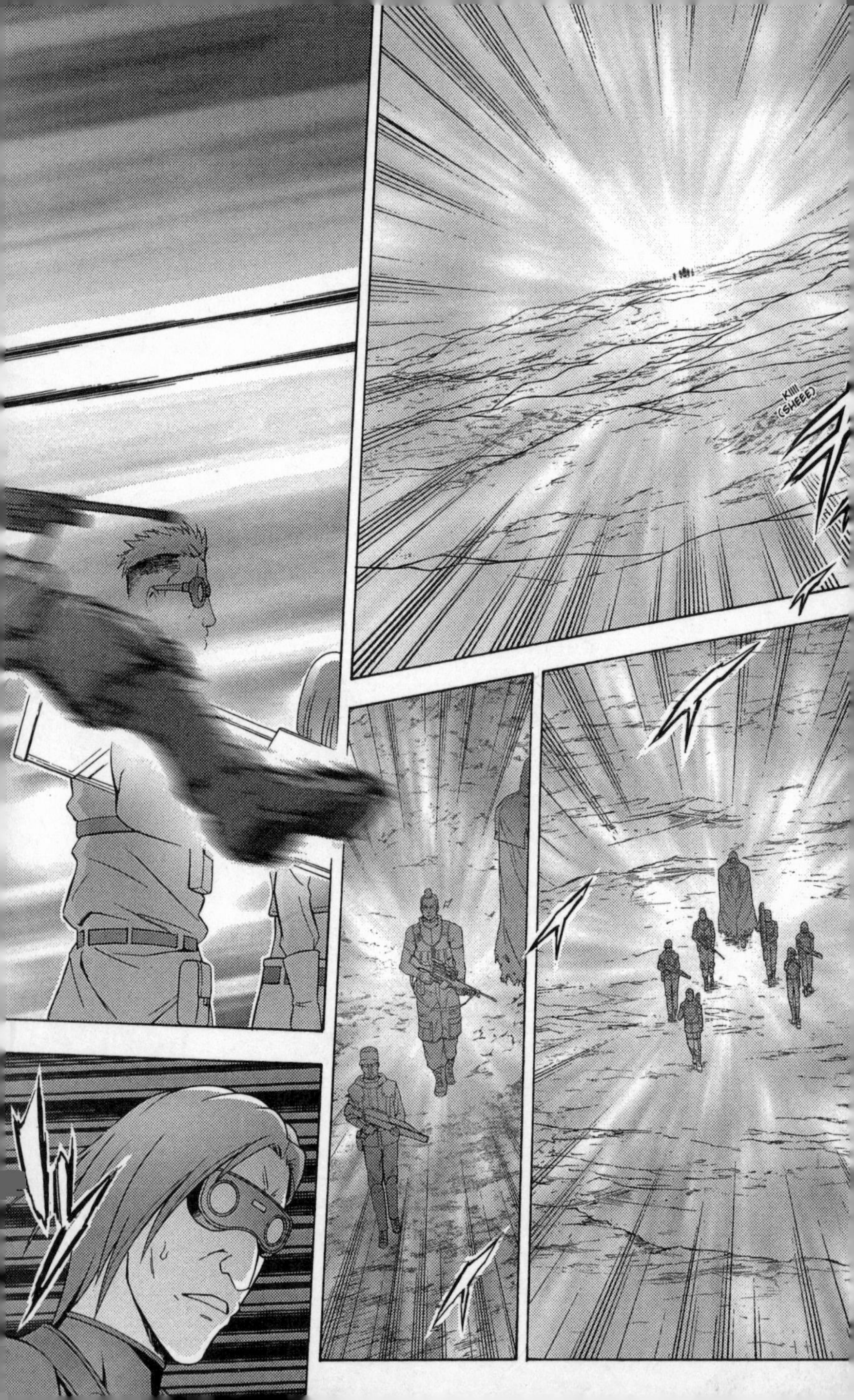
KIIII
(SHEEE)

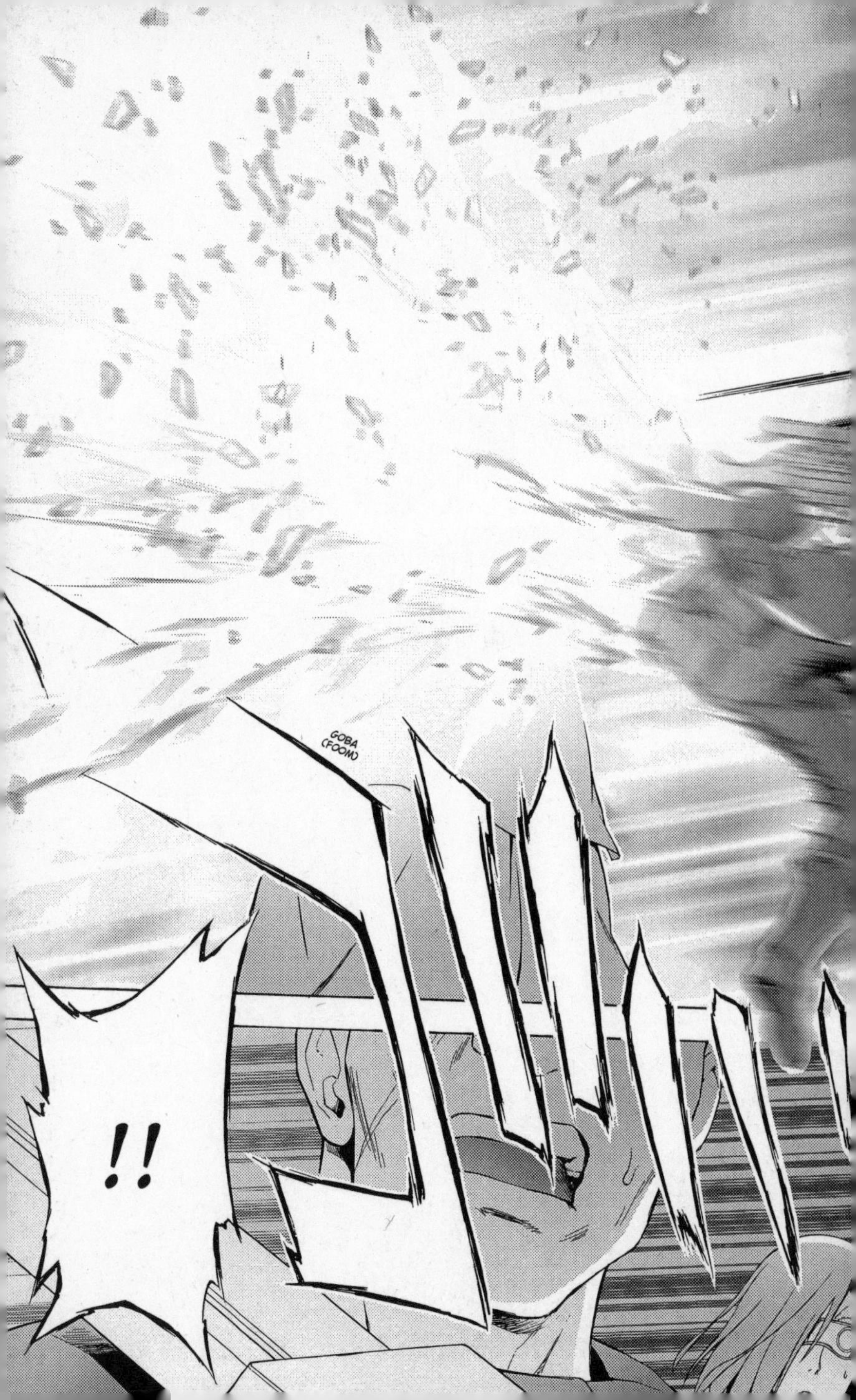
GOBA
(FOOM)
!!

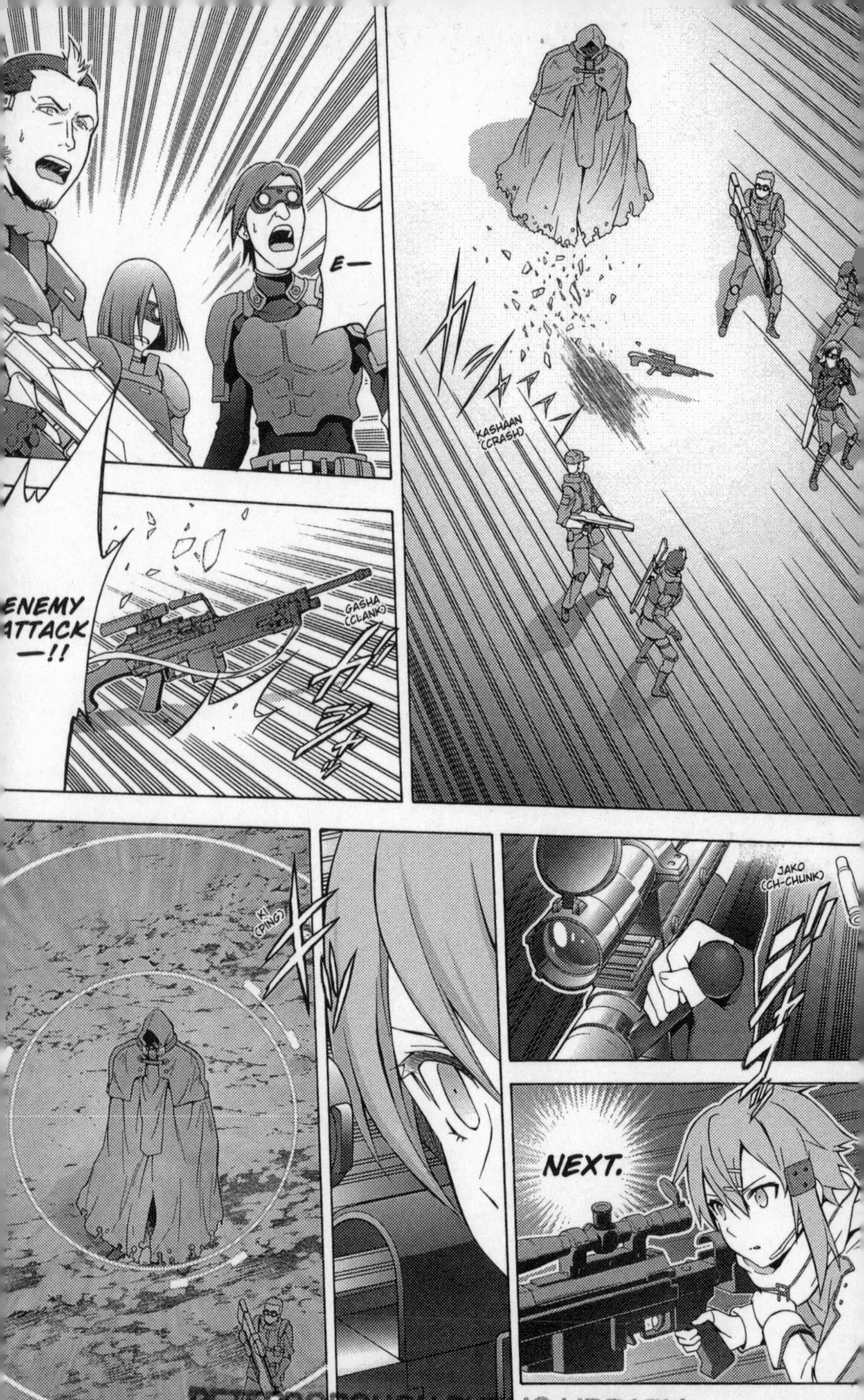
KASHAAN (CRASH)
E—
ENEMY ATTACK—!!
GASHA (CLANK)
JAKO (CH-CHUNK)
NEXT.
KI (PING)

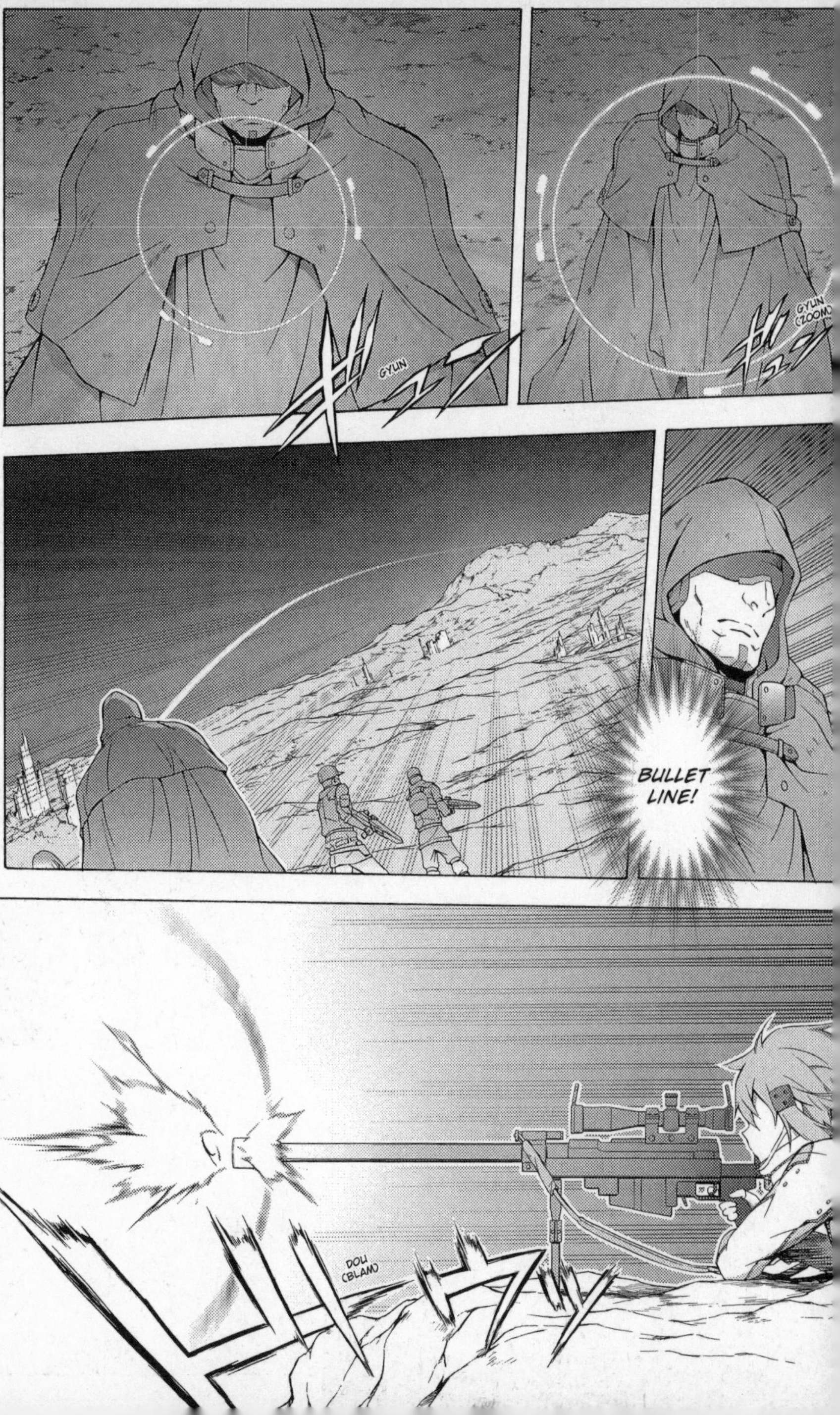
GYUN (ZOOM)
GYUN
BULLET LINE!
DOU (BLAM)

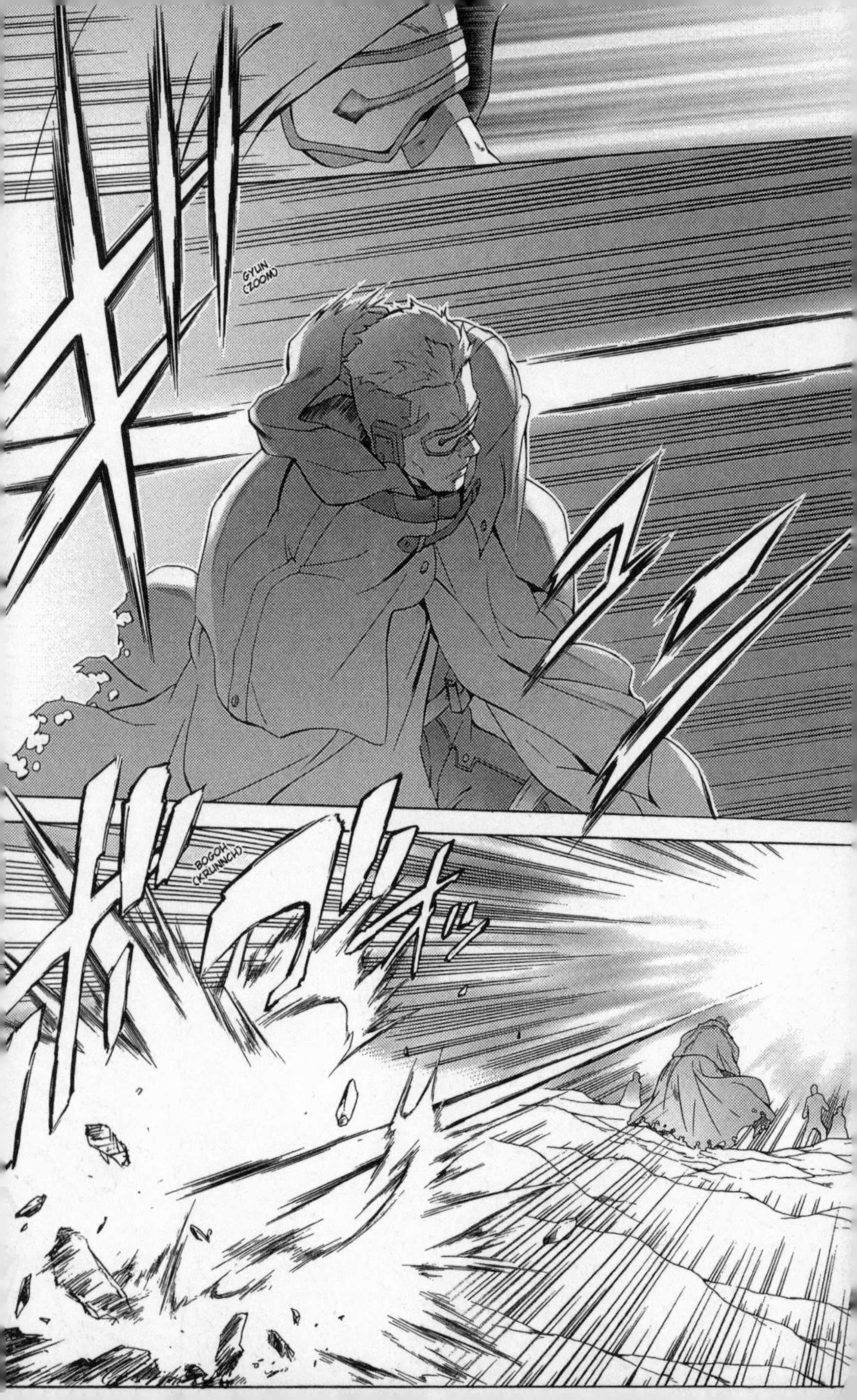
GYUN (ZOOM)
BOGOH (KRUNNCH)

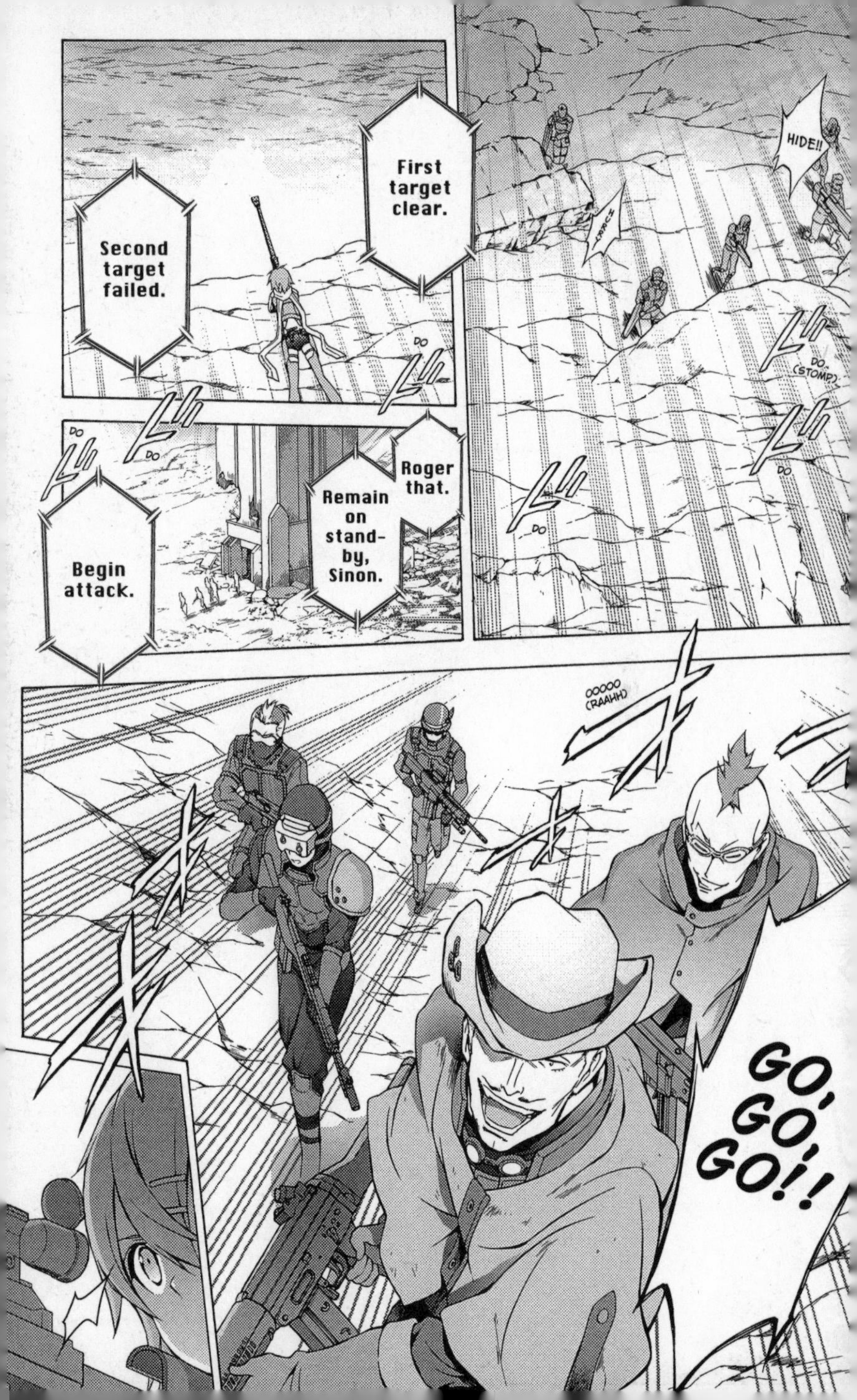
HIDE!!
DO.. (STOMP)
DO
DO
First target clear.
Second target failed.
DO
Roger that.
Remain on stand-by, Sinon.
DO
DO
Begin attack.
OOOOO (RAAHH)
GO, GO, GO!!

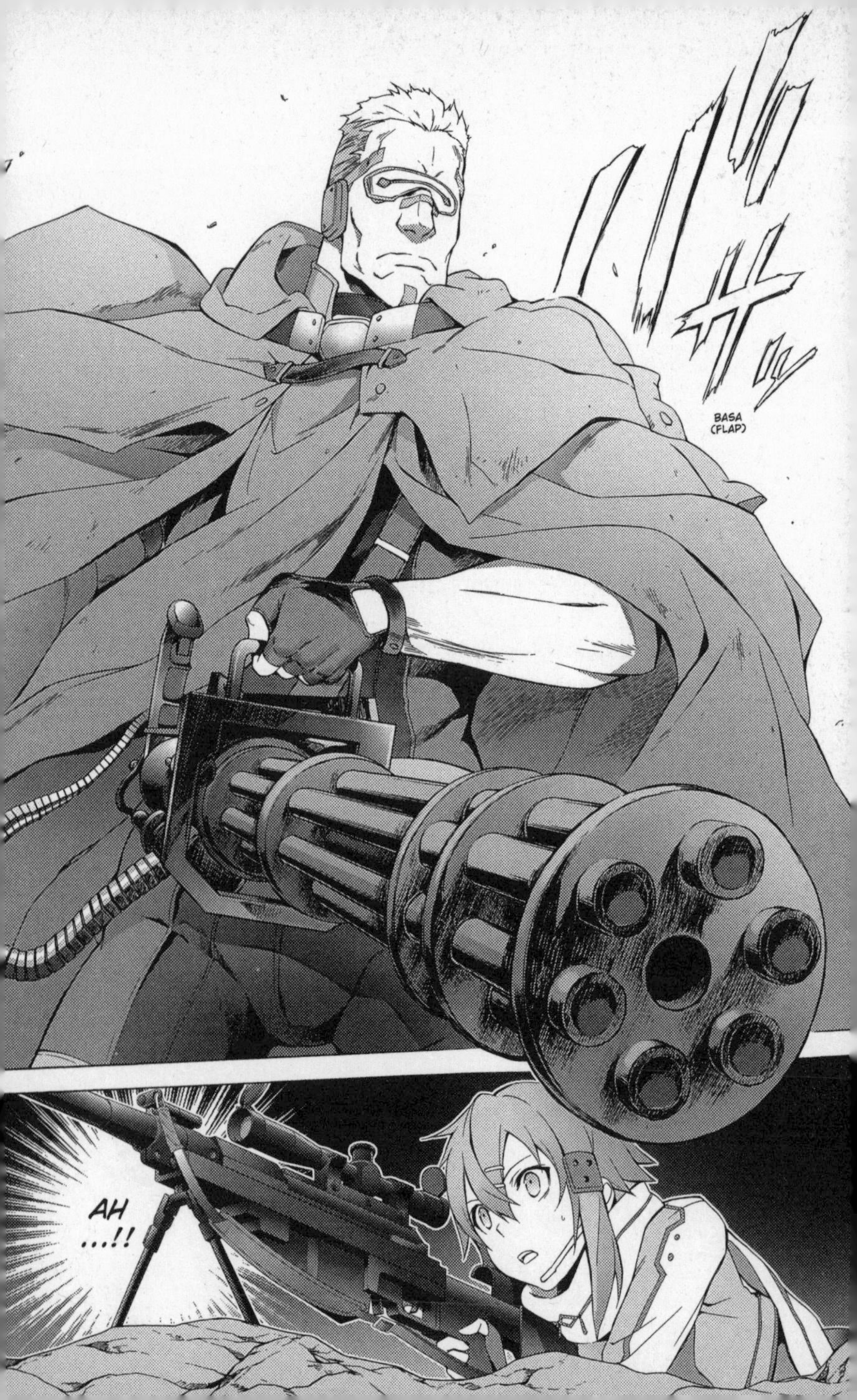
BASA
(FLAP)
AH
...!!

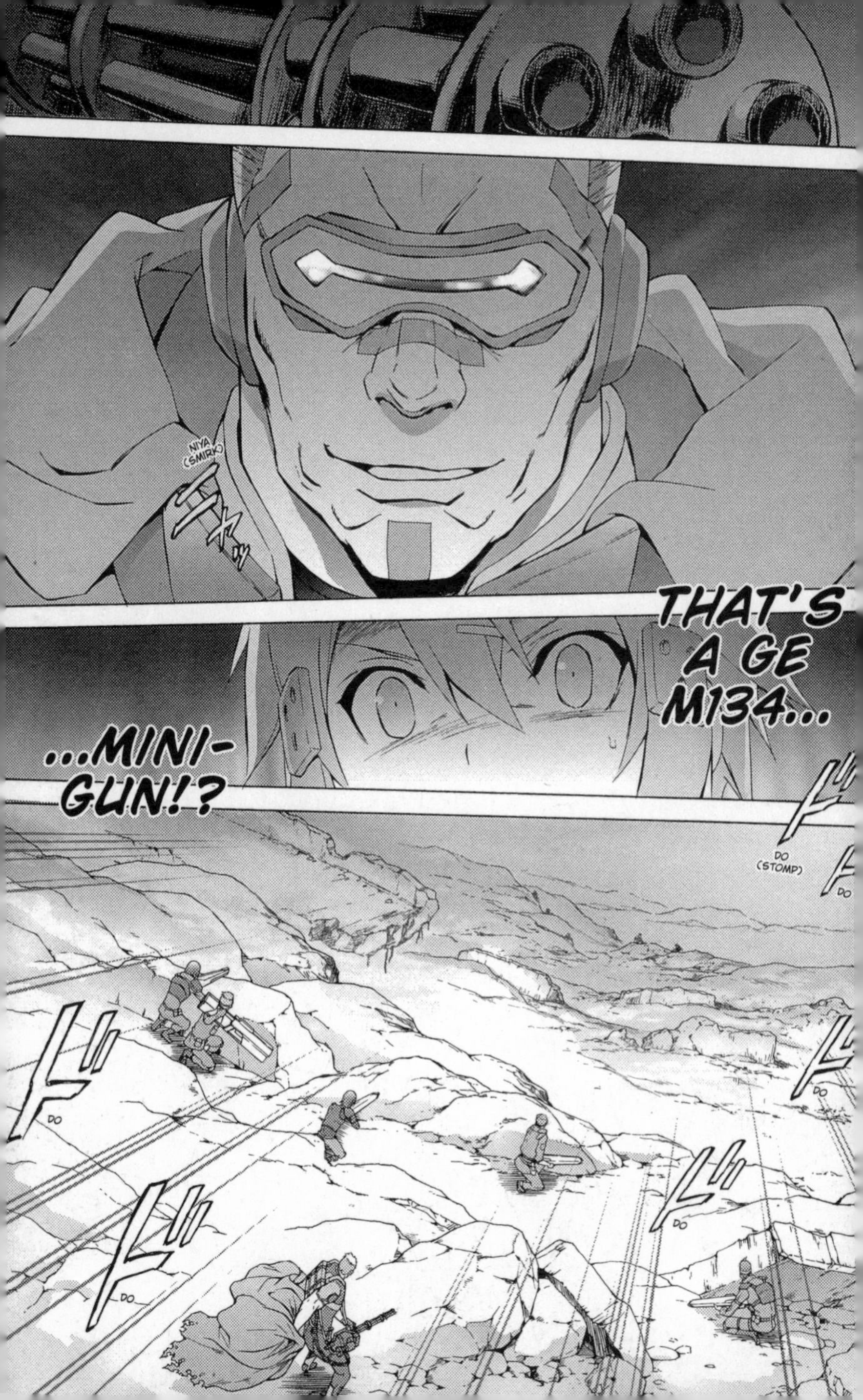
NIYA (SMIRK)
THAT'S A GE M134...
...MINI-GUN!?
DO (STOMP)
DO
DO
DO
DO
DO

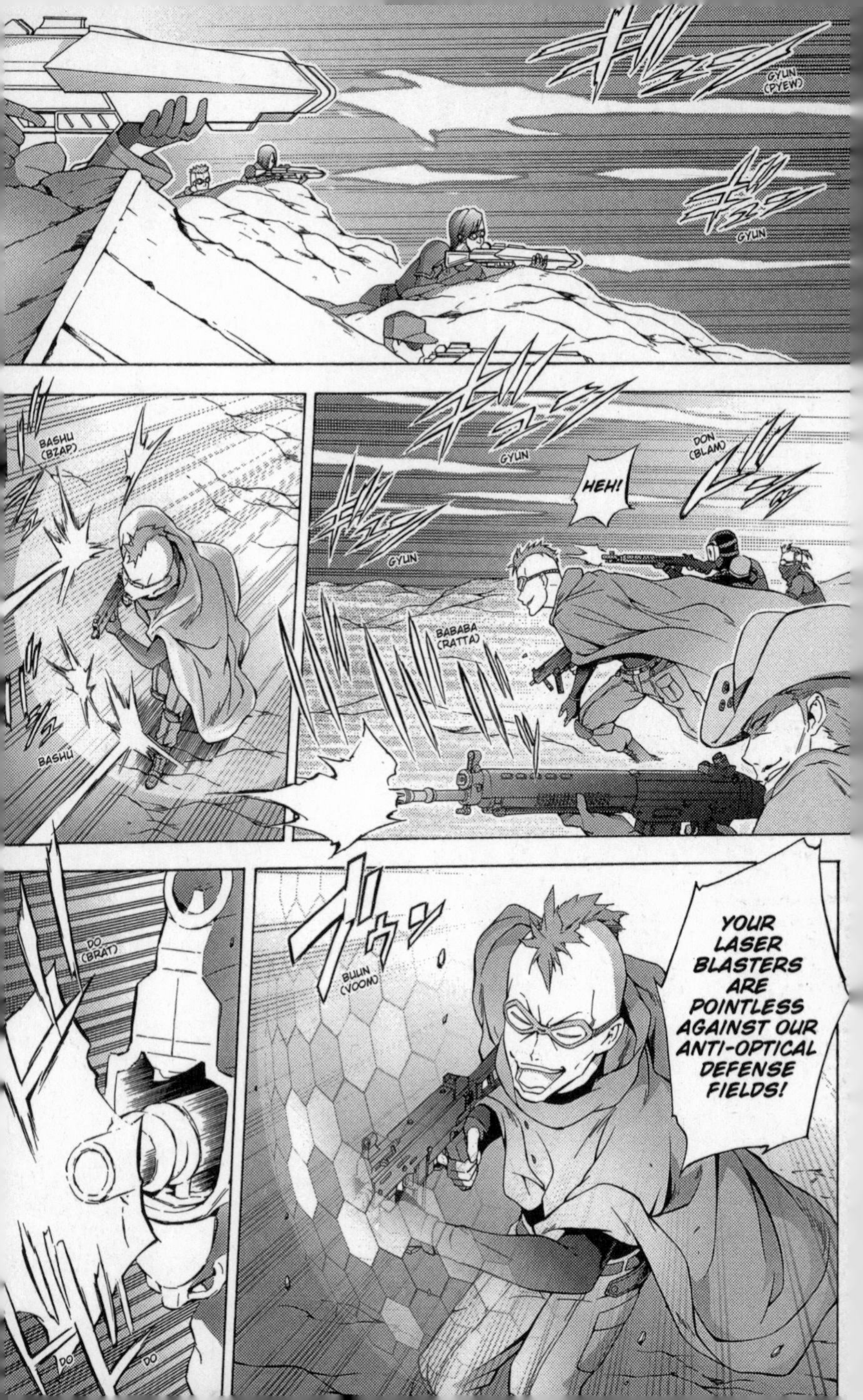
GYUN (PYEW)
GYUN
DON (BLAM)
HEH!
GYUN
GYUN
BABABA (RATTA)
BASHU (BZAP)
BASHU
YOUR LASER BLASTERS ARE POINTLESS AGAINST OUR ANTI-OPTICAL DEFENSE FIELDS!
BUUN (VOOM)
DO (BRAT)
DO
DO

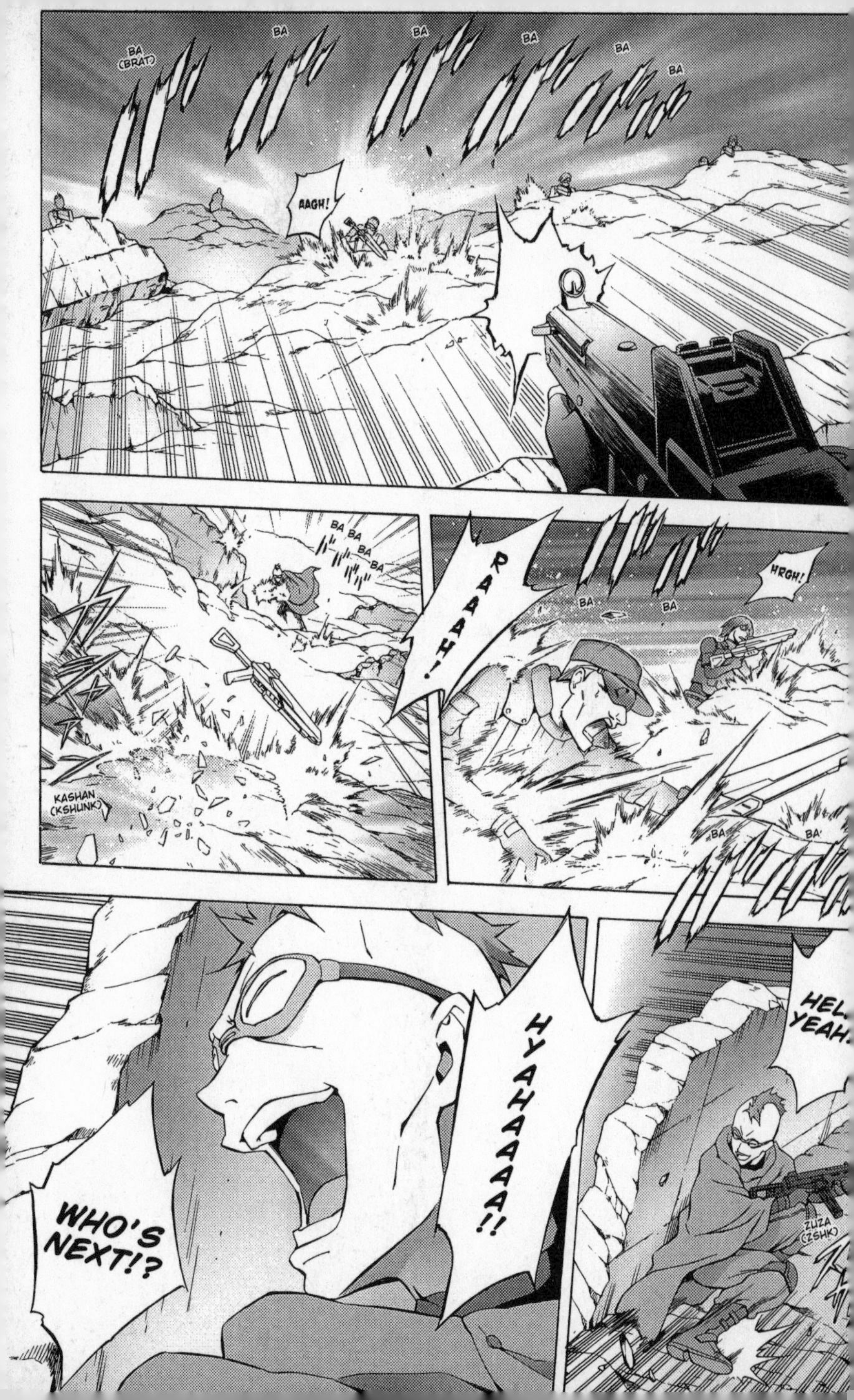
BA (BRAT)
BA
BA
BA
BA
BA
AAGH!
HRGH!
RAAAAH!
BA
BA
BA
BA
BA
BA
BA
BA
KASHAN (KSHUNK)
HEL YEAH.
ZUZA (ZSHK)
HYAHAAAAAA!!
WHO'S NEXT!?

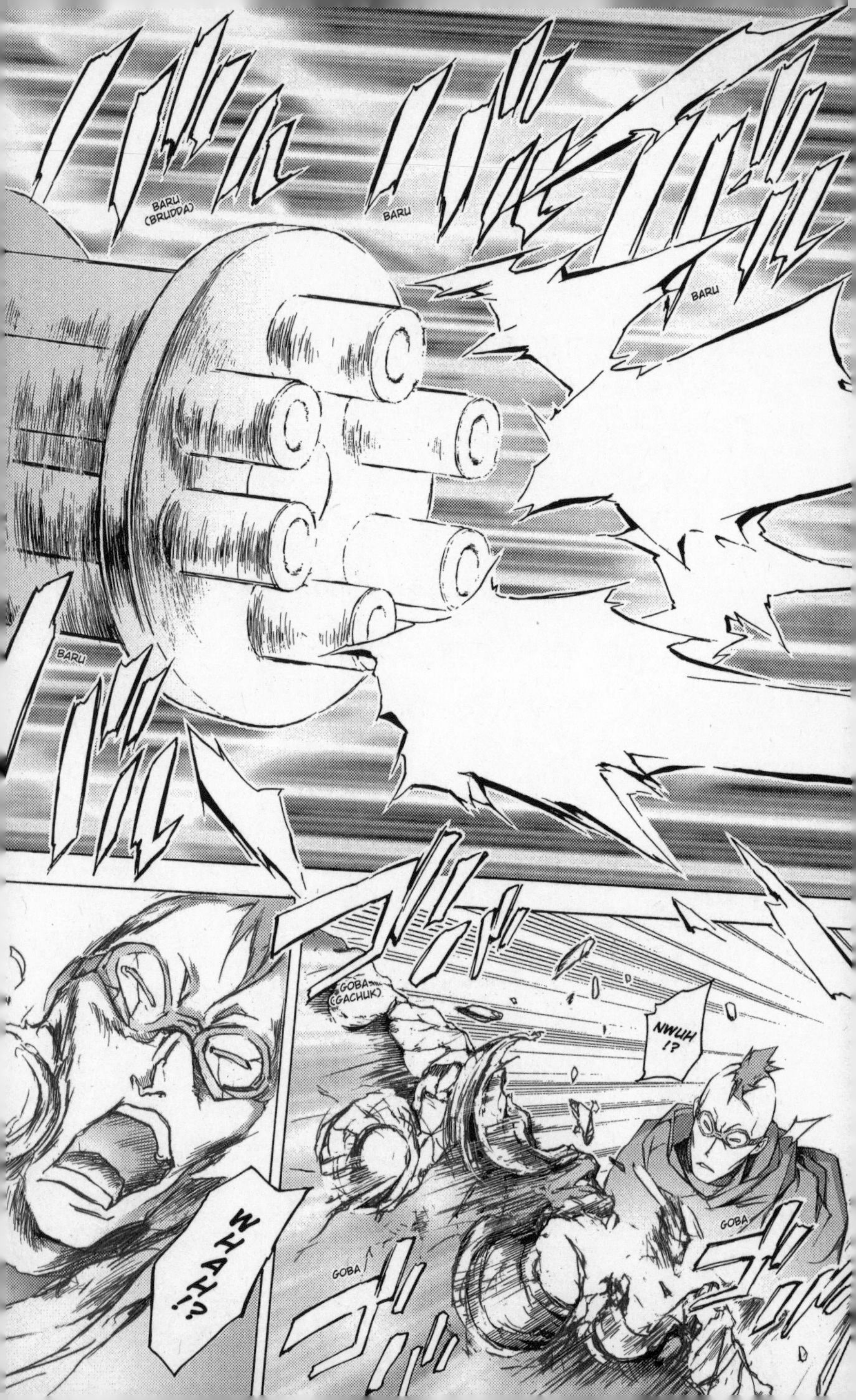
BARU
BARU
BARU (BRUDDA)
BARU
GOBA (GACHUK)
NWUH !?
GOBA
GOBA
WHAH!?

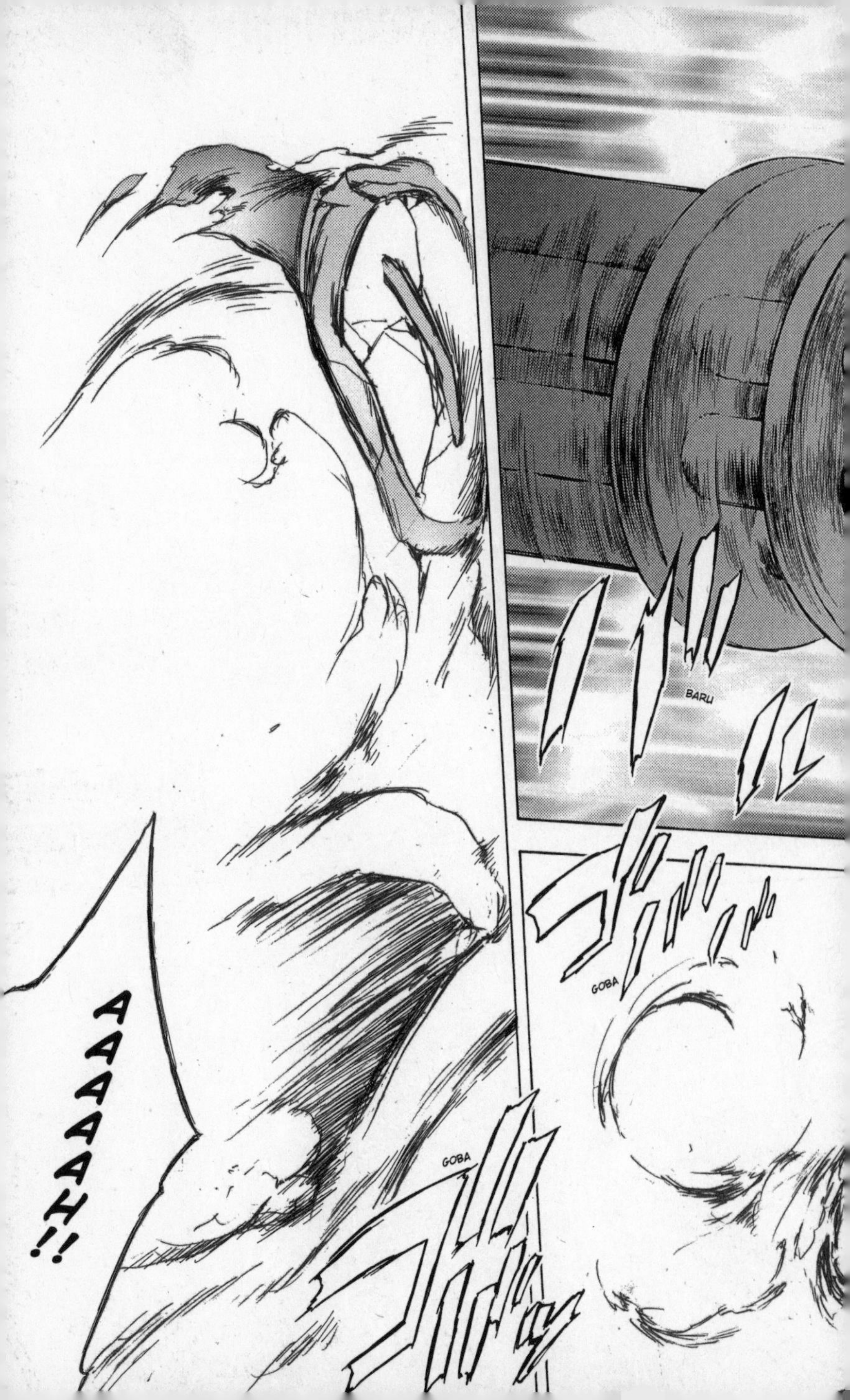
BARU
GOBA
AAAAAH!!
GOBA

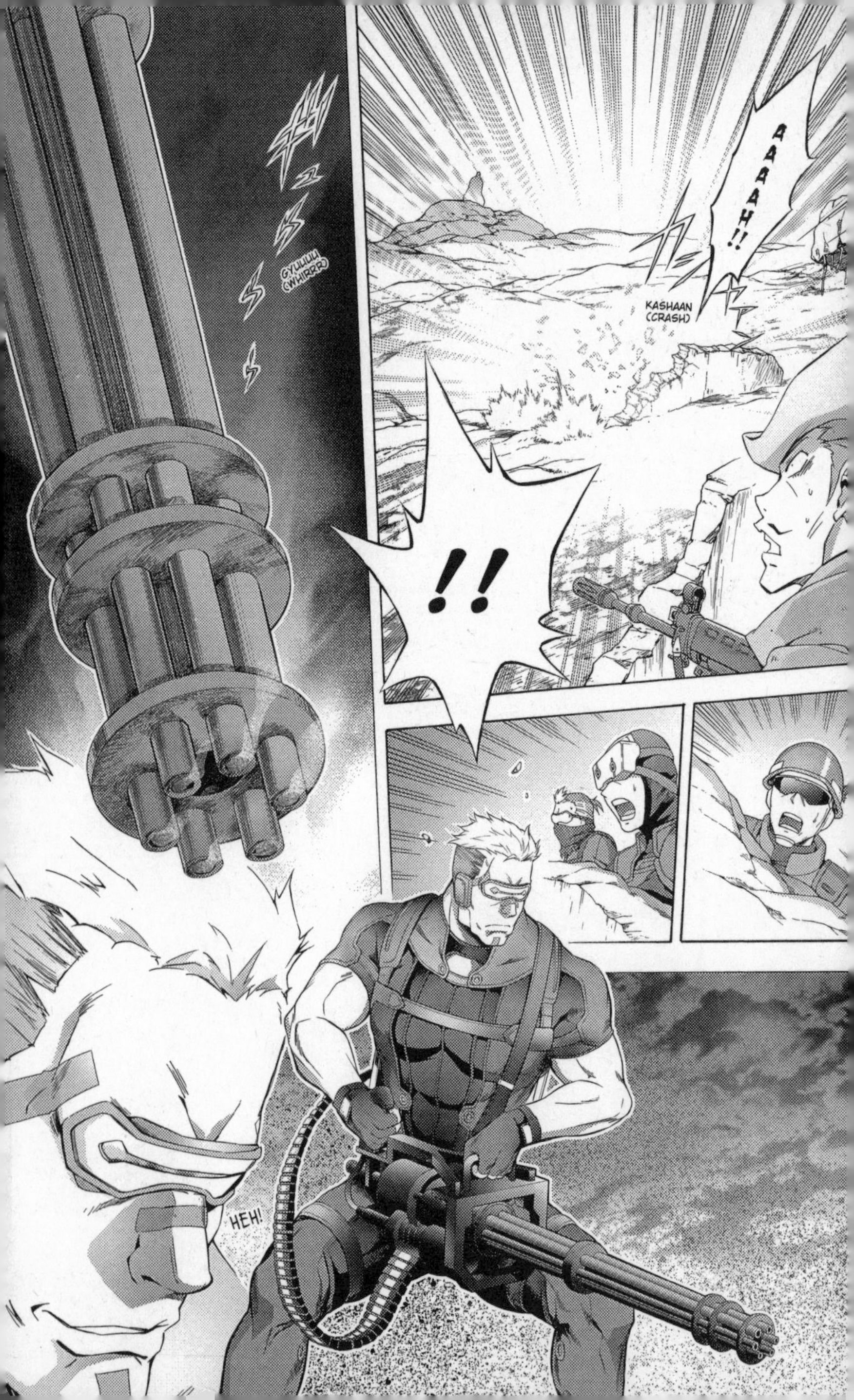
AAAAAH!!
KASHAAN (CRASH)
!!
GYULULU (WHIRRR)
HEH!

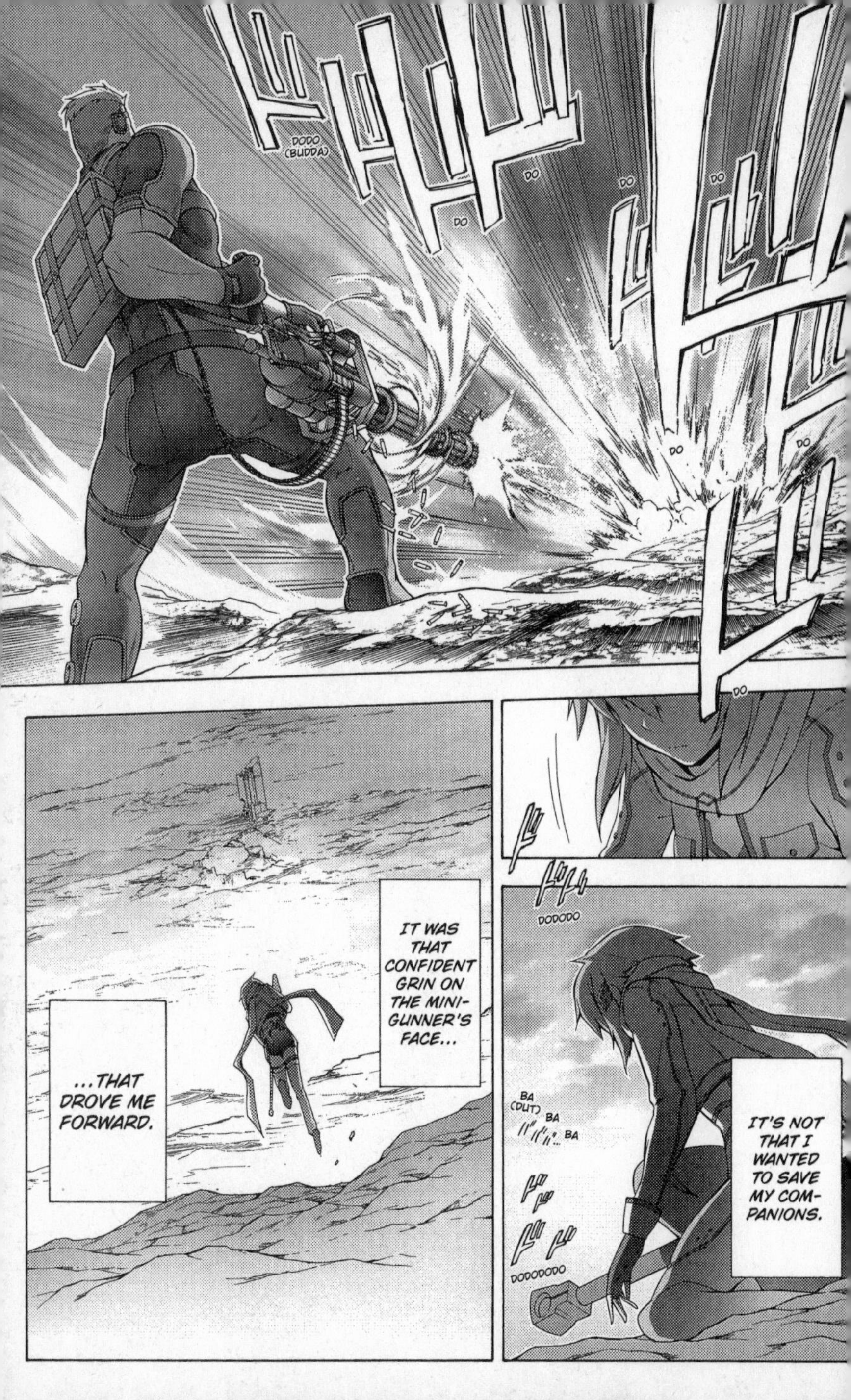
DODO (BUDDA)
DO
DO
DO
DO
DO
DO
DO
DODODO
BA (DUT) BA BA
DODODODO
IT'S NOT THAT I WANTED TO SAVE MY COMPANIONS.
IT WAS THAT CONFIDENT GRIN ON THE MINI-GUNNER'S FACE...
...THAT DROVE ME FORWARD.

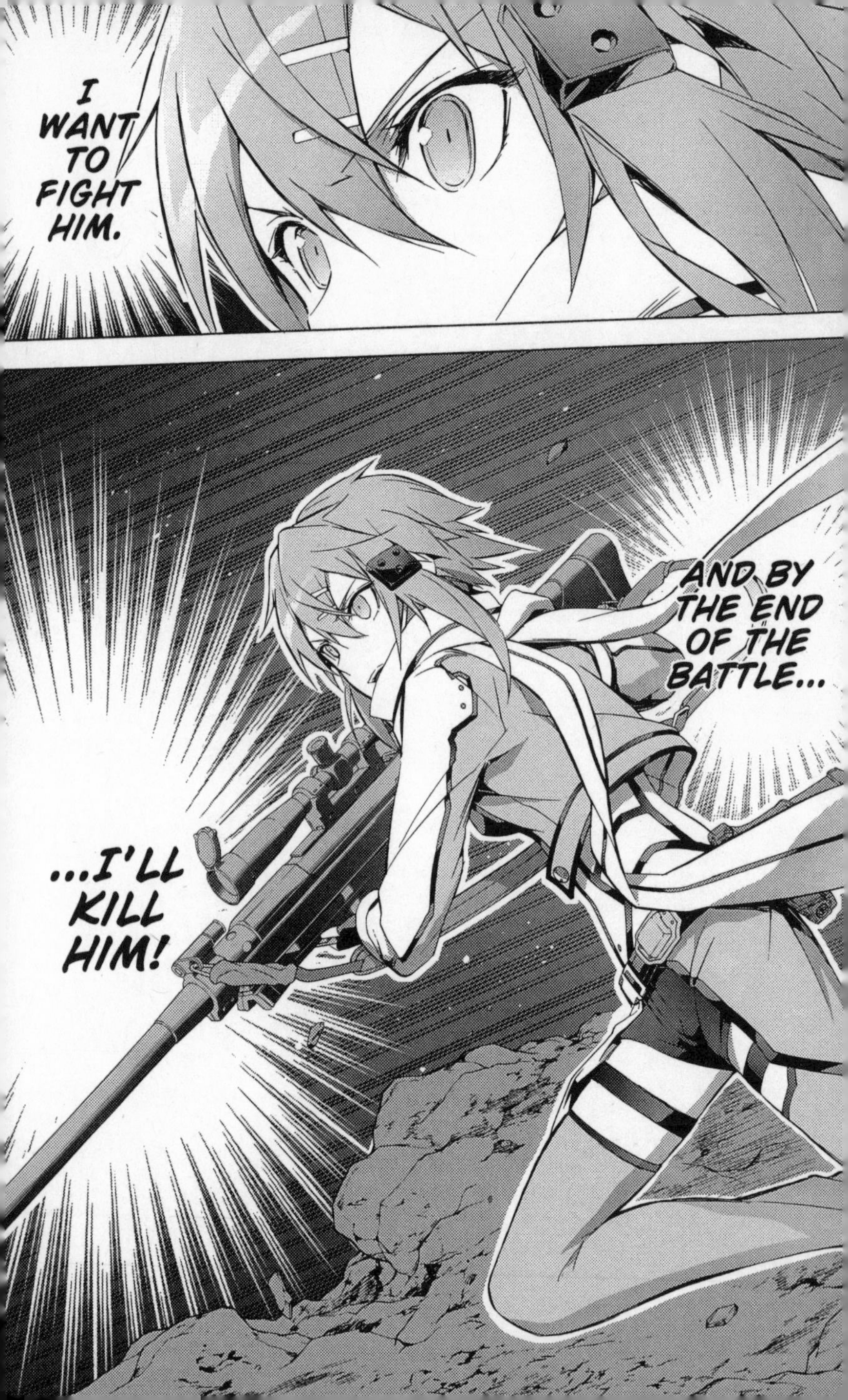
I WANT TO FIGHT HIM.
AND BY THE END OF THE BATTLE...
...I'LL KILL HIM!

SWORD ART ONLINE
phantom bullet

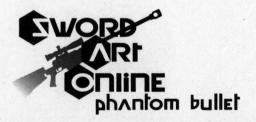

SWORD ART ONLINE
phantom bullet

003

check point!

GUN GALE ONLINE: WORLD

UNLIKE OTHER VRMMO WORLDS, THE BACK-STORY OF GGO IS VERY SPARSE, BUT BASED ON THE FINE DETAILS, IT APPEARS TO BE A SCI-FI SETTING OF A POST-COLLAPSE WORLD. THE "SBC" OF THE CAPITAL CITY SBC GLOCKEN STANDS FOR "SPACE BATTLE CRUISER," MEANING THE CITY ITSELF IS A LONG-DORMANT SPACESHIP. UNLIKE ALO, THE IN-GAME TIME IS SYNCHRONIZED WITH REAL TIME, BUT EVEN IN THE MIDDLE OF THE DAY, THE SKY IS A GLOOMY REDDISH YELLOW.

M134 MINIGUN: ITEM

AN AMERICAN 7.62 MM GATLING GUN DEVELOPED BY GENERAL ELECTRIC. IT'S A SMALLER VERSION OF THE 20 MM GATLING (VULCAN) LOADED ON FIGHTER JETS, MEANT TO HELP HELICOPTERS AND ARMORED VEHICLES PROVIDE SUPPRESSIVE FIRE. IT CAN FIRE 4,000 BULLETS A MINUTE. BUT THE BODY ALONE WEIGHS 40 POUNDS, AND WHEN AMMO AND BATTERY IS INCLUDED, IT CAN GO WELL OVER 100 POUNDS. SO IN REALITY, IT WOULD BE IMPOSSIBLE FOR INDIVIDUAL SOLDIERS LIKE BEHEMOTH TO USE IT.

COURTESY OF: A-1 PICTURES
©2014 REKI KAWAHARA/KADOKAWA ASCII MEDIA WORKS/SAO II PROJECT

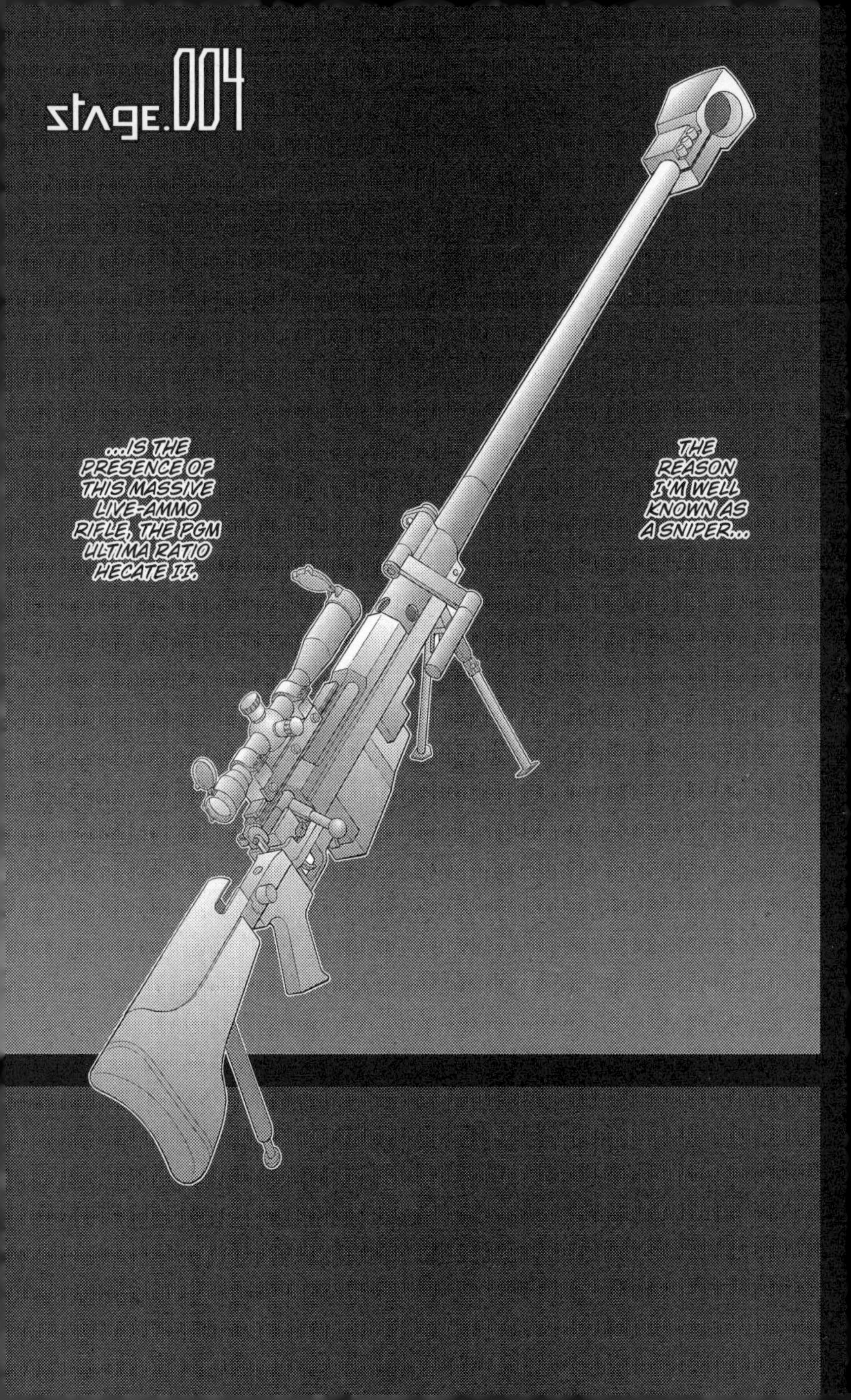
stage.004
THE REASON I'M WELL KNOWN AS A SNIPER...
...IS THE PRESENCE OF THIS MASSIVE LIVE-AMMO RIFLE, THE PGM ULTIMA RATIO HECATE II.

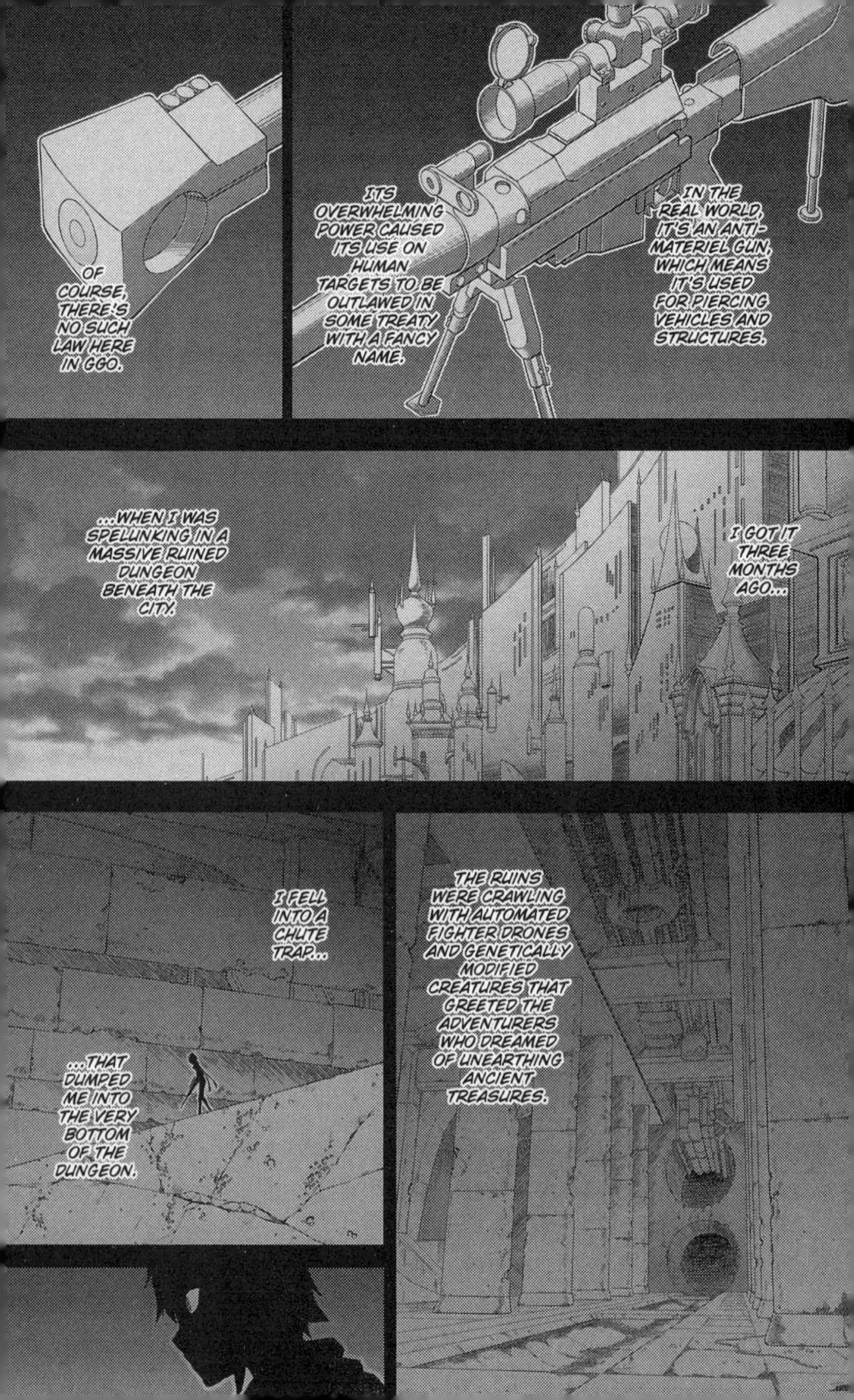
IN THE REAL WORLD, IT'S AN ANTI-MATERIEL GUN, WHICH MEANS IT'S USED FOR PIERCING VEHICLES AND STRUCTURES.
ITS OVERWHELMING POWER CAUSED ITS USE ON HUMAN TARGETS TO BE OUTLAWED IN SOME TREATY WITH A FANCY NAME.
OF COURSE, THERE'S NO SUCH LAW HERE IN GGO.
I GOT IT THREE MONTHS AGO...
...WHEN I WAS SPELUNKING IN A MASSIVE RUINED DUNGEON BENEATH THE CITY.
THE RUINS WERE CRAWLING WITH AUTOMATED FIGHTER DRONES AND GENETICALLY MODIFIED CREATURES THAT GREETED THE ADVENTURERS WHO DREAMED OF UNEARTHING ANCIENT TREASURES.
I FELL INTO A CHUTE TRAP...
...THAT DUMPED ME INTO THE VERY BOTTOM OF THE DUNGEON.

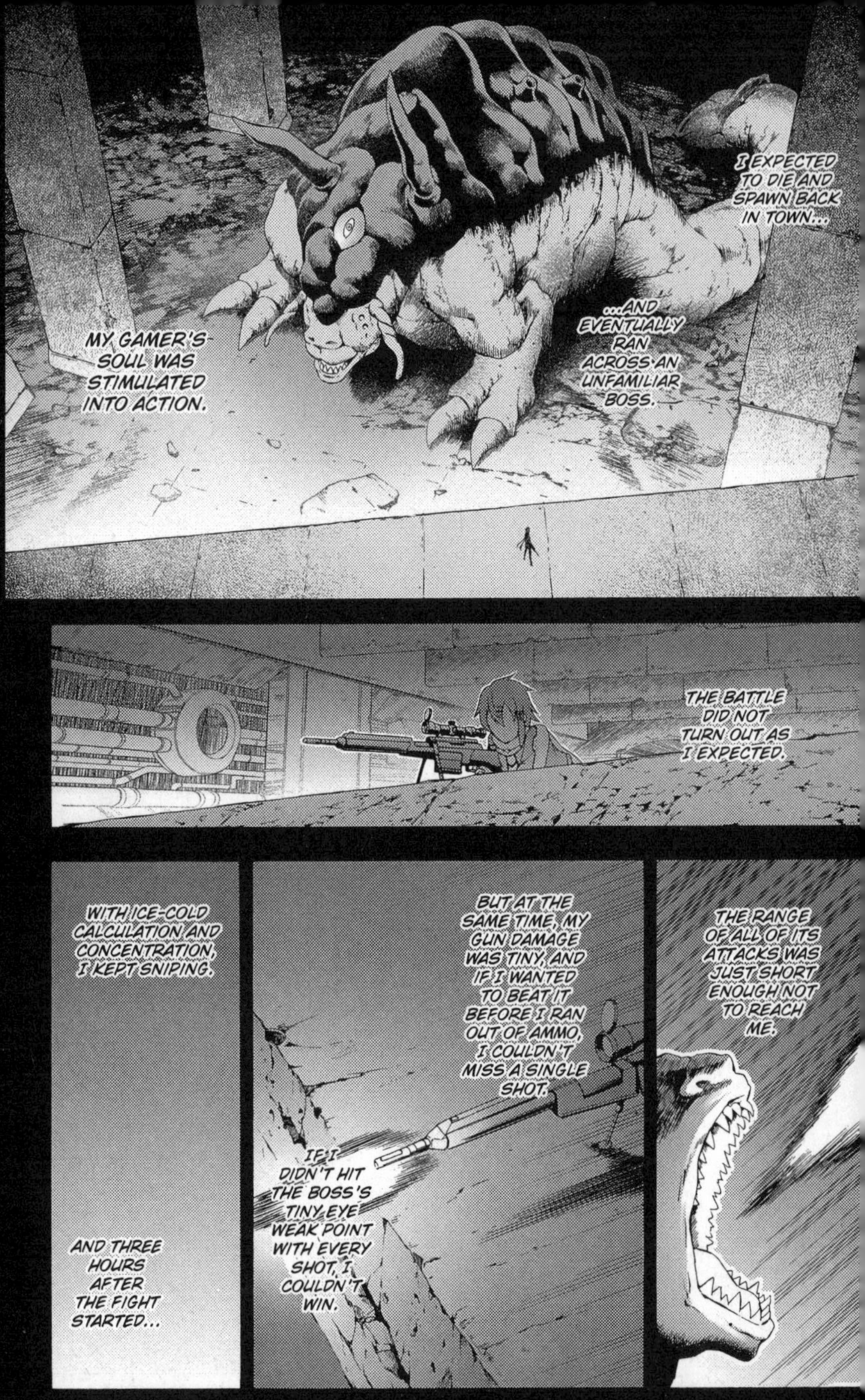
I EXPECTED TO DIE AND SPAWN BACK IN TOWN...
...AND EVENTUALLY RAN ACROSS AN UNFAMILIAR BOSS.
MY GAMER'S SOUL WAS STIMULATED INTO ACTION.
THE BATTLE DID NOT TURN OUT AS I EXPECTED.
THE RANGE OF ALL OF ITS ATTACKS WAS JUST SHORT ENOUGH NOT TO REACH ME.
BUT AT THE SAME TIME, MY GUN DAMAGE WAS TINY, AND IF I WANTED TO BEAT IT BEFORE I RAN OUT OF AMMO, I COULDN'T MISS A SINGLE SHOT.
IF I DIDN'T HIT THE BOSS'S TINY EYE WEAK POINT WITH EVERY SHOT, I COULDN'T WIN.
WITH ICE-COLD CALCULATION AND CONCENTRATION, I KEPT SNIPING.
AND THREE HOURS AFTER THE FIGHT STARTED...

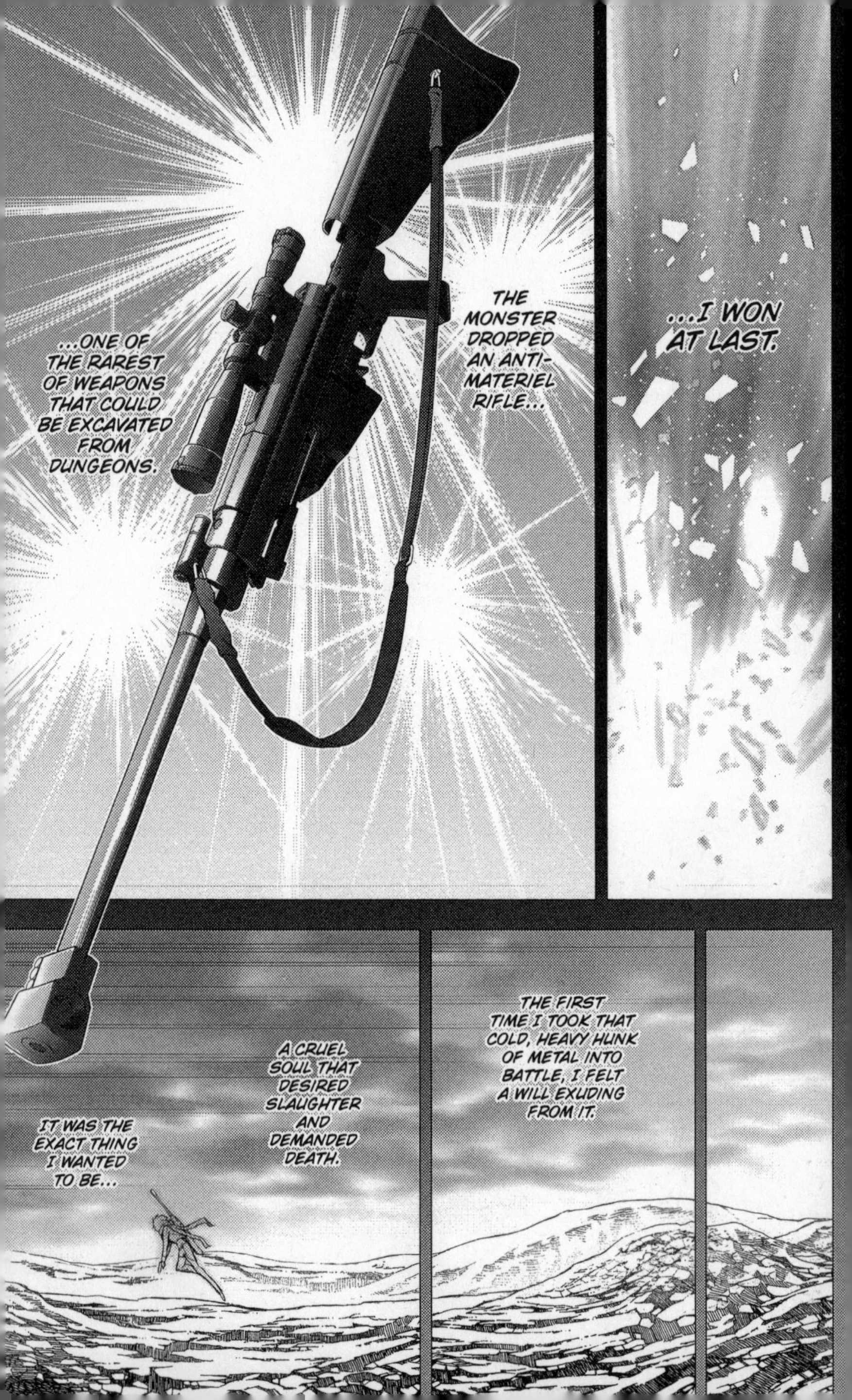
...I WON AT LAST.
THE MONSTER DROPPED AN ANTI-MATERIEL RIFLE...
...ONE OF THE RAREST OF WEAPONS THAT COULD BE EXCAVATED FROM DUNGEONS.
THE FIRST TIME I TOOK THAT COLD, HEAVY HUNK OF METAL INTO BATTLE, I FELT A WILL EXUDING FROM IT.
A CRUEL SOUL THAT DESIRED SLAUGHTER AND DEMANDED DEATH.
IT WAS THE EXACT THING I WANTED TO BE...

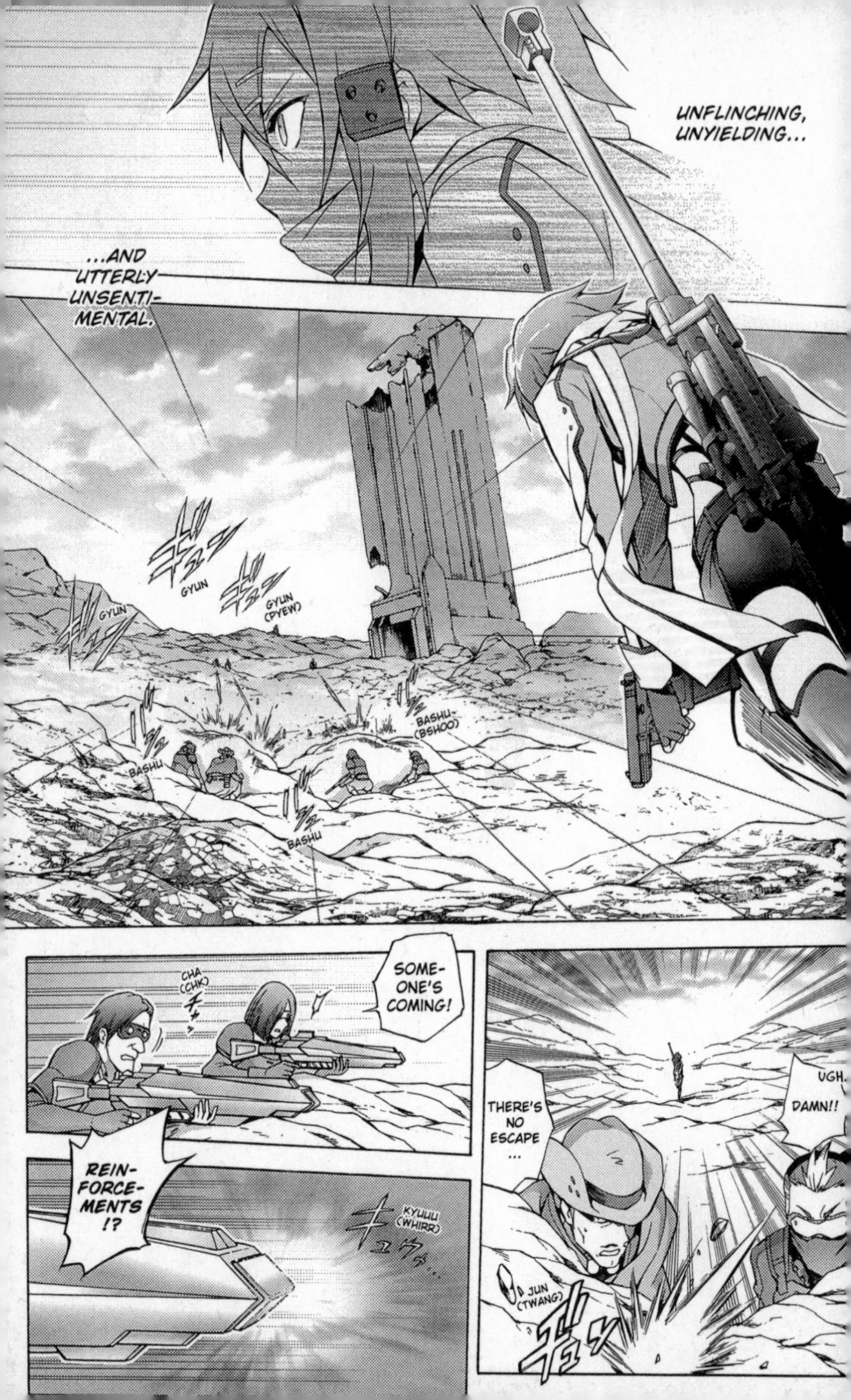
UNFLINCHING, UNYIELDING...
...AND UTTERLY UNSENTI-MENTAL.
GYUN
GYUN (PYEW)
GYUN
BASHU (BSHOO)
BASHU
BASHU
SOME-ONE'S COMING!
CHA (CHK)
REIN-FORCE-MENTS !?
KYUUU (WHIRR)
UGH.
DAMN!!
THERE'S NO ESCAPE ...
JUN (TWANG)

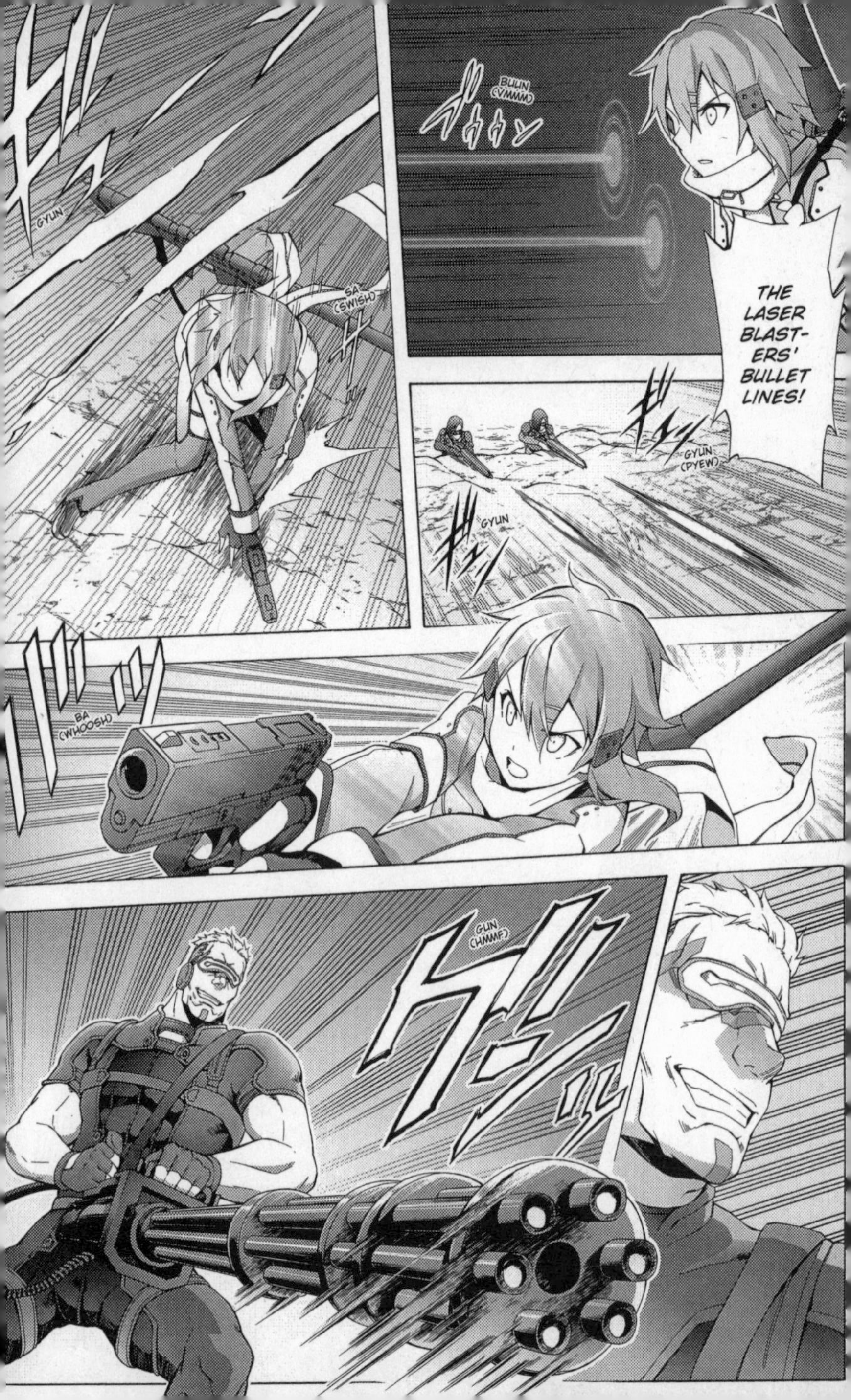
THE LASER BLAST-ERS' BULLET LINES!
BUUN (VMMM)
GYUN (PYEW)
GYUN
GYUN
SA (SWISH)
BA (WHOOSH)
GUN (HMMF)

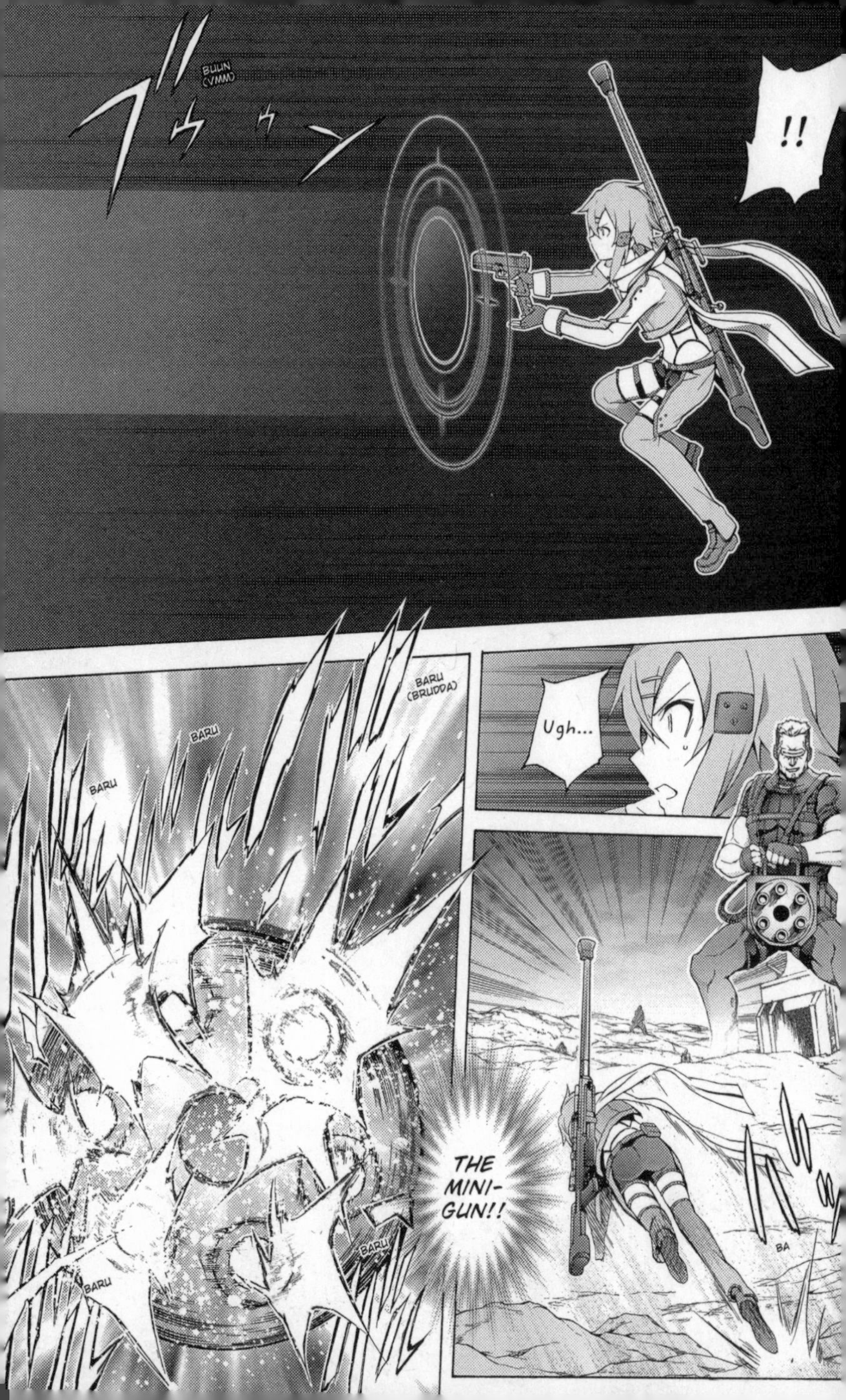
!!
BUUN (VMM)
Ugh...
THE MINI-GUN!!
BA
BARU (BRUDDA)
BARU
BARU
BARU
BARU

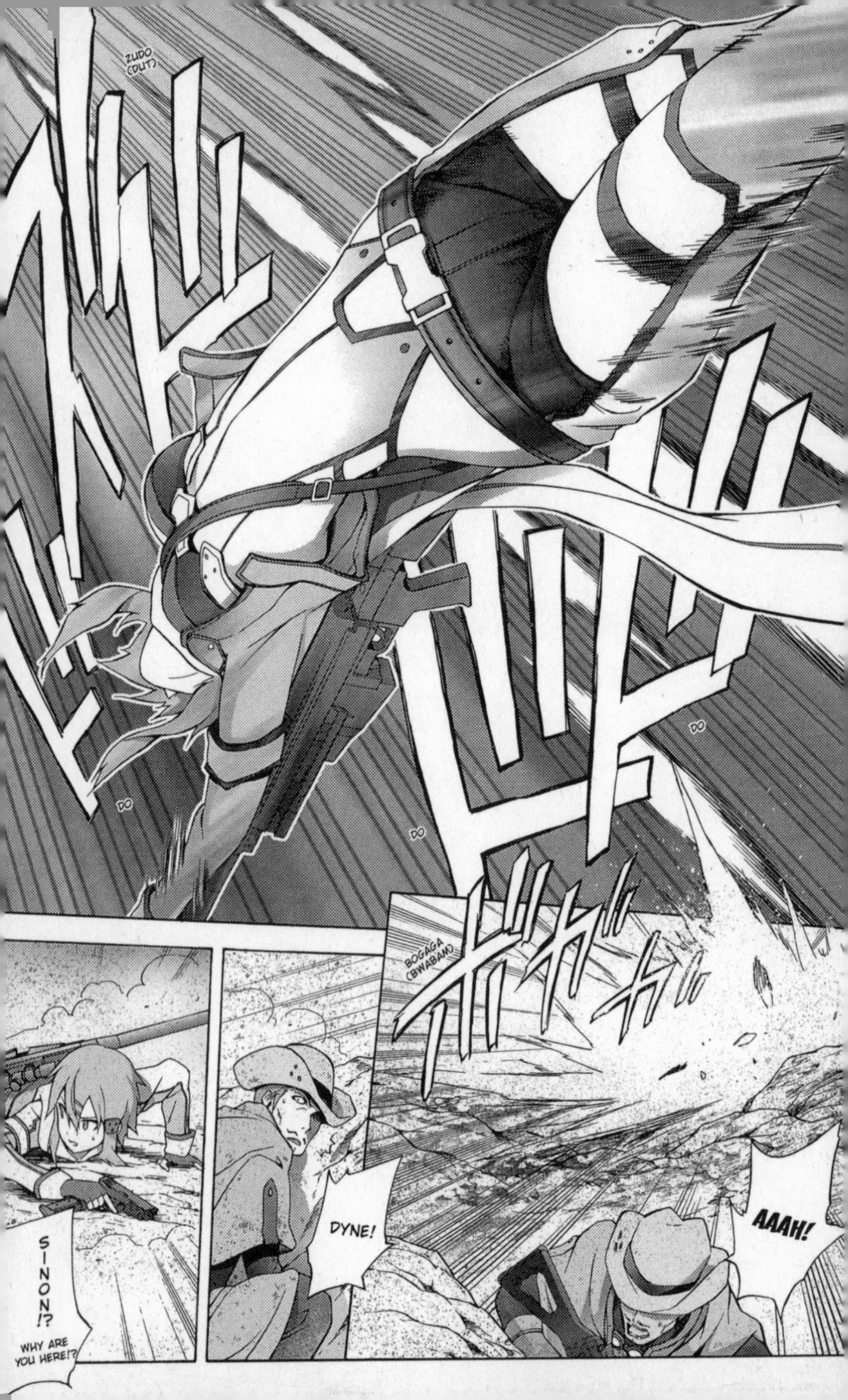
ZUDO (DUT)
DO
DO
DO
BOGAGA (BWABAM)
AAAH!
DYNE!
SINON!?
WHY ARE YOU HERE!?

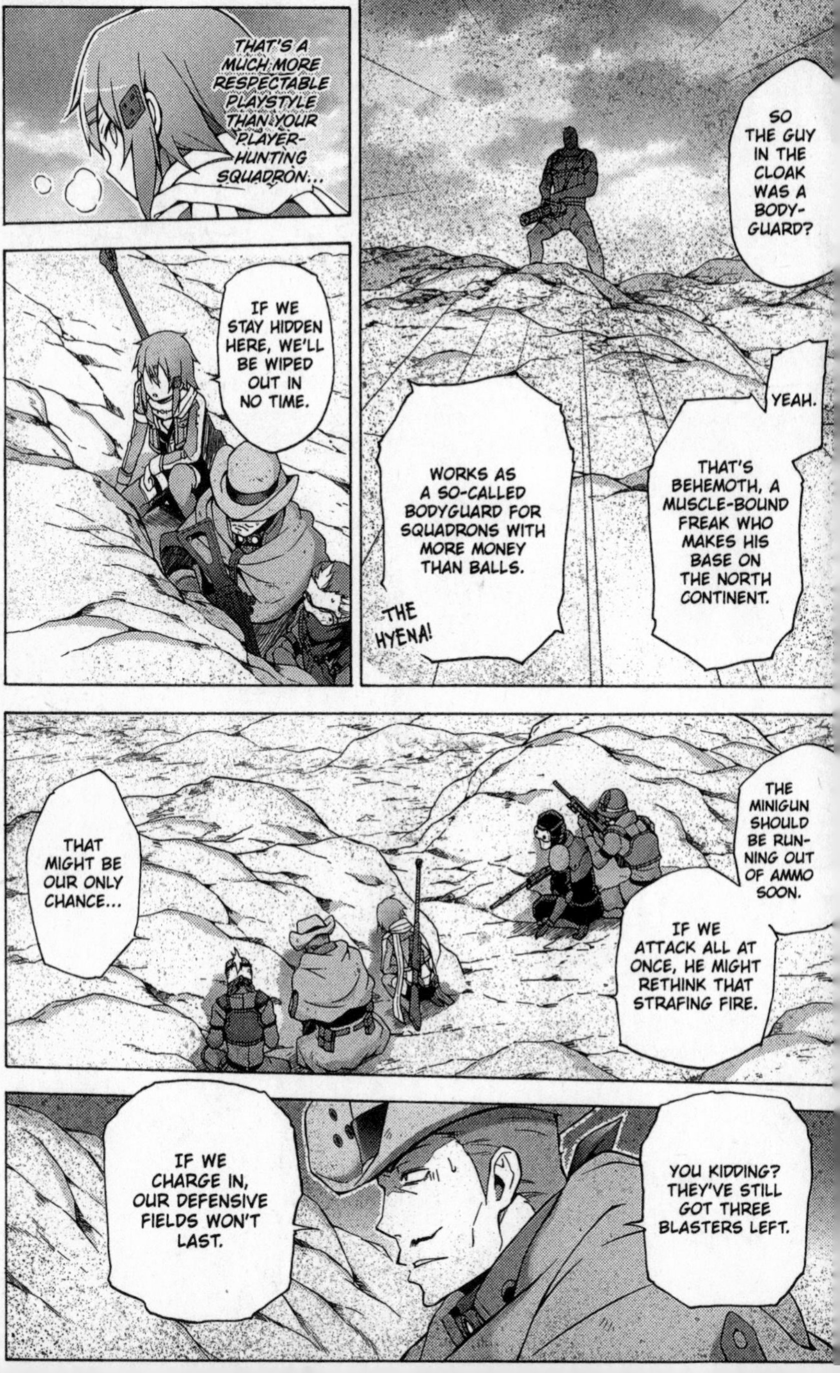
SO THE GUY IN THE CLOAK WAS A BODY-GUARD?
YEAH.
THAT'S BEHEMOTH, A MUSCLE-BOUND FREAK WHO MAKES HIS BASE ON THE NORTH CONTINENT.
WORKS AS A SO-CALLED BODYGUARD FOR SQUADRONS WITH MORE MONEY THAN BALLS.
THE HYENA!
THAT'S A MUCH MORE RESPECTABLE PLAYSTYLE THAN YOUR PLAYER-HUNTING SQUADRON...
IF WE STAY HIDDEN HERE, WE'LL BE WIPED OUT IN NO TIME.
THE MINIGUN SHOULD BE RUN-NING OUT OF AMMO SOON.
IF WE ATTACK ALL AT ONCE, HE MIGHT RETHINK THAT STRAFING FIRE.
THAT MIGHT BE OUR ONLY CHANCE...
YOU KIDDING? THEY'VE STILL GOT THREE BLASTERS LEFT.
IF WE CHARGE IN, OUR DEFENSIVE FIELDS WON'T LAST.

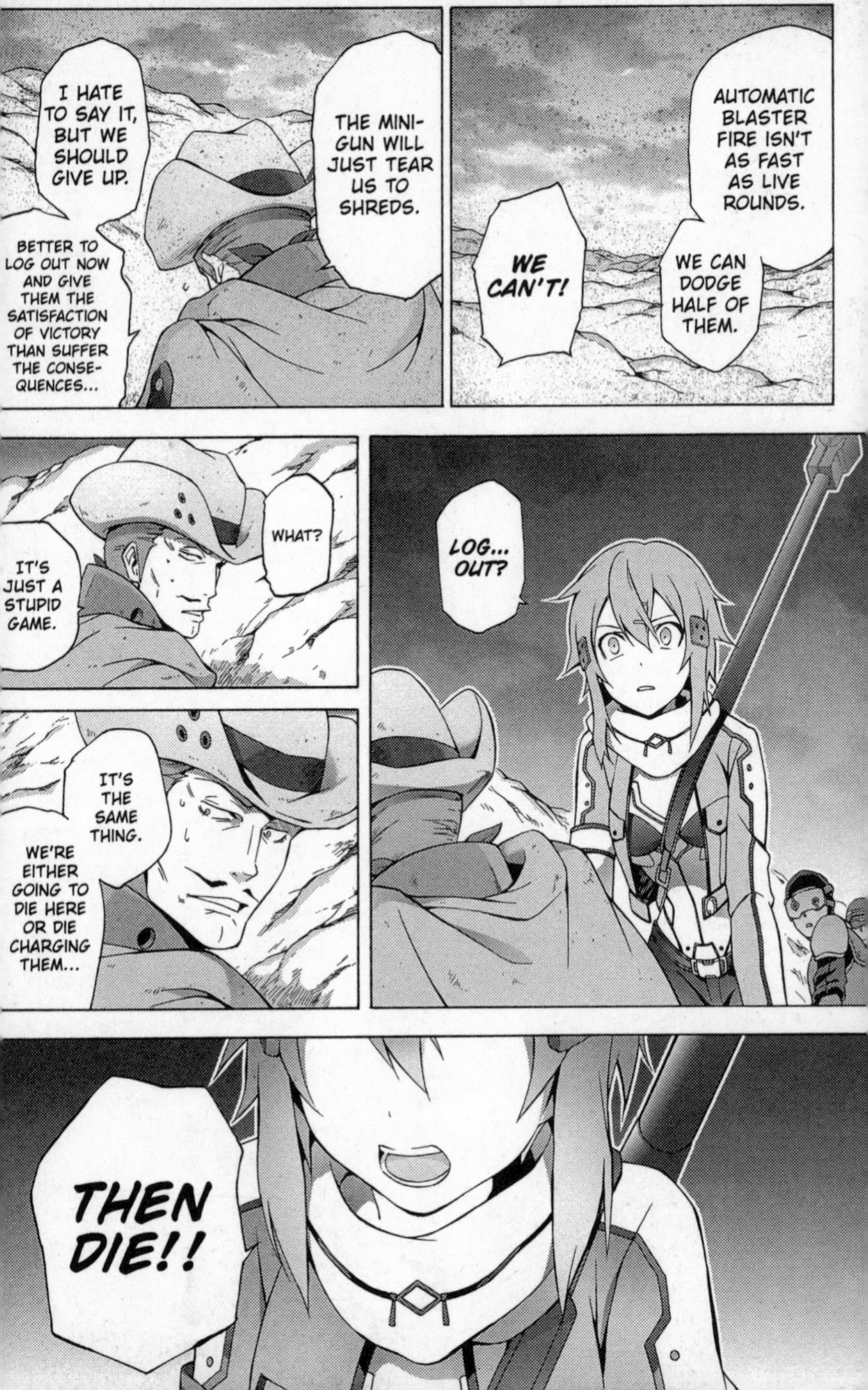
AUTOMATIC BLASTER FIRE ISN'T AS FAST AS LIVE ROUNDS.
WE CAN DODGE HALF OF THEM.
WE CAN'T!
THE MINI-GUN WILL JUST TEAR US TO SHREDS.
I HATE TO SAY IT, BUT WE SHOULD GIVE UP.
BETTER TO LOG OUT NOW AND GIVE THEM THE SATISFACTION OF VICTORY THAN SUFFER THE CONSEQUENCES...
LOG... OUT?
WHAT?
IT'S JUST A STUPID GAME.
IT'S THE SAME THING.
WE'RE EITHER GOING TO DIE HERE OR DIE CHARGING THEM...
THEN DIE!!

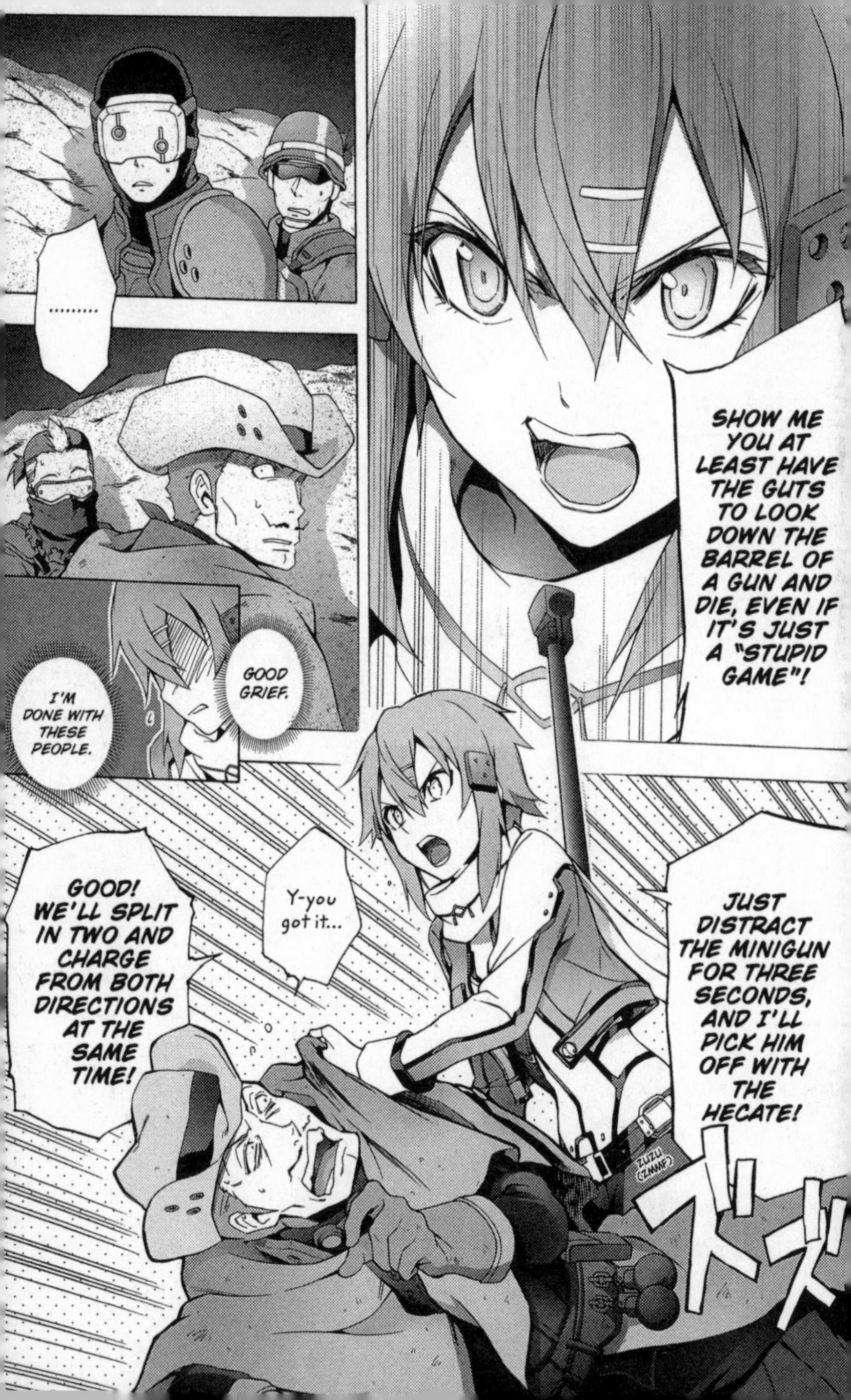
SHOW ME YOU AT LEAST HAVE THE GUTS TO LOOK DOWN THE BARREL OF A GUN AND DIE, EVEN IF IT'S JUST A "STUPID GAME"!
....
GOOD GRIEF.
I'M DONE WITH THESE PEOPLE.
JUST DISTRACT THE MINIGUN FOR THREE SECONDS, AND I'LL PICK HIM OFF WITH THE HECATE!
Y-you got it...
GOOD! WE'LL SPLIT IN TWO AND CHARGE FROM BOTH DIRECTIONS AT THE SAME TIME!
ZUZU (ZMMF)

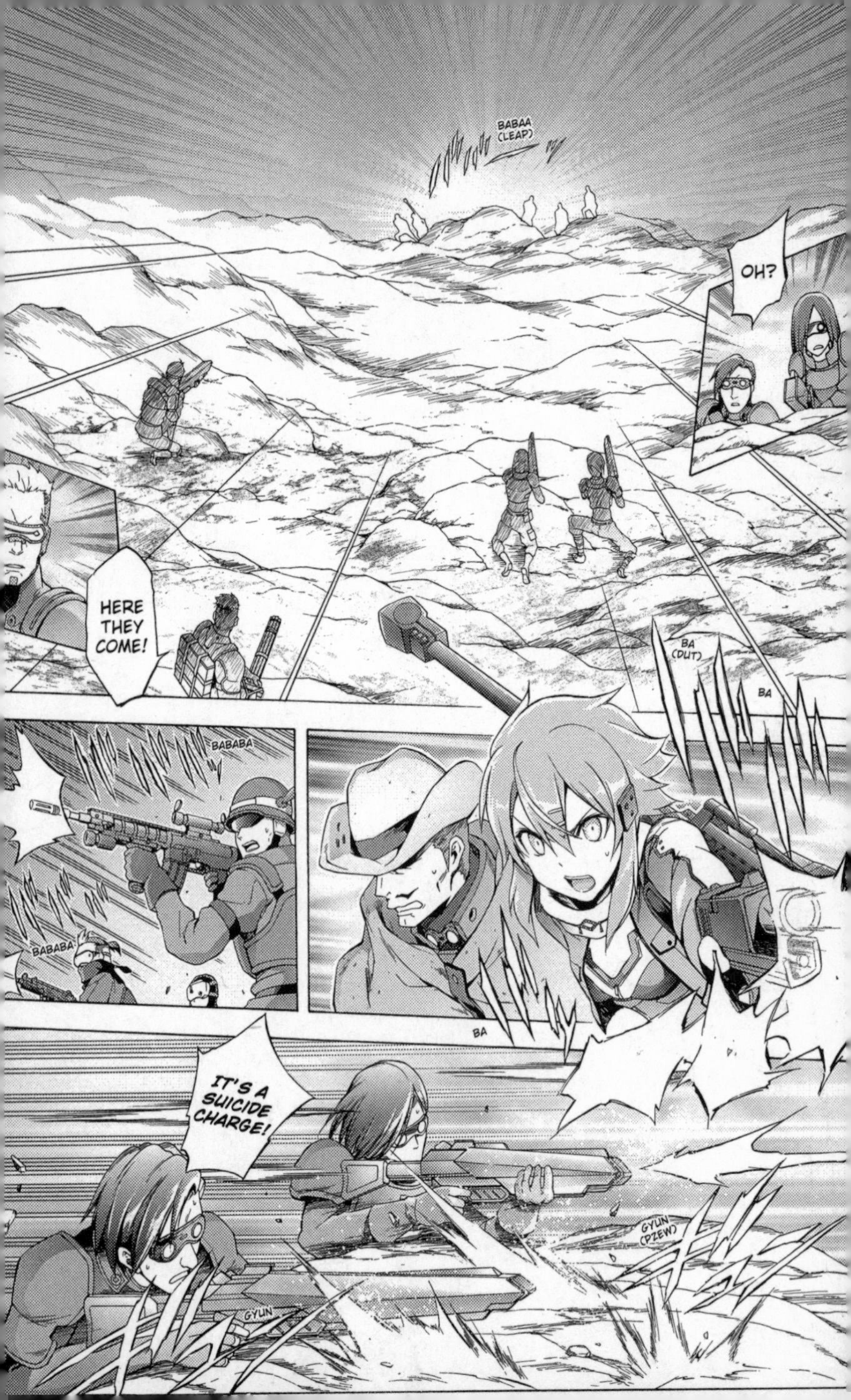
BABAA (LEAP)
OH?
HERE THEY COME!
BA (DUT)
BA
BA
BABABA
BABABA
IT'S A SUICIDE CHARGE!
GYUN (PZEW)
GYUN

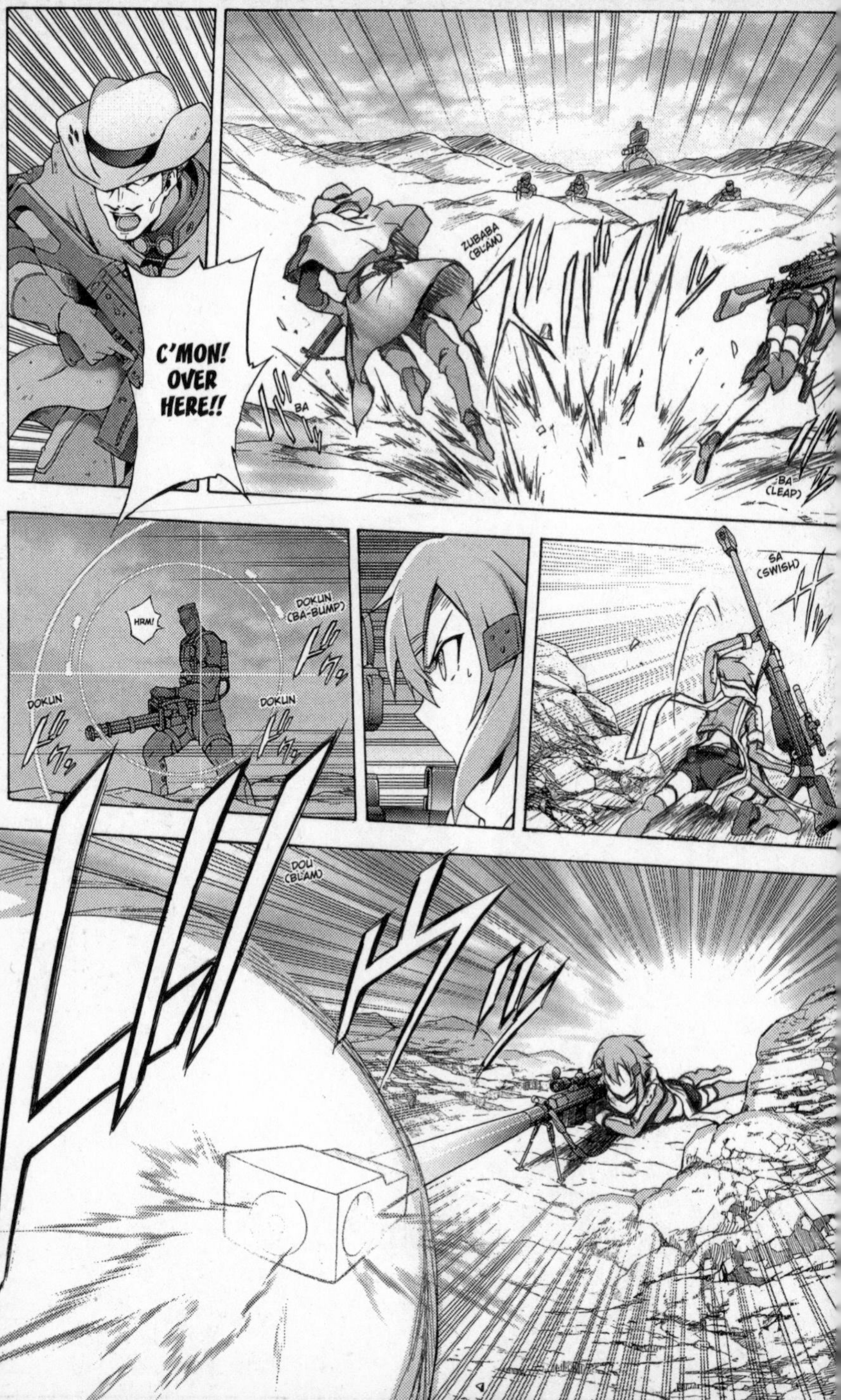
ZUBABA (BL'AM)
BA
BA (LEAP)
C'MON! OVER HERE!!
SA (SWISH)
DOKUN (BA-BUMP)
HRM!
DOKUN
DOKUN
DOU (BL'AM)

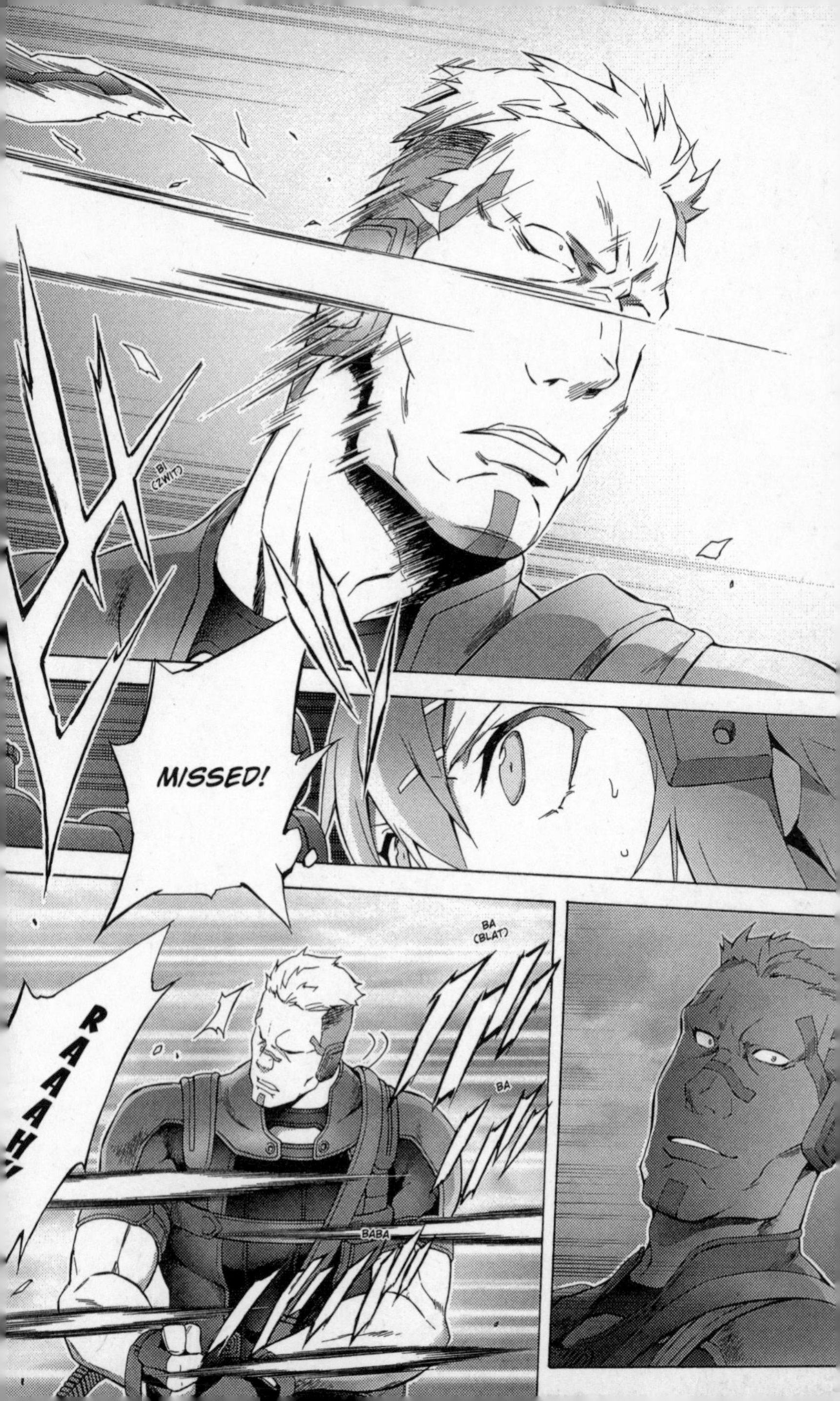
BI (ZWIT)
MISSED!
BA (BLAT)
BA
BABA
RAAAAH!!

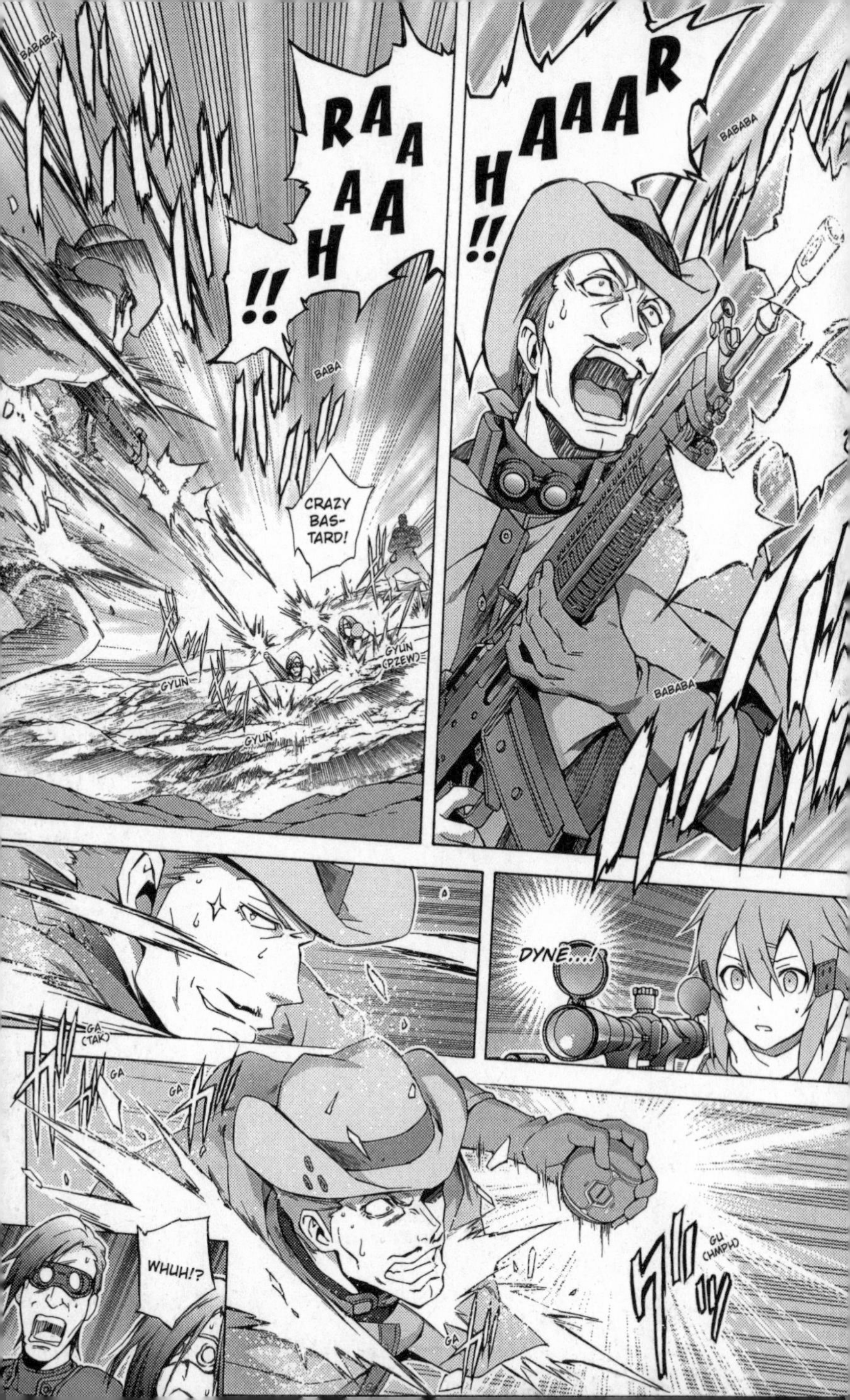
BABABA
HAAAR!!
BABABA
BABABA
RAAAAH!!
BABA
D...
CRAZY BASTARD!
GYUN (PZEW)
GYUN
GYUN
DYNE...!
GA (TAK)
GA
GA
GU CHMPHD
WHUH!?
GA

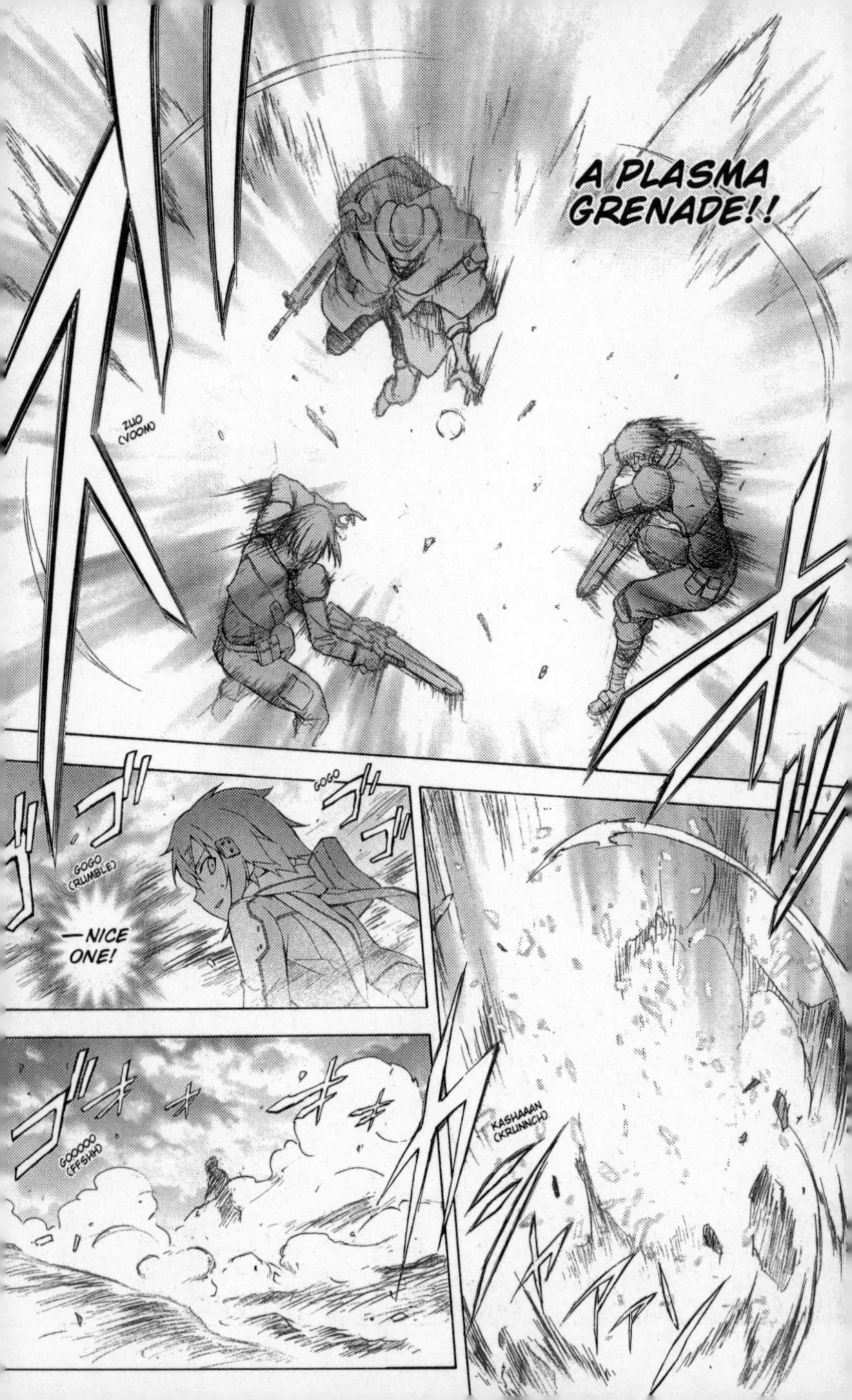
A PLASMA GRENADE!!
ZUO (VOOM)
KASHAAAN (KRUNNCH)
GOGO
GOGO (RUMBLE)
—NICE ONE!
GOOOOO (FFSHH)

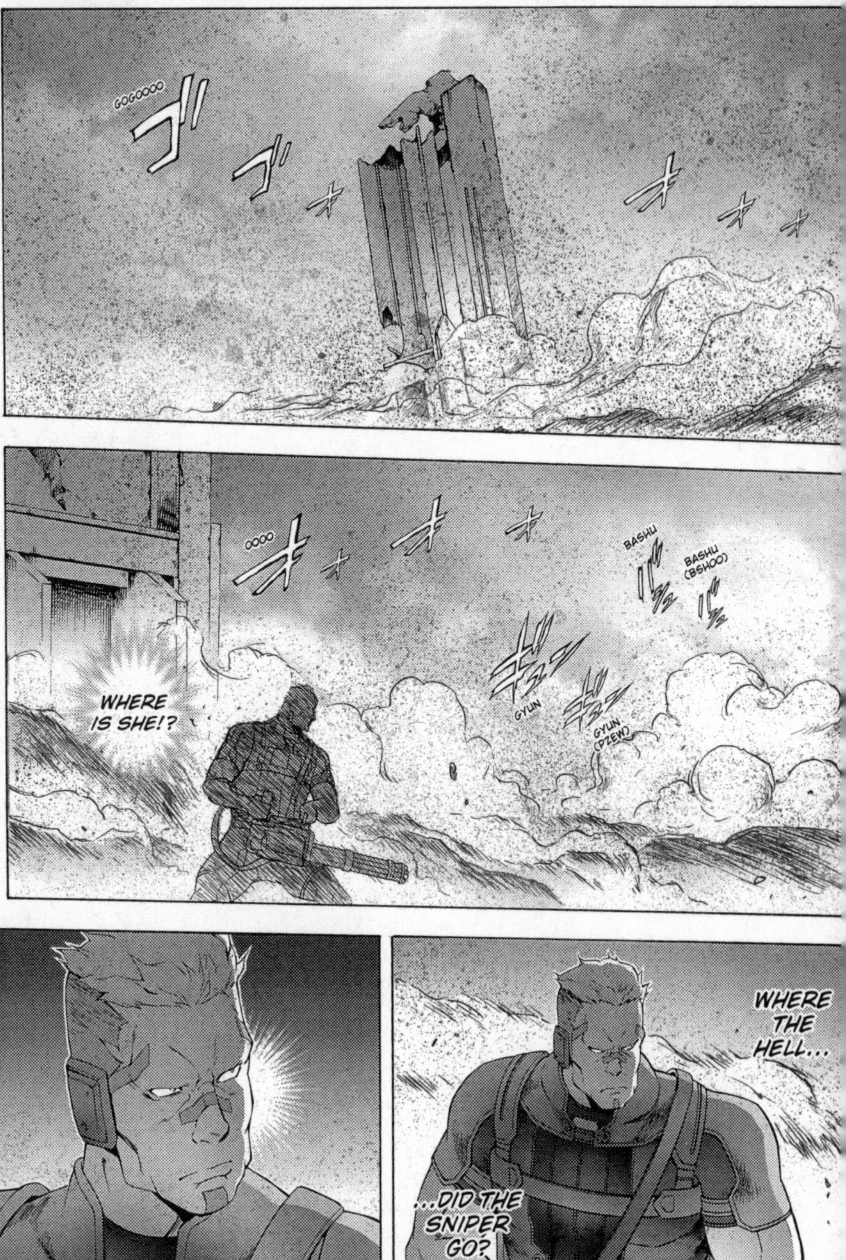
GOGOOOO
BASHU (BSHOO)
BASHU
OOOO
GYUN
GYUN (PZEW)
WHERE IS SHE!?
WHERE THE HELL...
...DID THE SNIPER GO?

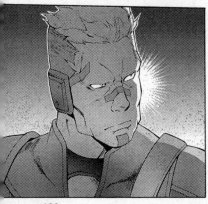

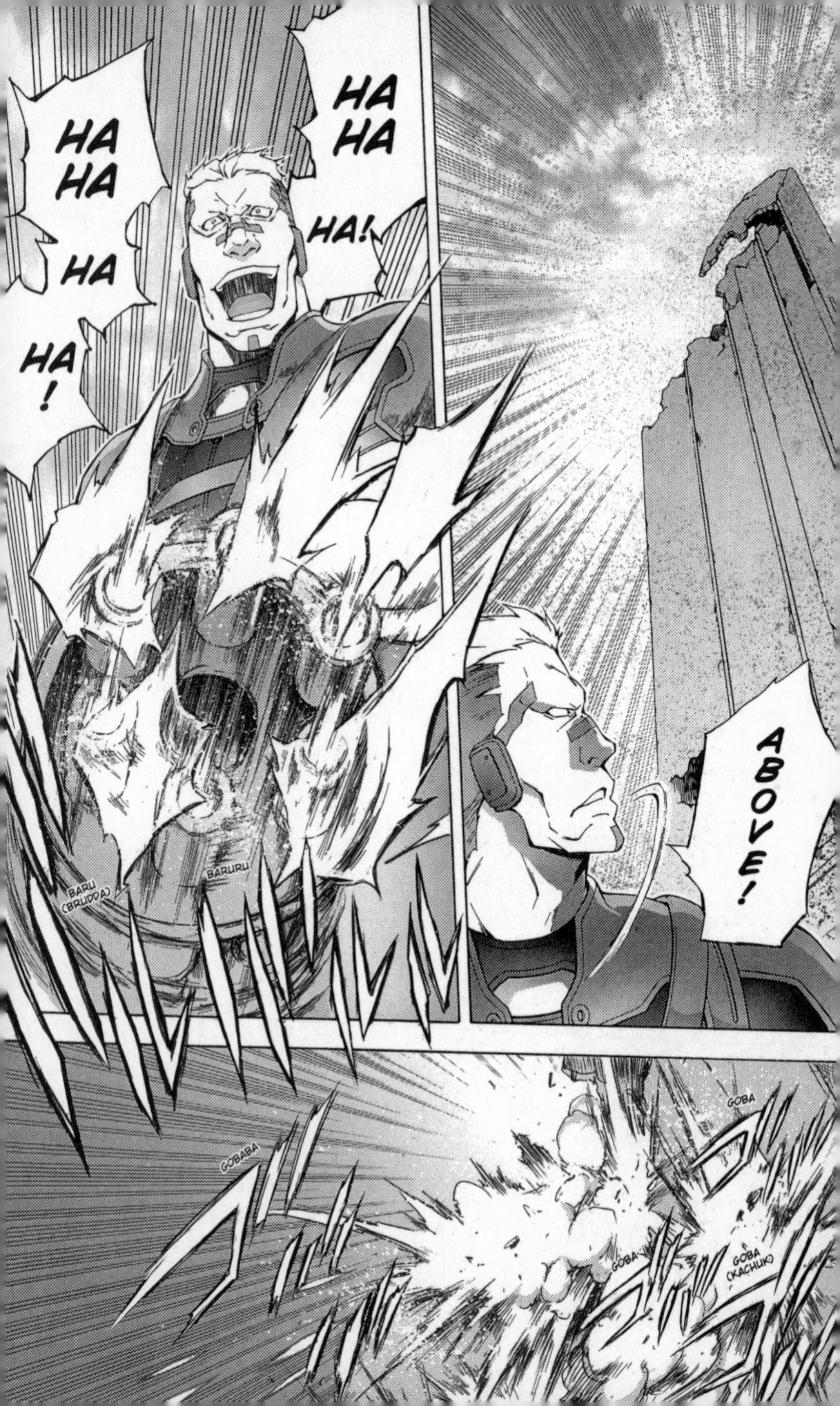
ABOVE!
HA HA HA!
HA HA HA HA!
BARURU
BARU (BRUDDA)
GOBA
GOBA (KACHUK)
GOBA
GOBABA

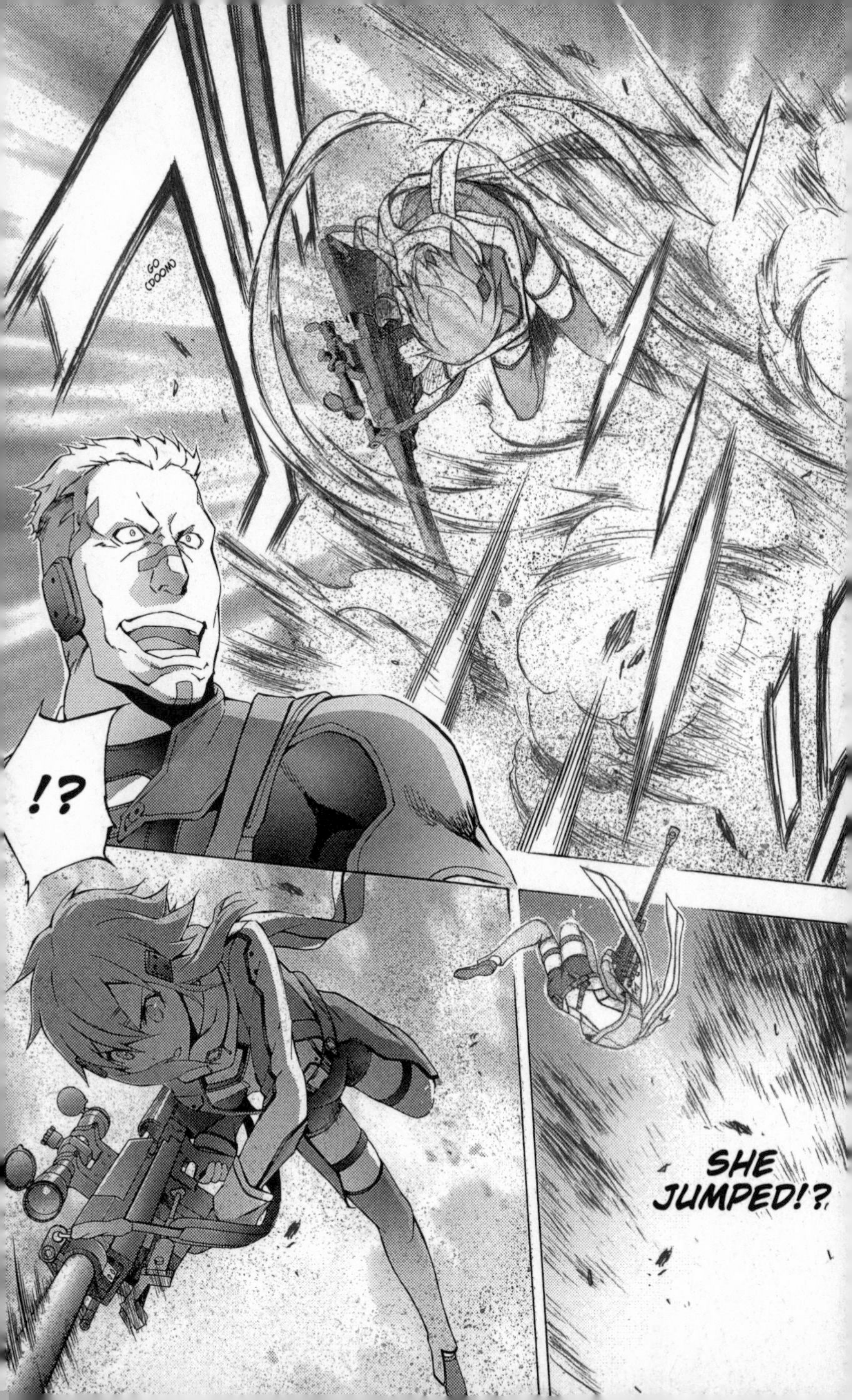
GO DOOM
!?
SHE JUMPED!?

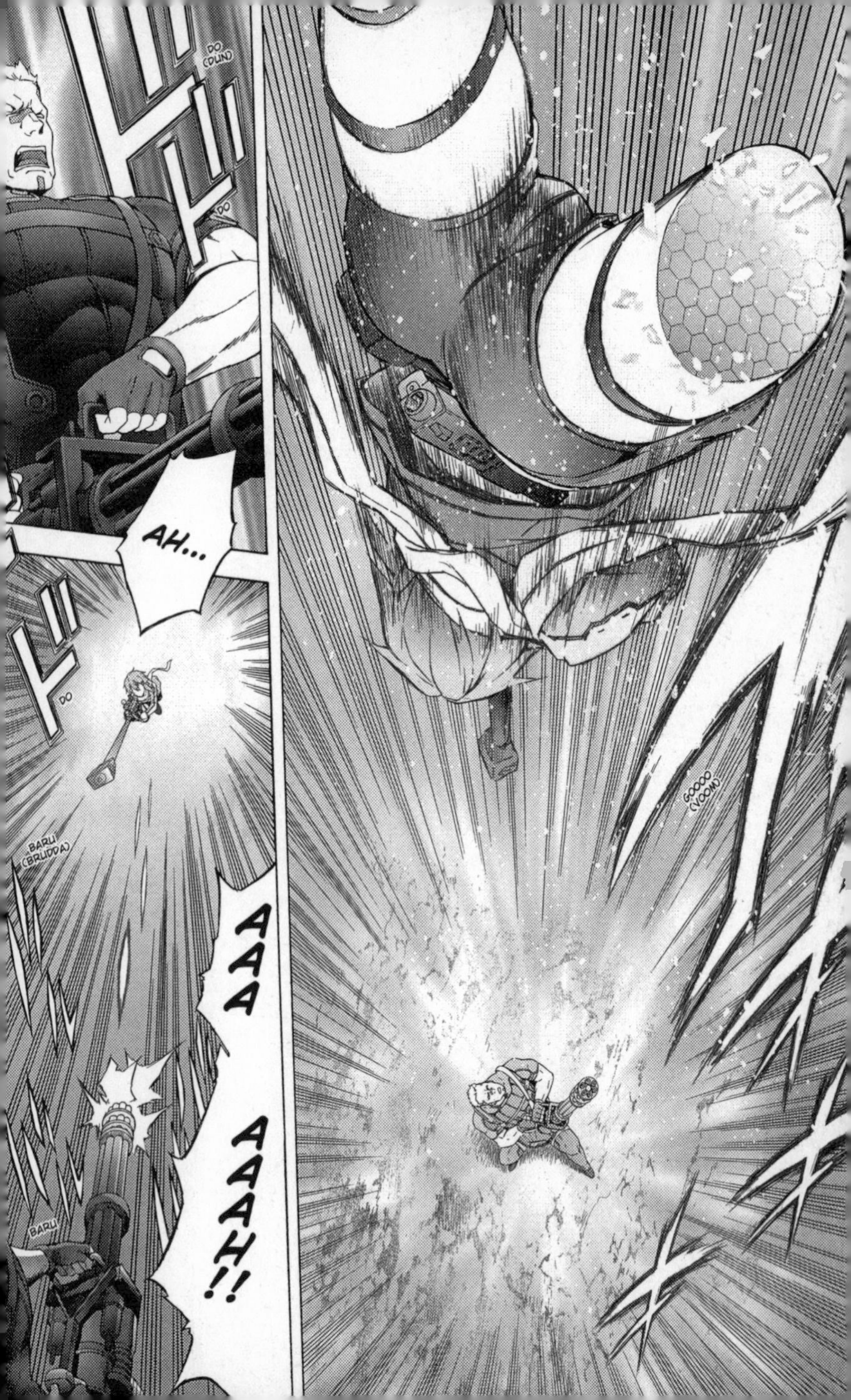
GOOOO (VOOM)
DO (DUN)
DO
AH...
DO
BARU (BRUDDA)
AAA AAAAH!!
BARU

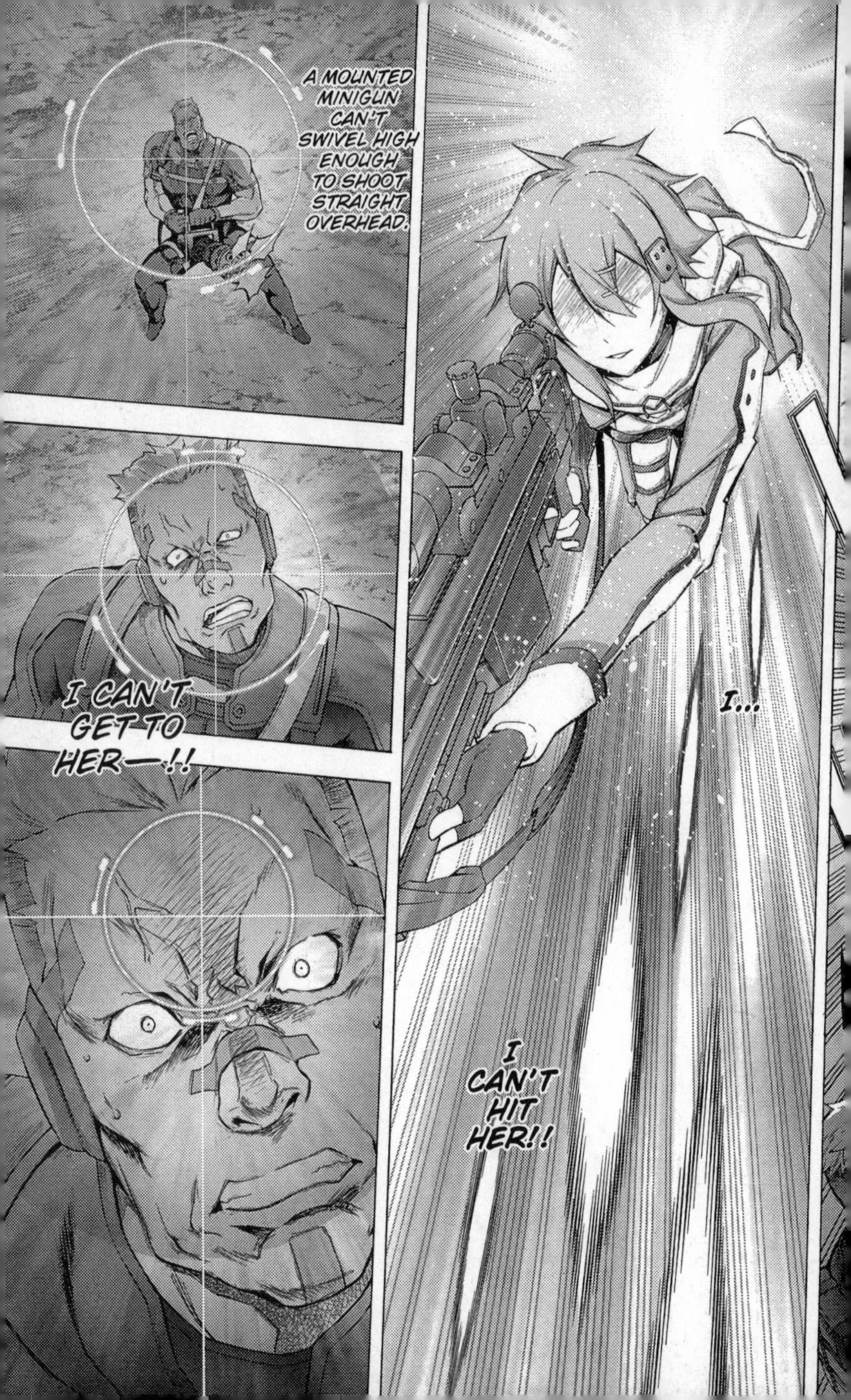
I...
I CAN'T HIT HER!!
A MOUNTED MINIGUN CAN'T SWIVEL HIGH ENOUGH TO SHOOT STRAIGHT OVERHEAD.
I CAN'T GET TO HER—!!

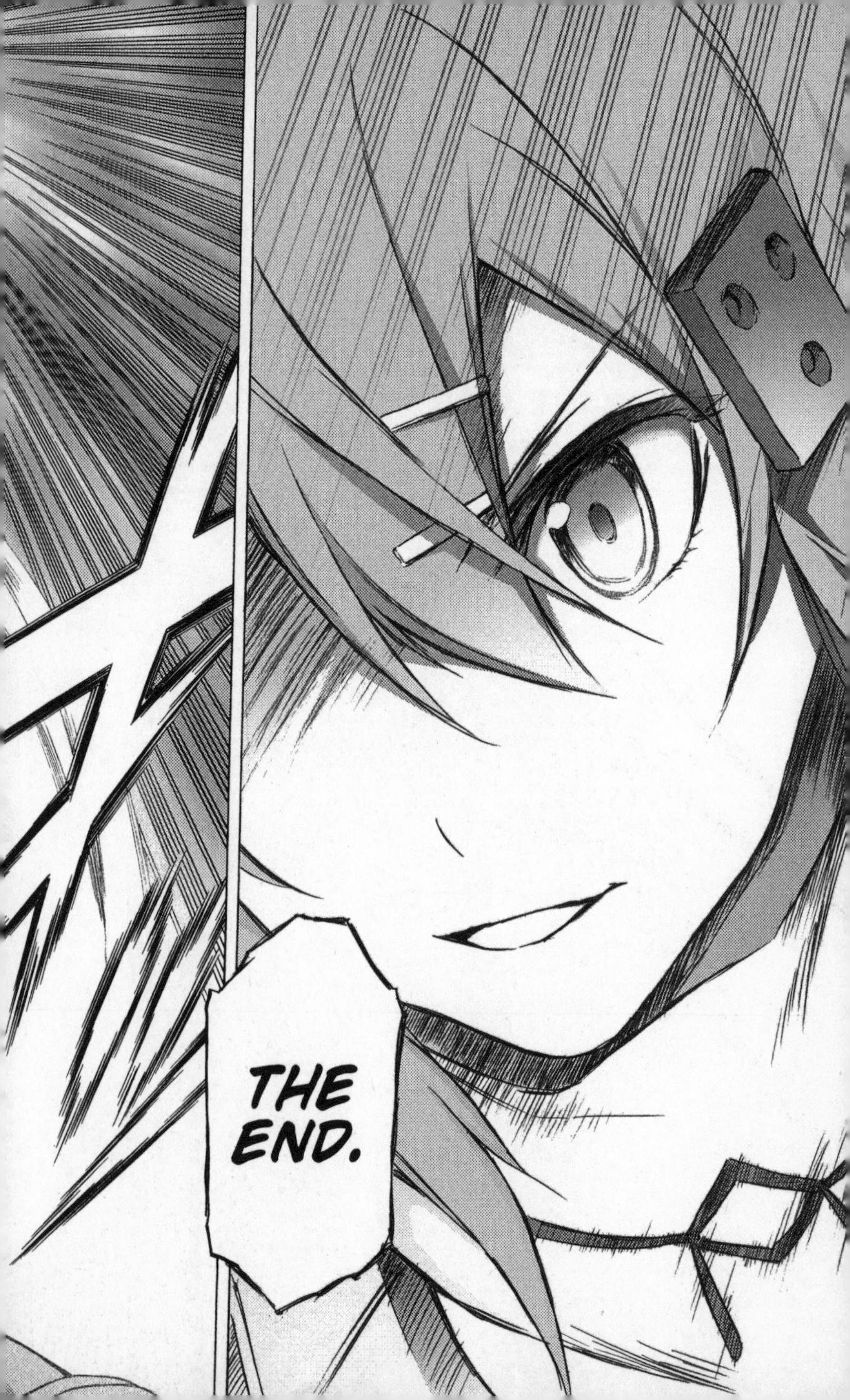
THE END.

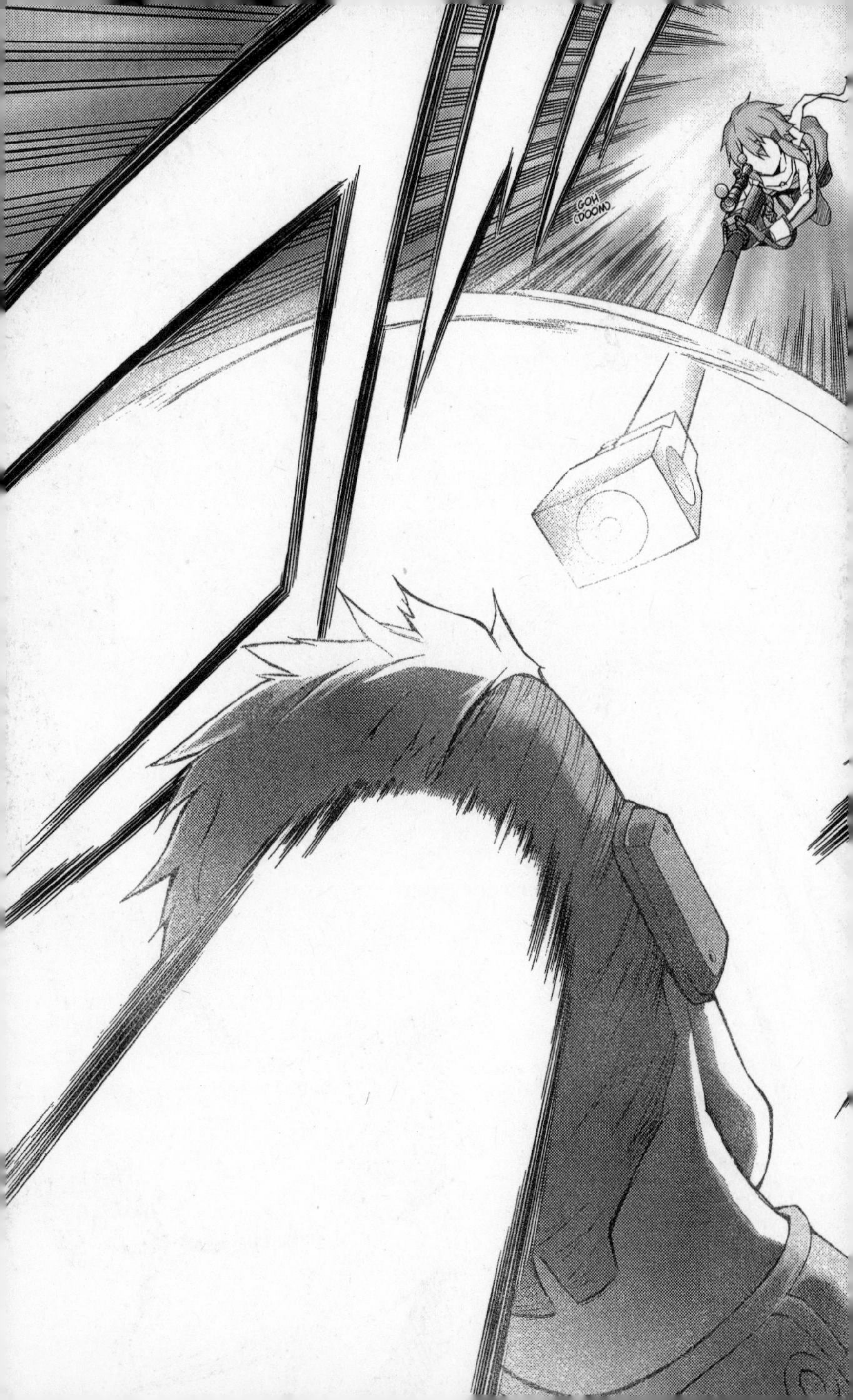
GOH (DOOM)

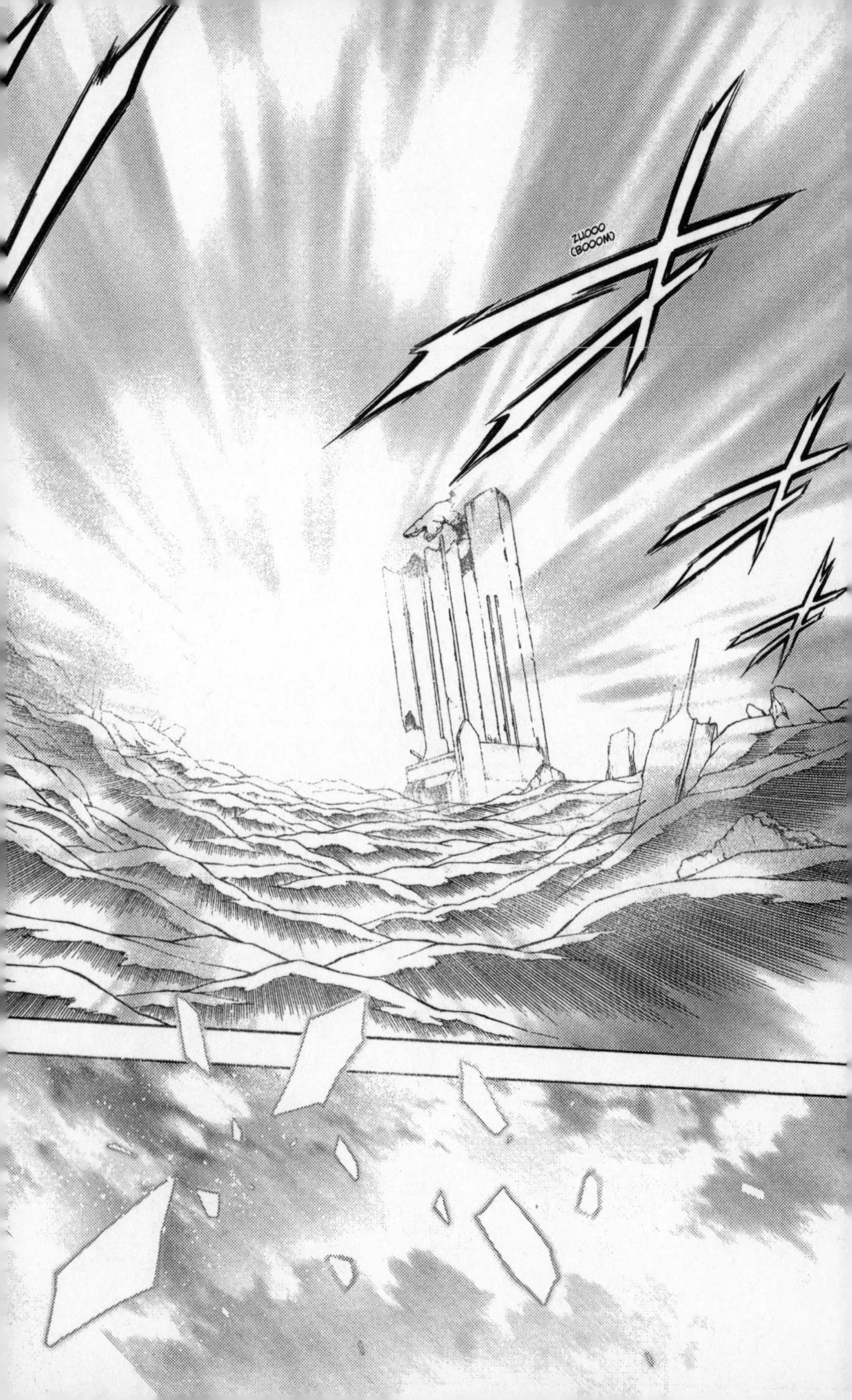
ZUOOO (BOOOM)

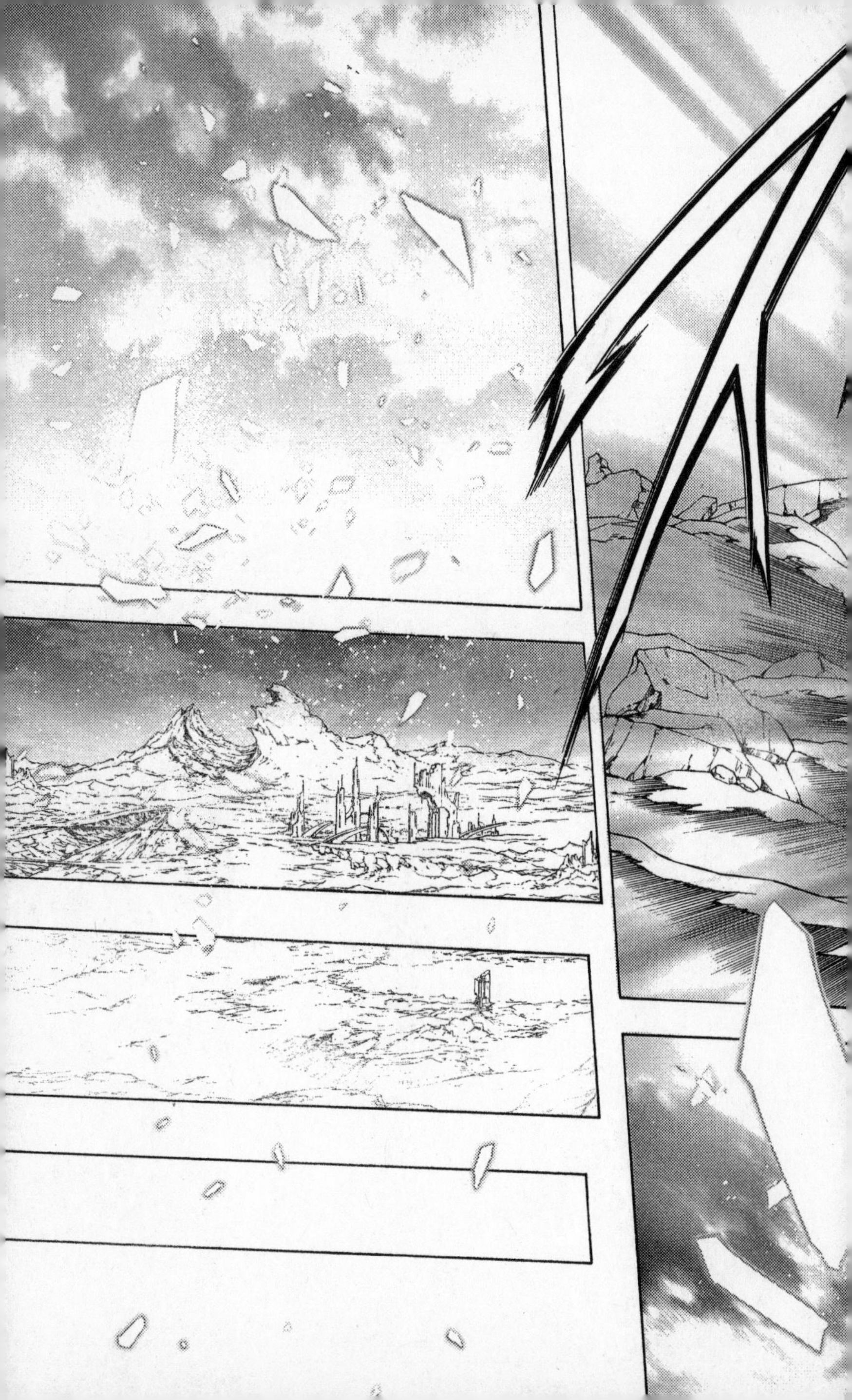

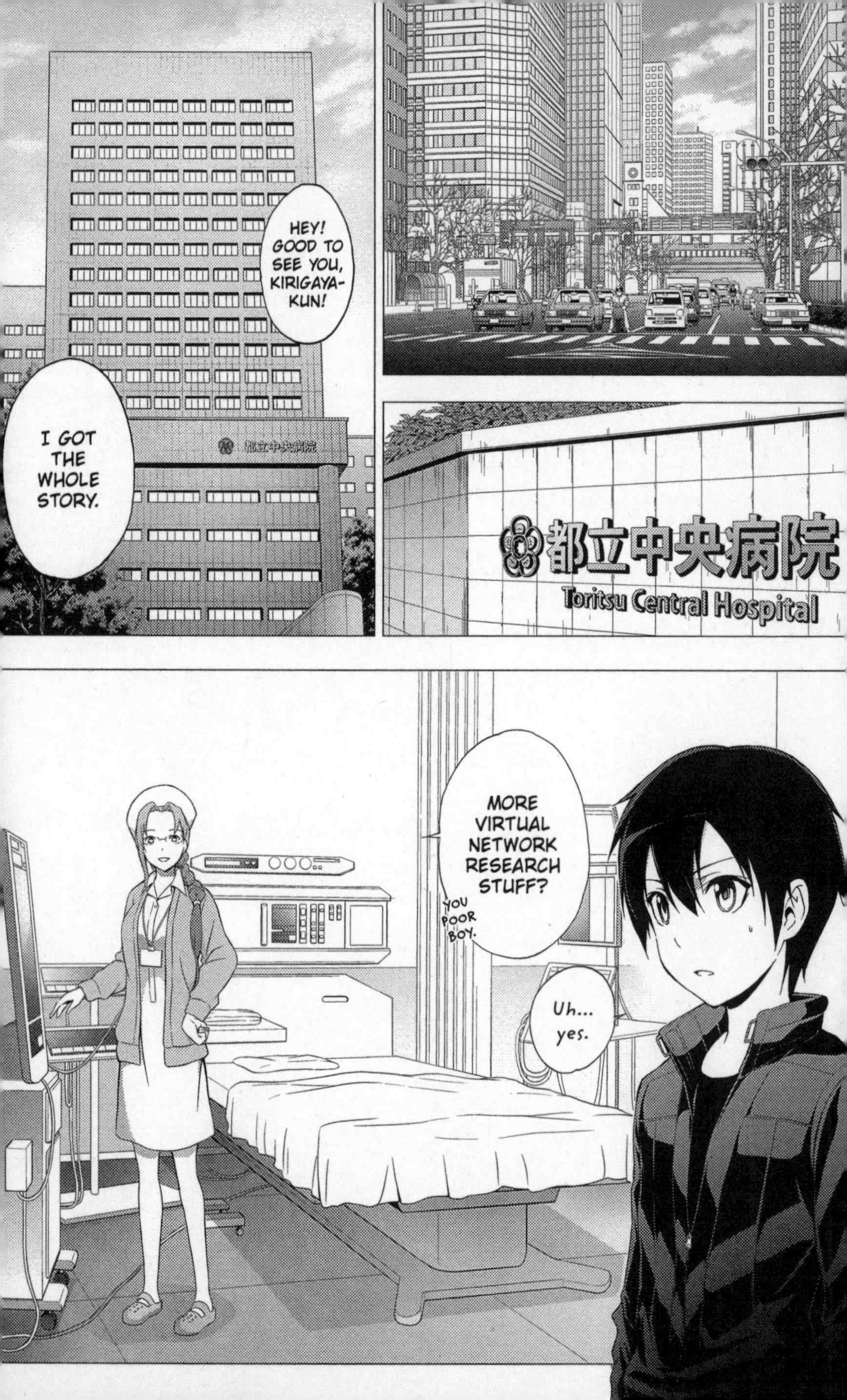
都立中央病院
Toritsu Central Hospital
HEY! GOOD TO SEE YOU, KIRIGAYA-KUN!
I GOT THE WHOLE STORY.
都立中央病院
MORE VIRTUAL NETWORK RESEARCH STUFF?
YOU POOR BOY.
Uh... yes.

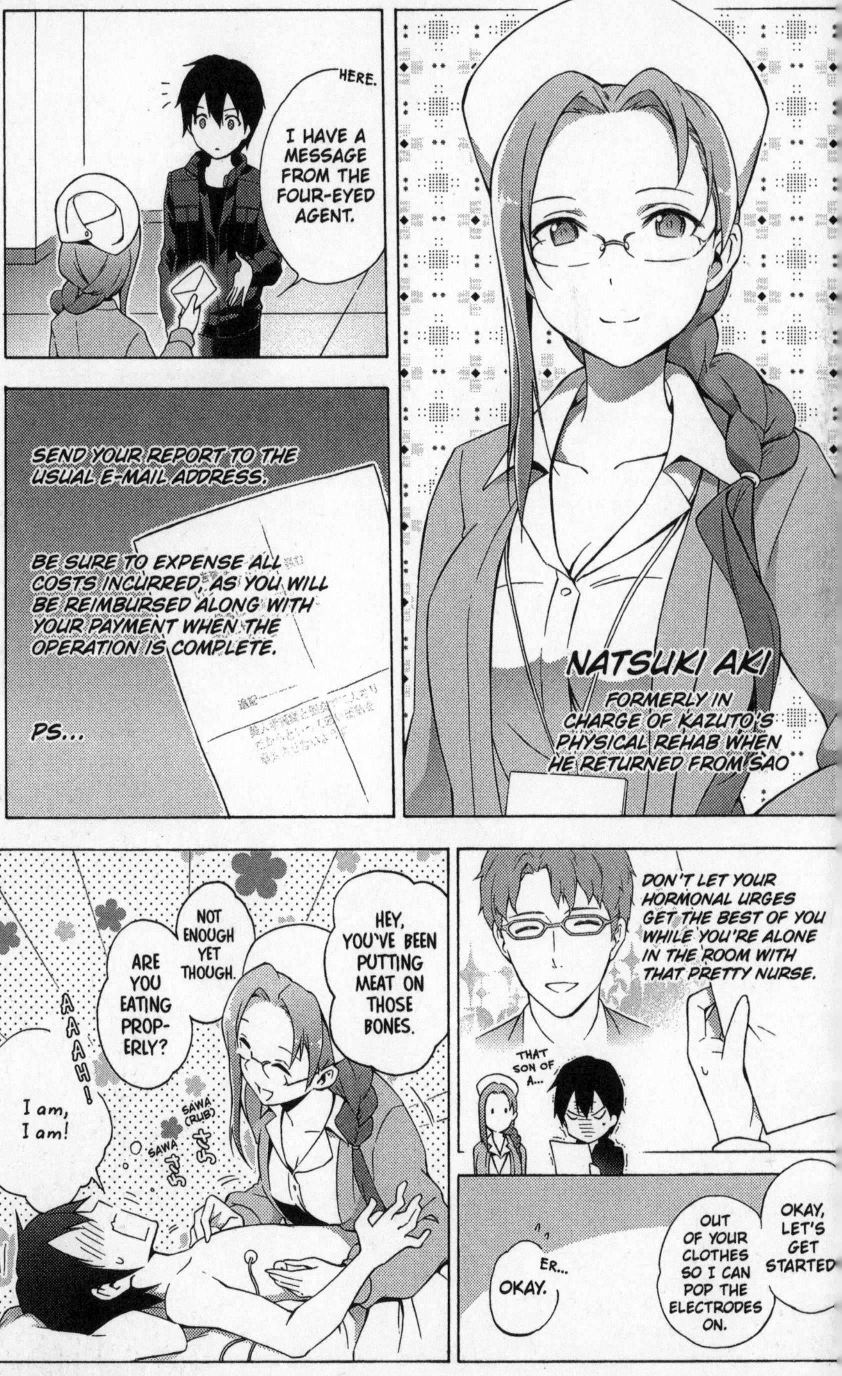
NATSUKI AKI
FORMERLY IN CHARGE OF KAZUTO'S PHYSICAL REHAB WHEN HE RETURNED FROM SAO
HERE.
I HAVE A MESSAGE FROM THE FOUR-EYED AGENT.
SEND YOUR REPORT TO THE USUAL E-MAIL ADDRESS.
BE SURE TO EXPENSE ALL COSTS INCURRED, AS YOU WILL BE REIMBURSED ALONG WITH YOUR PAYMENT WHEN THE OPERATION IS COMPLETE.
PS...
DON'T LET YOUR HORMONAL URGES GET THE BEST OF YOU WHILE YOU'RE ALONE IN THE ROOM WITH THAT PRETTY NURSE.
THAT SON OF A...
OKAY, LET'S GET STARTED
OUT OF YOUR CLOTHES SO I CAN POP THE ELECTRODES ON.
ER... OKAY.
HEY, YOU'VE BEEN PUTTING MEAT ON THOSE BONES.
NOT ENOUGH YET THOUGH.
ARE YOU EATING PROPERLY?
AAAH!
I am, I am!
SAWA (RUB)
SAWA

AND THAT SHOULD DO IT...

I'LL BE WATCHING YOUR BODY VERY CLOSELY, SO DON'T WORRY ABOUT ANYTHING BACK HERE.

TH... THANKS A LOT...

SUU (HAAH)

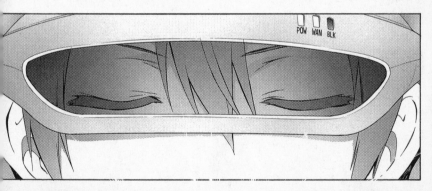

POW WAN BLK

LINK START!

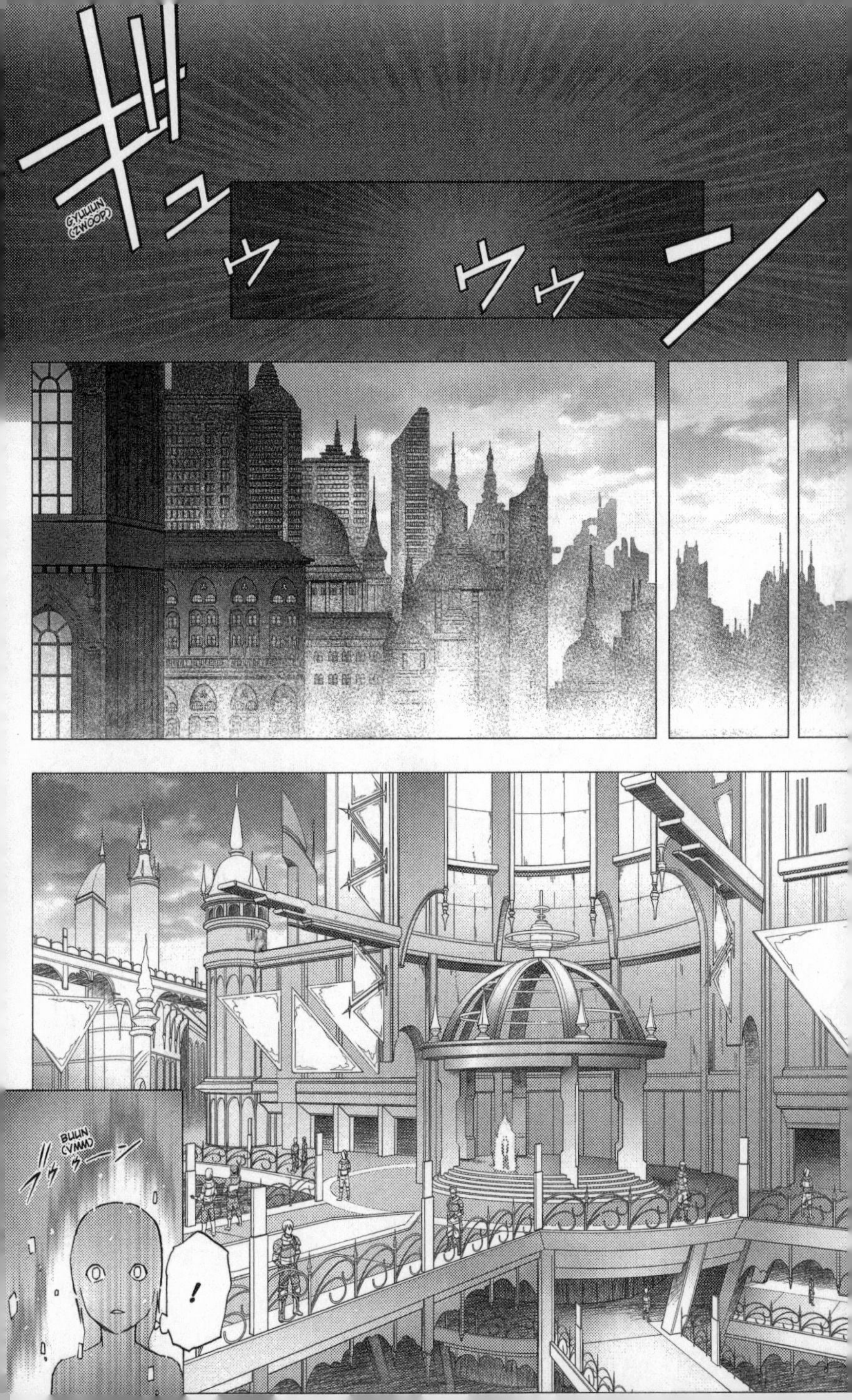
ギュウウゥン
GYUUUN (ZWOOP)
BUUN (VMM)
!

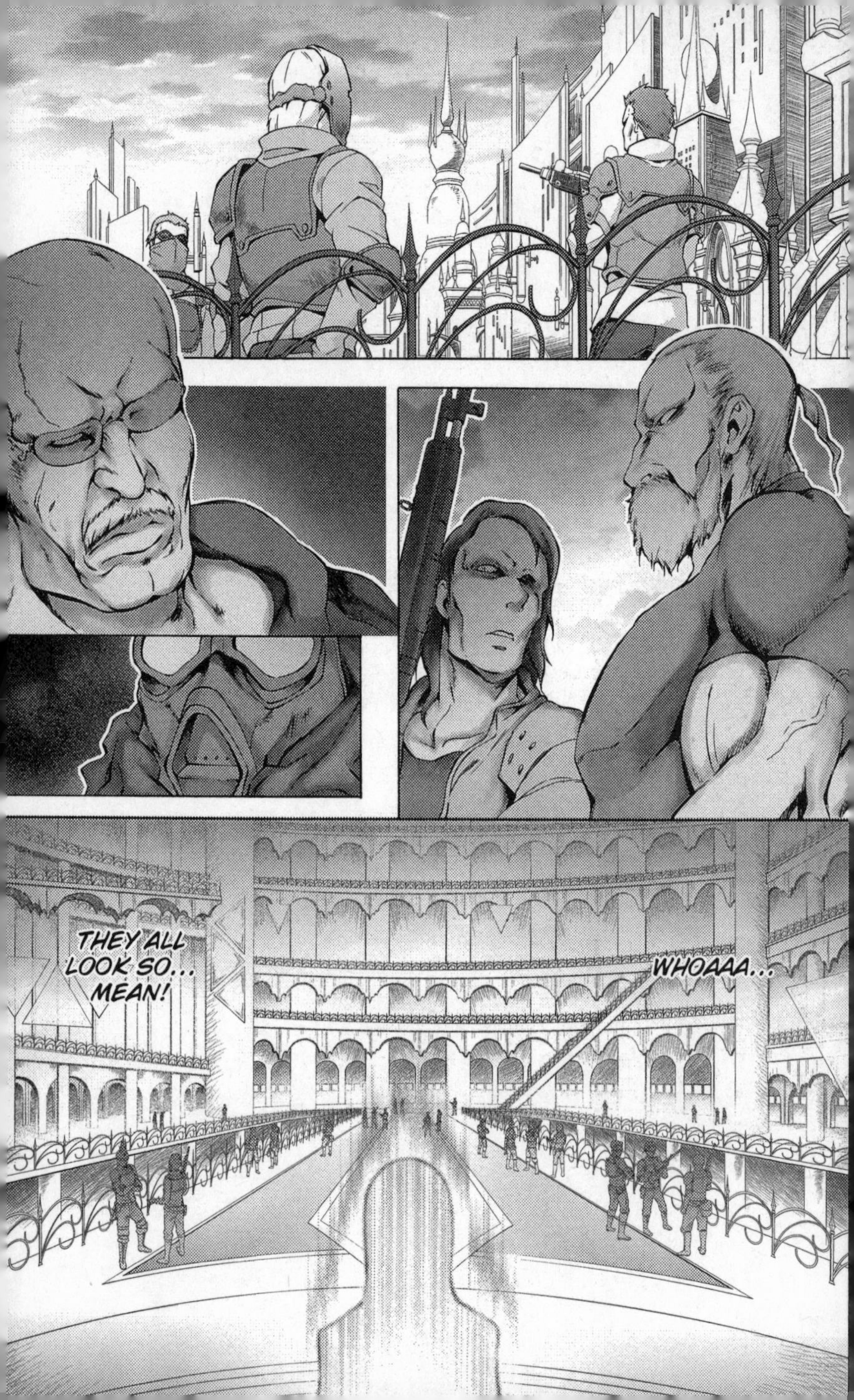
WHOAAA...
THEY ALL LOOK SO... MEAN!

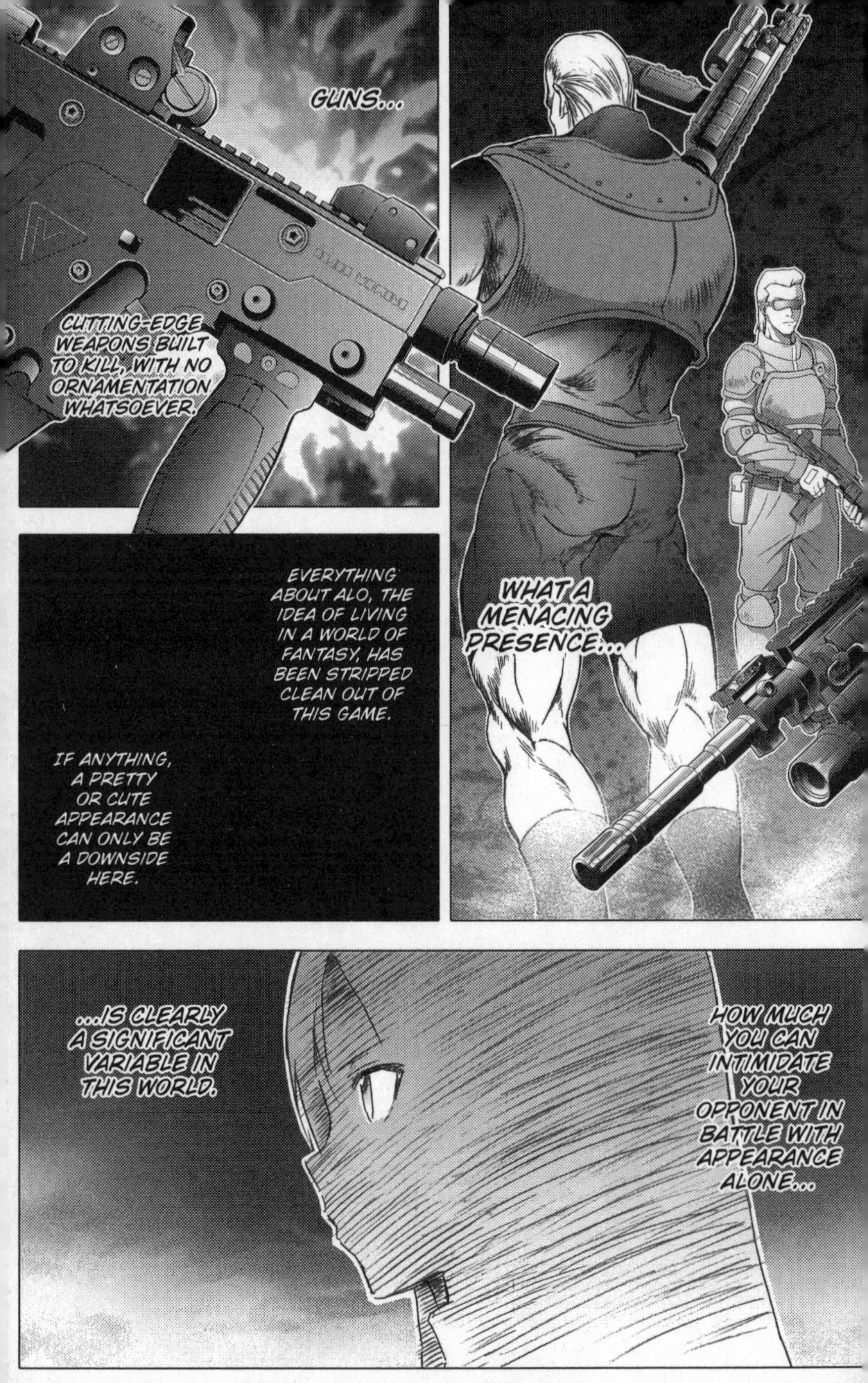
WHAT A MENACING PRESENCE...
GUNS...
CUTTING-EDGE WEAPONS BUILT TO KILL, WITH NO ORNAMENTATION WHATSOEVER.
EVERYTHING ABOUT ALO, THE IDEA OF LIVING IN A WORLD OF FANTASY, HAS BEEN STRIPPED CLEAN OUT OF THIS GAME.
IF ANYTHING, A PRETTY OR CUTE APPEARANCE CAN ONLY BE A DOWNSIDE HERE.
HOW MUCH YOU CAN INTIMIDATE YOUR OPPONENT IN BATTLE WITH APPEARANCE ALONE...
...IS CLEARLY A SIGNIFICANT VARIABLE IN THIS WORLD.

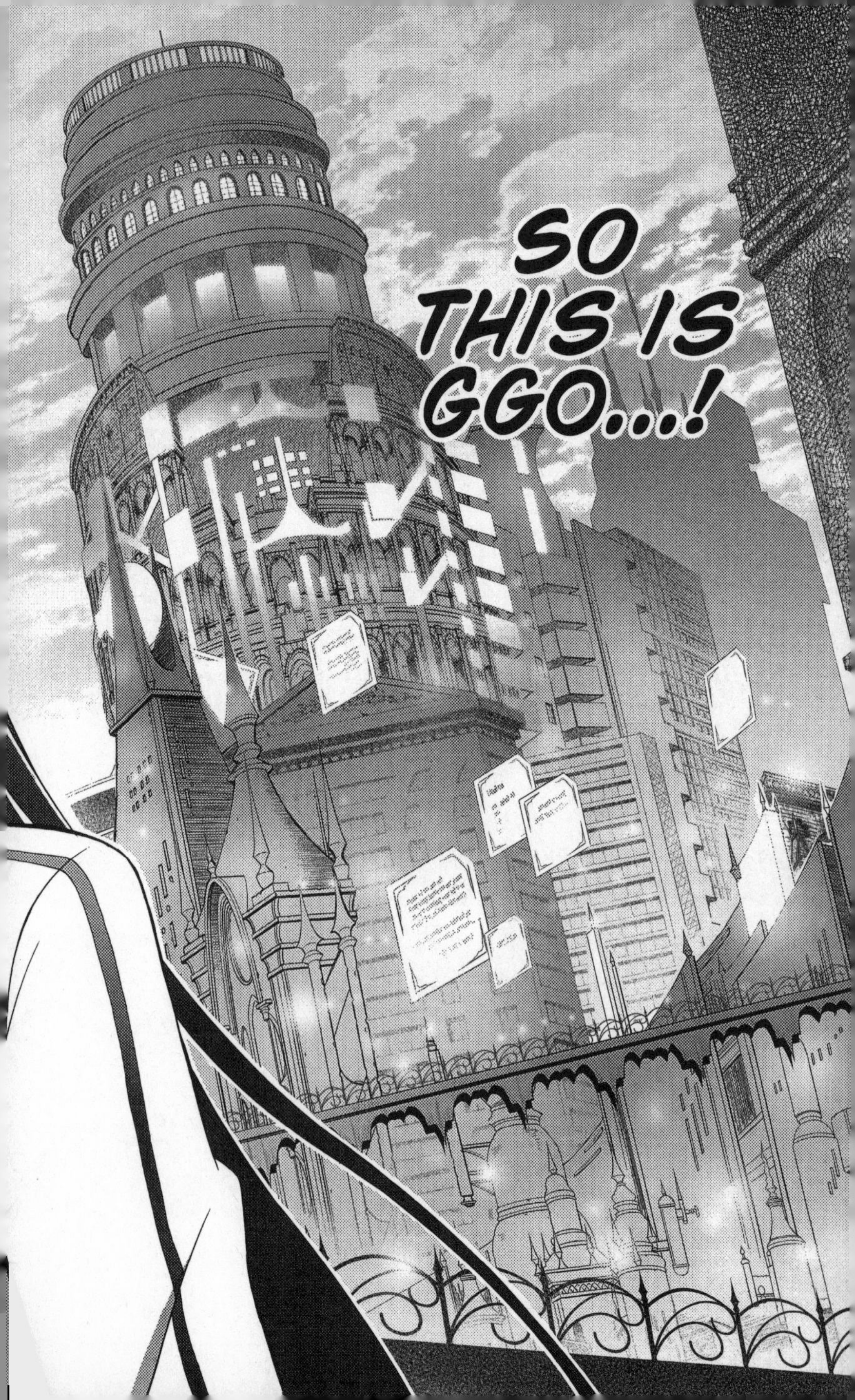
SO THIS IS GGO...!

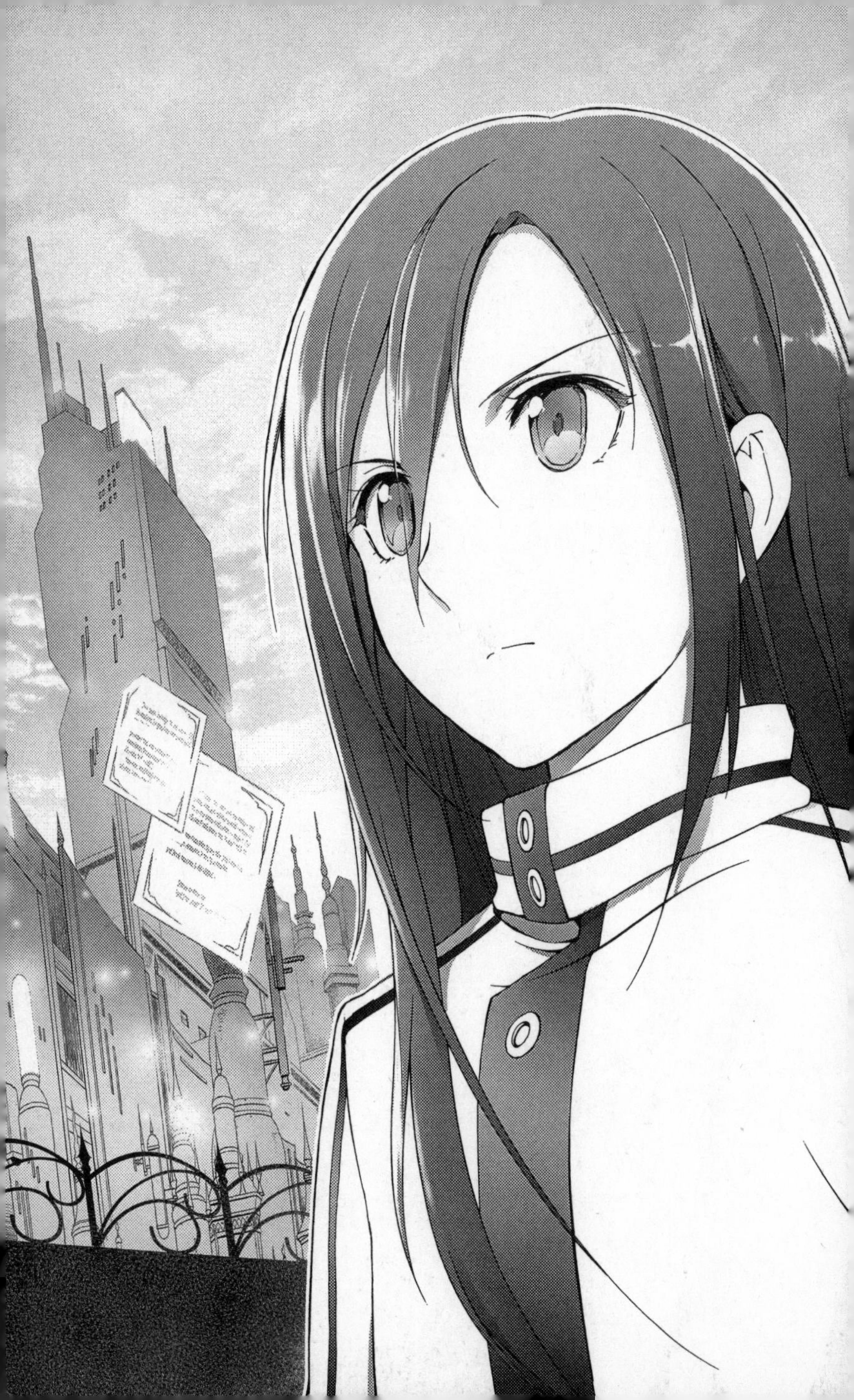

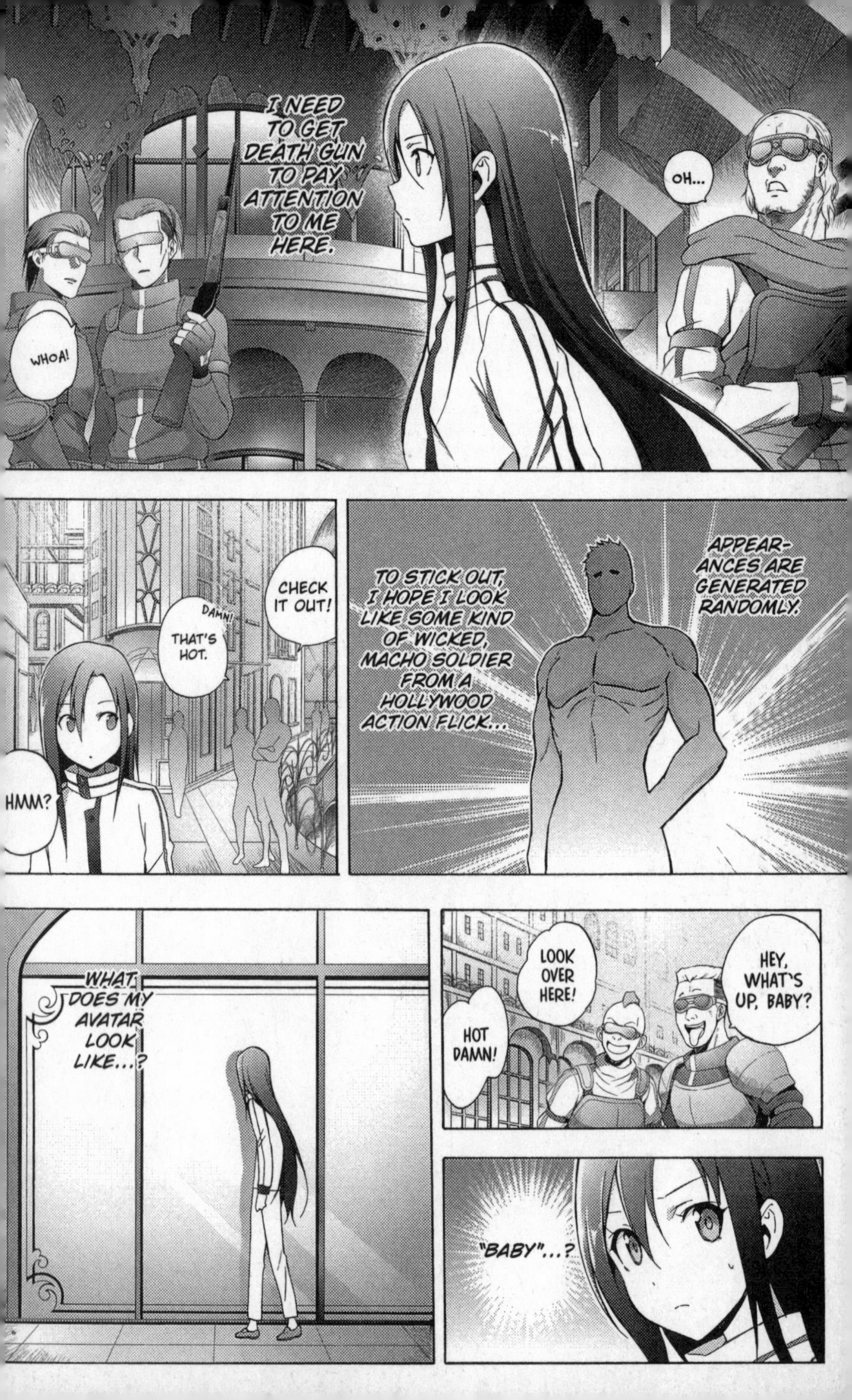
OH...
I NEED TO GET DEATH GUN TO PAY ATTENTION TO ME HERE.
WHOA!
APPEAR-ANCES ARE GENERATED RANDOMLY.
TO STICK OUT, I HOPE I LOOK LIKE SOME KIND OF WICKED, MACHO SOLDIER FROM A HOLLYWOOD ACTION FLICK...
CHECK IT OUT!
DAMN!
THAT'S HOT.
HMM?
HEY, WHAT'S UP, BABY?
LOOK OVER HERE!
HOT DAMN!
"BABY"...?
WHAT DOES MY AVATAR LOOK LIKE...?

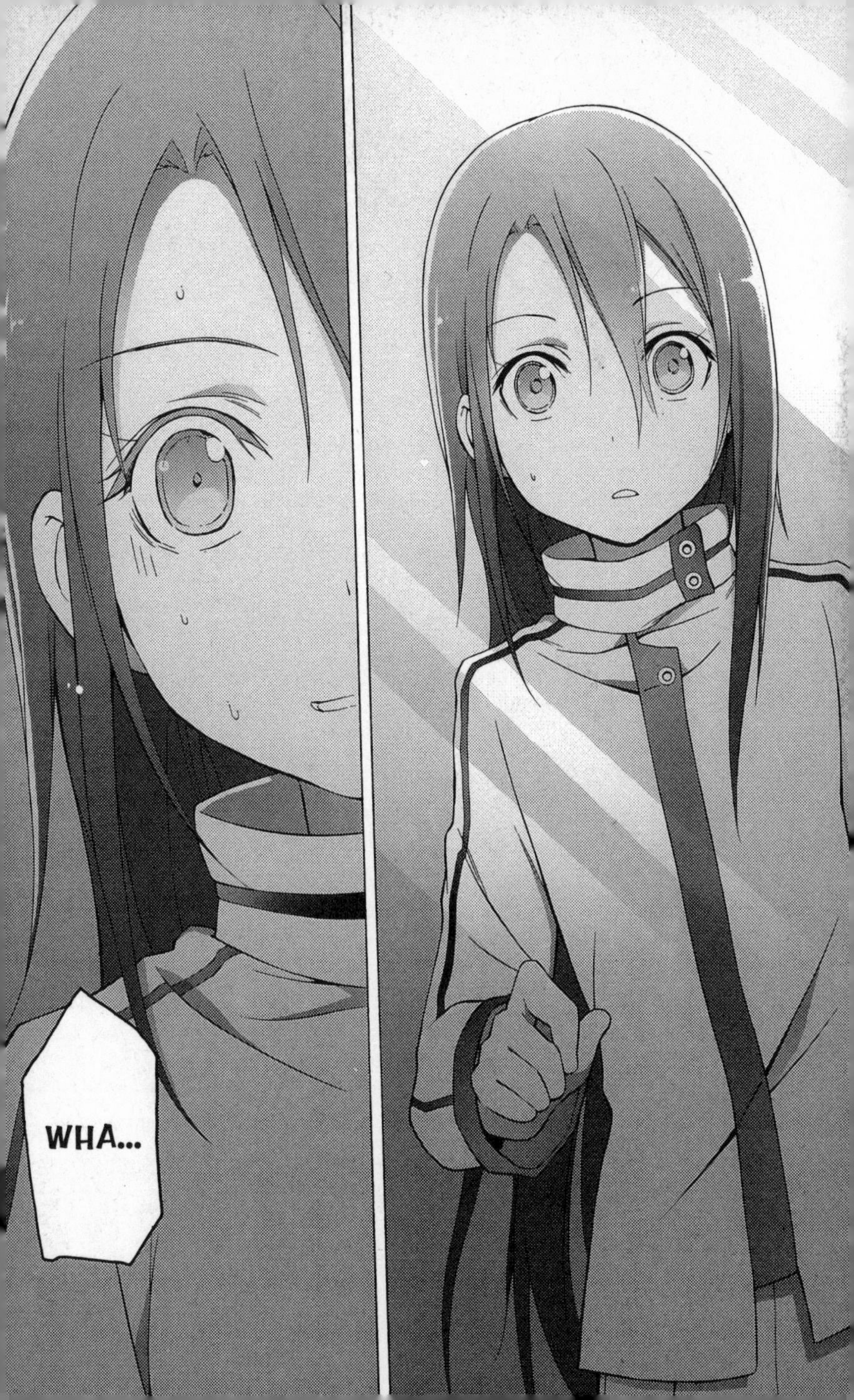
WHA...

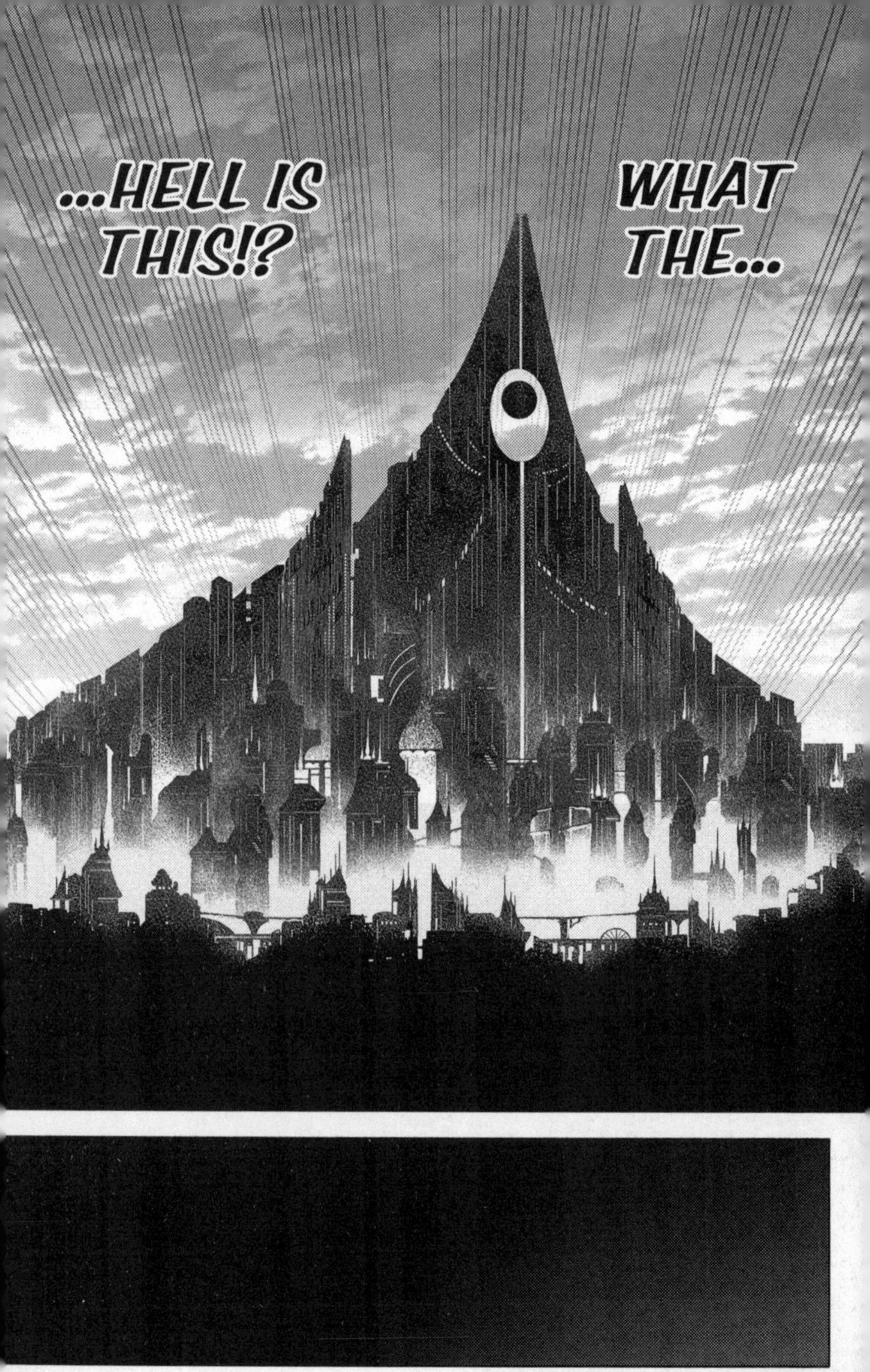
WHAT THE...
...HELL IS THIS!?

Sword Art Online: Phantom Bullet - To Be Continued

special comment

original story: reki kawahara

CONGRATULATIONS ON THE PUBLICATION OF THE FIRST VOLUME OF THE SERIES!

FIRST, I MUST THANK YAMADA-SAN FOR HIS GORGEOUS LINEWORK AND POWERFUL COMPOSITION IN DRAWING THAT QUICK DIGEST OF THE AINCRAD ARC, FOLLOWED IMMEDIATELY BY THE THRILLING EXCITEMENT OF THE *PHANTOM BULLET* INTRO! I'M SURE THAT ALL OF THE GUNS IN *GGO* WILL MAKE IT A MONUMENTAL TASK TO DRAW...BUT AS A READER, I CAN'T WAIT TO SEE IT ALL. MY PERSONAL FAVORITE ILLUSTRATION IS THE CLOSE-UP OF DEATH GUN ON PAGES 50 AND 51. I THINK IT'S THE COOLEST SCENE WE'VE WITNESSED YET! LOOKING FORWARD TO THE CONTINUATION OF THE SERIES!!

REKI KAWAHARA

special comment

character design: abec

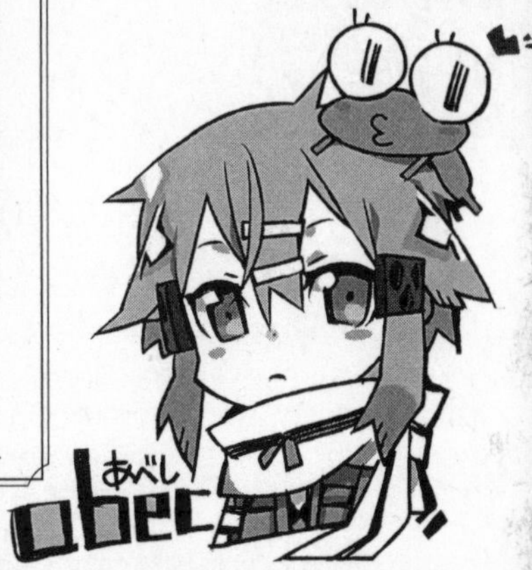
あべし
abec

CONGRATS ON THE RELEASE OF THE FIRST VOLUME! PERSONALLY, THE WORLD OF *GGO* WAS THE HARDEST FOR ME TO DEPICT IN THE *SAO* SERIES, SO I CAN'T WAIT TO SEE HOW YOU CONTINUE TO ADAPT IT FOR MANGA!

ABEC

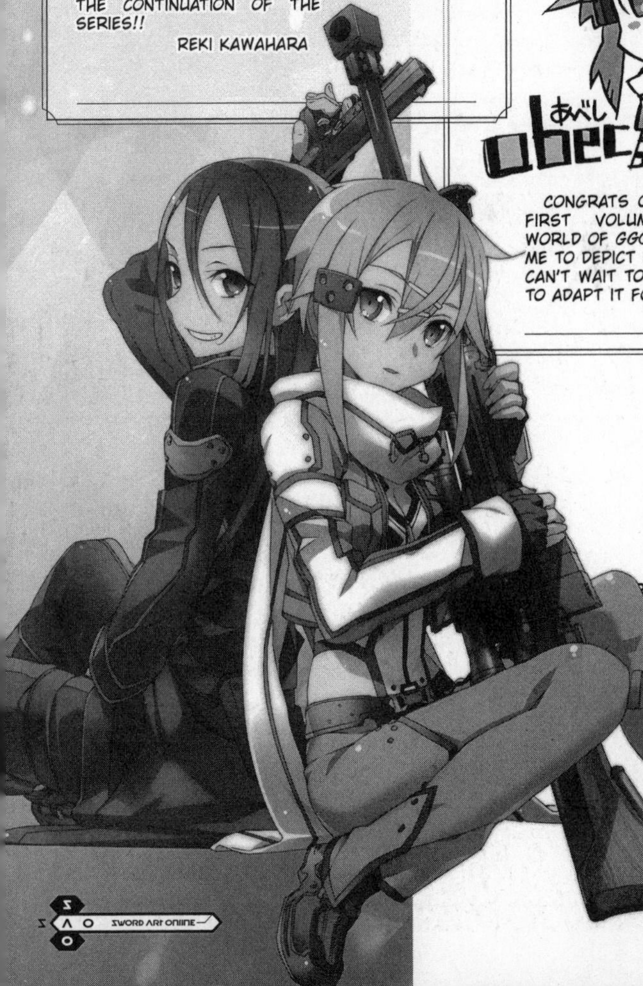

001

RD ART ONLINE phantom bulle

art: koutarou yamad
original story: reki kawahar
character design: abe

ILLUSTRATION/ABEC

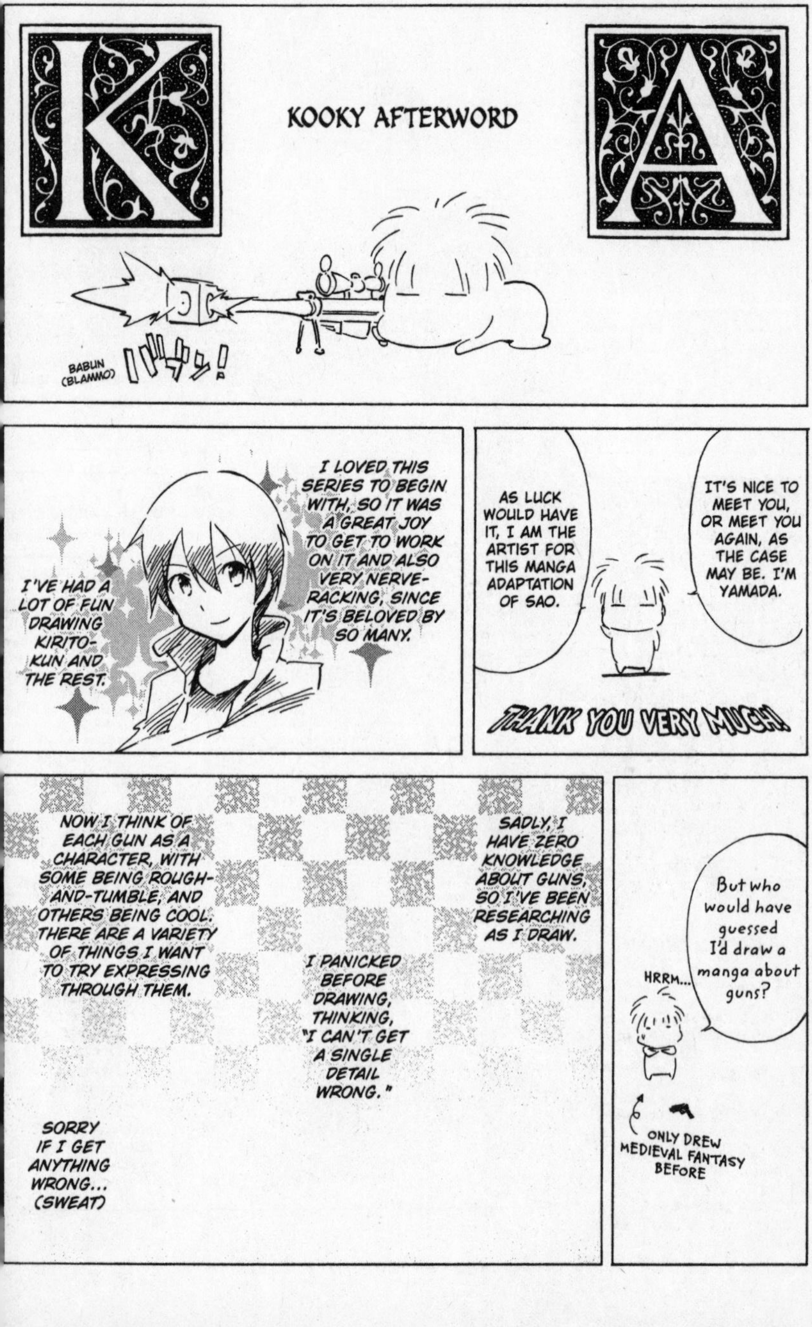
KOOKY AFTERWORD
BABUN (BLAMMO)
IT'S NICE TO MEET YOU, OR MEET YOU AGAIN, AS THE CASE MAY BE. I'M YAMADA.
AS LUCK WOULD HAVE IT, I AM THE ARTIST FOR THIS MANGA ADAPTATION OF SAO.
THANK YOU VERY MUCH!
I LOVED THIS SERIES TO BEGIN WITH, SO IT WAS A GREAT JOY TO GET TO WORK ON IT AND ALSO VERY NERVE-RACKING, SINCE IT'S BELOVED BY SO MANY.
I'VE HAD A LOT OF FUN DRAWING KIRITO-KUN AND THE REST.
But who would have guessed I'd draw a manga about guns?
HRRM...
ONLY DREW MEDIEVAL FANTASY BEFORE
SADLY, I HAVE ZERO KNOWLEDGE ABOUT GUNS, SO I'VE BEEN RESEARCHING AS I DRAW.
I PANICKED BEFORE DRAWING, THINKING, "I CAN'T GET A SINGLE DETAIL WRONG."
NOW I THINK OF EACH GUN AS A CHARACTER, WITH SOME BEING ROUGH-AND-TUMBLE, AND OTHERS BEING COOL. THERE ARE A VARIETY OF THINGS I WANT TO TRY EXPRESSING THROUGH THEM.
SORRY IF I GET ANYTHING WRONG... (SWEAT)

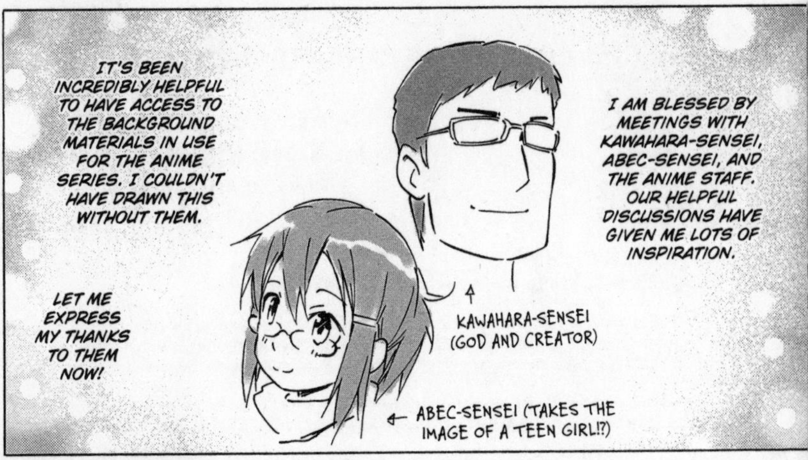
I AM BLESSED BY MEETINGS WITH KAWAHARA-SENSEI, ABEC-SENSEI, AND THE ANIME STAFF. OUR HELPFUL DISCUSSIONS HAVE GIVEN ME LOTS OF INSPIRATION.
IT'S BEEN INCREDIBLY HELPFUL TO HAVE ACCESS TO THE BACKGROUND MATERIALS IN USE FOR THE ANIME SERIES. I COULDN'T HAVE DRAWN THIS WITHOUT THEM.
KAWAHARA-SENSEI (GOD AND CREATOR)
LET ME EXPRESS MY THANKS TO THEM NOW!
ABEC-SENSEI (TAKES THE IMAGE OF A TEEN GIRL!?)

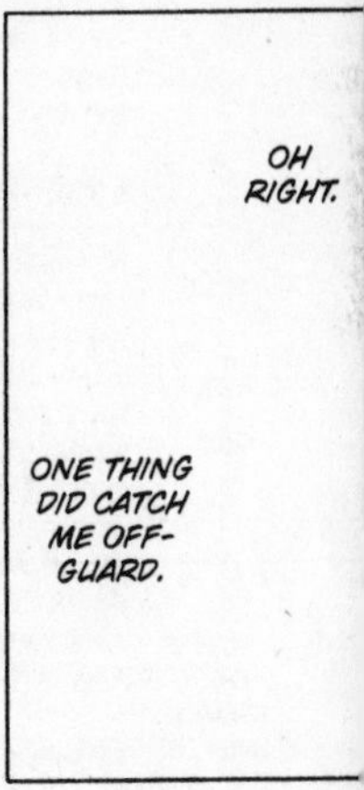
OH RIGHT.
ONE THING DID CATCH ME OFF-GUARD.

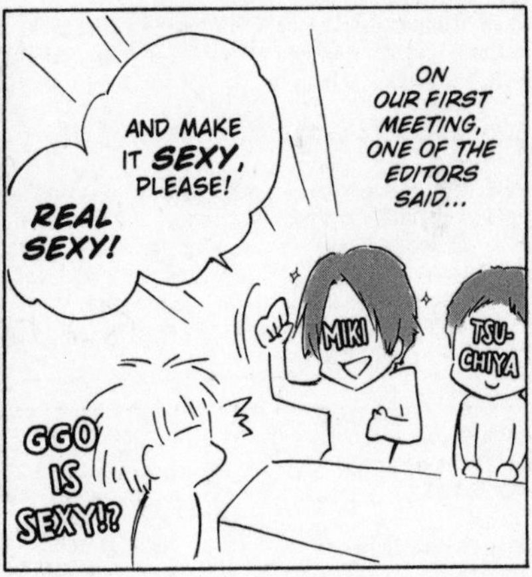
ON OUR FIRST MEETING, ONE OF THE EDITORS SAID...
AND MAKE IT SEXY, PLEASE!
REAL SEXY!
MIKI
TSU-CHIYA
GGO IS SEXY!?

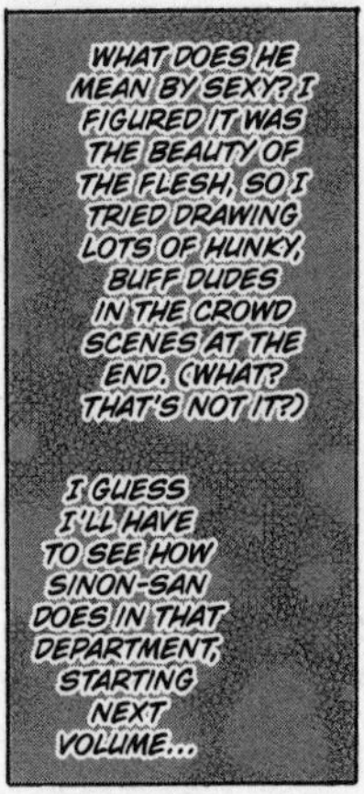
WHAT DOES HE MEAN BY SEXY? I FIGURED IT WAS THE BEAUTY OF THE FLESH, SO I TRIED DRAWING LOTS OF HUNKY, BUFF DUDES IN THE CROWD SCENES AT THE END. (WHAT? THAT'S NOT IT?)
I GUESS I'LL HAVE TO SEE HOW SINON-SAN DOES IN THAT DEPARTMENT, STARTING NEXT VOLUME...

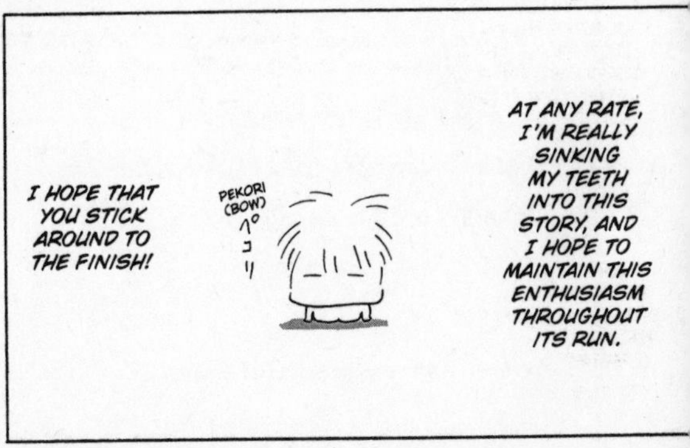
AT ANY RATE, I'M REALLY SINKING MY TEETH INTO THIS STORY, AND I HOPE TO MAINTAIN THIS ENTHUSIASM THROUGHOUT ITS RUN.
PEKORI (BOW)
I HOPE THAT YOU STICK AROUND TO THE FINISH!

—SPECIAL THANKS—

NAKAMURA-SAN

SAITOU-SAN, TAURA-SAN
SHINO-SAN, TAKAYA-SAN

OKOMEKEN

REKI KAWAHARA-SENSEI,
ABEC-SENSEI
THE MEMBERS OF THE
ANIME STAFF

KAZUMA MIKI-SAMA
TOMOYUKI TSUCHIYA-SAMA

SWORD ART ONLINE: PHANTOM BULLET 1

ART: KOUTAROU YAMADA
ORIGINAL STORY: REKI KAWAHARA
CHARACTER DESIGN: abec

Translation: Stephen Paul
Lettering: Brndn Blakeslee and Lys Blakeslee

This book is a work of fiction. Names, characters, places, and incidents are the product of the author's imagination or are used fictitiously. Any resemblance to actual events, locales, or persons, living or dead, is coincidental.

SWORD ART ONLINE: Phantom Bullet
© REKI KAWAHARA/KOUTAROU YAMADA 2014
All rights reserved.
Edited by ASCII MEDIA WORKS
First published in Japan in 2014 by KADOKAWA CORPORATION, Tokyo.
English translation rights arranged with KADOKAWA CORPORATION, Tokyo, through Tuttle-Mori Agency, Inc., Tokyo.

English translation © 2016 by Hachette Book Group, Inc.

All rights reserved. In accordance with the U.S. Copyright Act of 1976, the scanning, uploading, and electronic sharing of any part of this book without the permission of the publisher is unlawful piracy and theft of the author's intellectual property. If you would like to use material from the book (other than for review purposes), prior written permission must be obtained by contacting the publisher at permissions@hbgusa.com. Thank you for your support of the author's rights.

Yen Press
Hachette Book Group
1290 Avenue of the Americas
New York, NY 10104

www.HachetteBookGroup.com
www.YenPress.com

Yen Press is an imprint of Hachette Book Group, Inc. The Yen Press name and logo are trademarks of Hachette Book Group, Inc.

First Yen Press Edition: January 2016

Library of Congress Control Number: 2015952590

ISBN: 978-0-316-26888-2

10 9 8 7 6 5 4 3 2 1

BVG

Printed in the United States of America

YN
$12.40

PETERBOROUGH PUBLIC LIBRARY   JUL - - 2016